Toolkit Texts

Selected by **Anne Goudvis** and **Stephanie Harvey**

Short Nonfiction for American History
Westward Expansion

| 1800 | 1820 | 1840 | 1860 | 1880 |

Women's Voices From the Trail

The Celestials' Railroad

Growing Up Native American

EXODUSTERS

Caught in the Crossfire

Mr. Jefferson's Expedition
The Journey of Lewis and Clark

Heinemann

DEDICATED TO TEACHERS™

Heinemann
361 Hanover Street
Portsmouth, NH 03801-3912
www.heinemann.com

Offices and agents throughout the world

Library of Congress Cataloging-in-Publication Data
Name: Harvey, Stephanie, author. | Goudvis, Anne, author.
Title: Short nonfiction for American history : westward expansion / by Stephanie Harvey
    and Ann Goudvis.
Description: Portsmouth, NH : Heinemann, 206. | Series: Toolkit texts
    Includes bibliographical references.
Identifiers: LCCN 2016037300 | ISBN 9780325048840
Subjects: LCSH: United States—Territorial expansion—Sources—Juvenile literature. |
    United States—Territorial expansion—Study and teaching (Elementary). | West (U.S.)
    History—Sources—Juvenile literature. |West (U.S.)—History—Study and teaching
    (Elementary). | CYAC: United States—Territorial expansion—Sources. | West
    (U.S.)—History—Sources.
Classification: LCC E179.5 .H278 2016 | DDC 978/.02—dc23

LC record available at https:lccn.loc.gov/2016037300

ISBN: 978-0-325-04884-0

Editor: Heather Anderson
Production: Patty Adams and Stephanie J. Levy
Cover Design: Suzanne Heiser
Typesetters: Eclipse Publishing Services, Gina Poirier Design, Kim Arney
Manufacturing: Steve Bernier

Printed in the United States of America on acid-free paper
20 19 18 17 16 EBM 1 2 3 4 5

Acknowledgments

As longtime history buffs, we are deeply fascinated by American history. Our *Short Nonfiction for American History* texts, part of The Comprehension Toolkit series, couldn't have come to fruition without the commitment, diligence, and hard work of our Heinemann team. Most of all, we are extremely grateful to our fabulous editor Heather Anderson for her prodigious research skills, sharp eye for engaging material, and boundless enthusiasm. Patty Adams, Stephanie Levy, Tina Miller, Anita Gildea, Lisa Fowler, Julie Kreiss, Lauren Audet, Suzanne Heiser, and Steven Bernier put forth the energy, creative thinking, and hard work that has brought this resource to life. A special thanks to Mark Corsey and Ruth Linstromberg for their talented design work for this series. We thank the entire Heinemann team for their ongoing support of our work.

— Anne and Steph

Contents

Lessons for Close Reading in History

Articles

Library of Congress

Westward Expansion was a period of excitement and growth for the United
States. But it was also a time of conflict, between those who felt it was the United
States' destiny to expand into the west, and those whose people had lived there for
thousands of years.

NATIVE AMERICAN LIFE AND EARLY EXPLORERS

What was it like to grow up as part of a Native American tribe?

Library of Congress

Library of Congress

Library of Congress

© Mark Gilliland/Houghton Mifflin Harcourt/HIP

Library of Congress

From the New York Public Library

SETTLING THE WEST

Gates Frontiers Fund
Colorado Collection within the
Carol M. Highsmith Archive,
Library of Congress, Prints
and Photographs Division.

North Wind Picture Archives

Yale University Art Gallery

History Colorado:
Tin Lunchbox: #H.6200.673

Library of Congress

Nebraska State
Historical Society

Cate Fitzgerald-Rice

Yale University Art Gallery

THE DANCE AFTER THE HUSKING.

Margaret Lindmark

CONFLICT BETWEEN SETTLERS AND NATIVE AMERICANS

North Wind Picture Archives

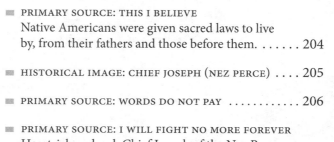

Library of Congress

Library of Congress

The **DIGITAL COMPANION RESOURCE** includes:

- all of the articles in full color,
- primary source documents,
- a full-color bank of additional historical images not included in the book, and
- "Teaching for Historical Literacy," by Anne Goudvis and Stephanie Harvey (*Educational Leadership*, March 2012).

For instructions on how to access the Digital Companion Resource, turn to
page xxi.

Introduction

Reading, writing, viewing, listening, talking, doing, and investigating are the hallmarks of active literacy. Throughout the school day and across the curriculum, kids are actively inferring, questioning, discussing, debating, inquiring, and generating new ideas. An active literacy classroom fairly bursts with enthusiastic, engaged learning.

The same goes for our history and social studies classrooms: They, too, must be thinking- and learning-intensive (President and Fellows of Harvard College 2007). To build intrigue, knowledge, and understanding in history, students read and learn about the events, mysteries, questions, controversies, issues, discoveries, and drama that are the real stuff of history.

Disciplinary Literacy

When students acquire knowledge in a discipline such as history and think about what they are learning, new insights and understandings emerge and kids generate new knowledge. Fundamental to this understanding is the idea that there's a difference between information and knowledge. Kids have to construct their own knowledge: only they can turn information into knowledge by thinking about it. But we educators must provide the environment, resources, and instruction so kids become curious, active learners.

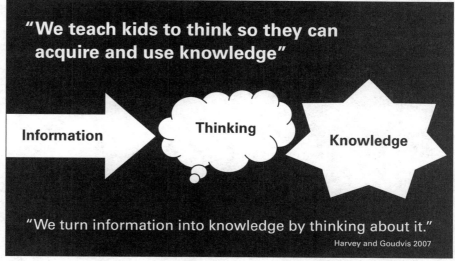

From Anne Goudvis, Stephanie Harvey, Brad Buhrow, and Anne Upczak-Garcia, 2012. *Scaffolding the Comprehension Toolkit for English Language Learners.* Portsmouth, NH: Heinemann.

But too often students experience history as a passive slog through the textbook, with a "coverage" curriculum that's a mile wide and an inch deep. Instead, students should be reading and actively responding to a wide range of historical sources; viewing and analyzing images; reading historical fiction, first-person accounts, letters, and all manner of sources; and engaging in simulations so they can understand and empathize with the experiences of people who lived "long ago and far away."

In this approach to disciplinary literacy, students use reading and thinking strategies as tools to acquire knowledge in history, science, and other subject areas. P. David Pearson and colleagues (Pearson, Moje, and Greenleaf 2010) suggest that:

> Without systematic attention to reading and writing in subjects like science and history, students will leave schools with an impoverished sense of what it means to use the tools of literacy for learning or even to reason within various disciplines (460).

Reading and thinking about historical sources and introducing students to ways of thinking in the discipline of history teaches them that there are many ways to understand the people, events, issues, and ideas of the past. But we also want students to understand the power and potential of their own thinking and learning so that they learn to think for themselves and connect history to their own lives.

CONTENT MATTERS

Cervetti, Jaynes, and Hiebert (2009) suggest that reading for understanding is the foundation for students acquiring and using knowledge. In the figure below, Cervetti et al. explain the reciprocal relationship between knowledge and comprehension—how background knowledge supports comprehension and in turn, through comprehension/reading for understanding, we "build new knowledge" (83).

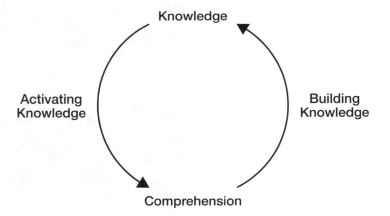

Research (Anderson and Pearson 1984) has long supported the strong relationship between background knowledge and school learning: Students' prior knowledge about content supports their new learning. From our perspective, history, more than many subjects, demands that students have a context for their learning, that they understand the essential ideas that emerge within a larger time span, and that they can discern the big picture.

But activating background knowledge is just the beginning. Researchers emphasize the knowledge-building side of this figure, which underscores the idea that when we comprehend, we add to and enhance our store of knowledge. "Knowledge, from this perspective, does not refer to a litany of facts, but rather to the discipline-based conceptual understanding . . . (which) engage students in becoming experts on the world around them" (Cervetti, Jaynes, and Hiebert 2009).

This is a reciprocal process that occurs as students build their knowledge in many content areas and disciplines. P. David Pearson sums it up well with his quip: "Today's new knowledge is tomorrow's background knowledge." The more students know, the more they will learn, and even more important, the more they will want to learn!

Historical Literacy

Our approach is to embed reading and thinking strategies in our social studies and history instruction, so that comprehension and thinking strategies become tools for learning and understanding content. Teaching historical literacy means we merge thoughtful, foundational literacy practices with challenging, engaging resources to immerse kids in historical ways of thinking.

What might this look like?

Students:

- read and reason through many different kinds of sources about the past, connecting to the experiences, dilemmas, discoveries, and reflections of people from other times and places

- ask their own authentic questions, just like historians do

- learn to read critically—to understand different purposes and perspectives, asking, "Who wrote this? Why did they write it? What are the authors' biases, points of view, and purposes?"

- try out ways of thinking about history—inferring, analyzing, and interpreting facts and evidence to surface themes and important ideas.

We believe these practices, above all, promote engagement with the discipline and motivate kids to want to find out more. When kids actively read, think, debate, discuss, and investigate, they have the best shot at becoming enthusiastic students of history. Not incidentally, zeroing in on content literacy in this way will go a long way in helping students meet district and state standards, including the Common Core State Standards (CCSS), which focus on 21st-century skills and learning across disciplines. The instructional practices advocated in this resource are supported by research that emphasizes a content-rich, standards-based approach:

A multisource, multigenre curriculum. We envision the active literacy classroom awash in engaging historical resources of all kinds: maps, timelines, artifacts, songs, poems, journals, letters, feature articles, biographies, and so on. Allington and Johnston (2002) found that students evidenced higher achievement when their classroom focused on a multisource, multigenre, multiperspective curriculum rather than a one-size-fits-all coverage approach. This research fits the bill.

Standards-based. The CCSS, as well as many state standards, highlight the importance of reading in the disciplines and reading for deeper meaning. Comprehension and thinking strategies are foundational for many of these standards. We don't "teach the standards," of course; we design instruction that supports students to read, reason, and respond so that they meet the appropriate standards. This resource includes ways in which comprehension and thinking strategies further the active use of knowledge and greater understanding in history and social studies.

Social studies strands. This resource provides a range of reading in the different social studies strands: history, culture, economics, government, and geography. A chart correlating the articles to the social studies strands appears on pages xix and xx.

History is the study of people, events, and achievements in the past. Learning about history helps students understand how people and societies behave. It also allows students to make connections between themselves and others who lived long ago. In addition, history helps students to understand the process of change and better prepare themselves for changes they will encounter in their lives.

Culture is the customs, traditions, habits, and values of a group of people. Learning about culture helps students to better understand and relate to others. By examining their own cultural traditions, students can understand the values of their society. By examining the cultural institutions of other groups, students can gain an appreciation of people who live differently from themselves and also see similarities they might not have otherwise realized.

Economics is the study of production, distribution, and consumption of goods and services. When students learn about economics, they learn how individuals, groups, and governments all make choices to satisfy their needs and wants. Understanding economics helps students to make better financial decisions in their own lives and also helps them to make sense of the economic world we live in.

Government is a system for making laws and keeping order in a city, state, or country. By learning about government, students are preparing themselves to be good citizens and take part in their political system. Not only does understanding government help students understand the modern-day world and its events, it also gives them the power to change that world through public actions.

Geography is the study of the Earth's surface and features and of the ways in which those features affect people around the world. Understanding geography helps students understand the physical world in which they live. It helps them see how different parts of their environment are connected and how all of those parts impact their lives and the lives of others.

Text Matters
SHORT TEXTS FOR LEARNING ABOUT THE WESTWARD EXPANSION

Kids need engaging texts and resources they can sink their teeth into. Just as with previously published *Toolkit Text* collections of articles, these articles on the Westward Expansion offer rich, engaging content that paints a vivid "big picture" of this time period. In this resource, we have included families of articles on a common topic or theme, with the understanding that the more widely kids read on a common topic, the more they learn and understand. The CCSS and other state standards expect that children will read a variety of texts on a common topic and synthesize the ideas and information across those texts.

Included here are informational articles in a number of genres: first-person accounts, plays, historical fiction, and feature articles. Images, portraits, and paintings, and all kinds of features, such as maps, charts, and timelines, provide visual interest and additional information in the articles. Primary sources, including historical speeches, images, and documents, can be found for each topic. We have also included a short bibliography of books, magazines, documentaries, and websites for investigation. We encourage you to add as many other texts and images on a topic as you can find, to bring history to life and encourage important research skills and practices.

WHY THESE SELECTIONS?

We considered the following criteria in selecting the articles, primary sources, and images:

Interest/content Kids love to learn about the quirky, the unusual, the unexpected, and the surprises that are essential to the study of history! Here we highlight those important but often lesser-known or unrecognized perspectives and voices from the past, for example, young people, women, Native Americans, and others. These are compelling voices, and we anticipate that these articles will ignite kids' interest as they explore historical ideas and issues.

Visual literacy Visual literacy is an essential 21st-century skill, so included here are primary sources, such as historical images, paintings, and maps. Other information-filled features in the articles include diagrams, timelines, charts, and photographs, all of which encourage interpretation, analysis, and comparison across texts and images. Images also provide another entry point for students to access historical texts. You may consider projecting the color versions of the historical images or articles rich with art for students to view closely as one way to generate a conversation about students' background knowledge. We also use images to introduce a particular theme or concept and model interpretation and analysis. Historical images with explanations are located throughout the book; additional historical images can be accessed on the Digital Companion Resource or through further research online.

Writing quality and accuracy When we think back to history class, we remember writing that was dull and voiceless—too often full of the generalizations and information overload common to textbook writing. To get kids excited about history and motivated to dig deeper and learn more, we searched for articles that had vibrant language and active voice. Variety makes a difference, so we include a rich assortment of nonfiction texts and visual features, as well as a bibliography of additional well-written, authentic resources.

Our knowledge of historical times and people is ever-changing as historians learn more and unearth additional artifacts and sources. Each article has been carefully vetted for accuracy by content experts and historical researchers.

Reading level/complexity Differentiation is key. Included in the collection are articles at a variety of reading levels to provide options for student practice. For example, there are shorter, more accessible articles and longer, more in-depth ones on the same or similar topics. All articles have carefully chosen images designed to enhance the content. This allows for differentiation according to students' reading proficiency levels as well as their interest levels.

We have also carefully selected primary source documents that will give students an authentic view of and unique insights into this time period. Arcane or unusual vocabulary and unfamiliar sentence structures can present significant reading challenges. We recommend building background knowledge and historical context (see Lesson 3) before digging into these authentic documents with your students. We offer strategies for approaching the close reading of primary source documents with your students in Lesson 4.

Assigning a grade level to a particular text is arbitrary, especially with content-rich selections, particularly in nonfiction with all of its supportive features. We suggest you look carefully at all the articles and choose from them based on your kids' interests and tastes as well as their reading levels.

CORRELATION CHART TO SOCIAL STUDIES STRANDS

Read across the chart to determine which social studies strands are covered in each article.

Article	History	Culture	Economics	Geography	Government
Overview: Westward Expansion, Promises and Destinies					
Native American Life and Early Explorers					
Growing Up Native American					
Spirits All Around: The Beliefs of the Plains Indians					
The Sacred Buffalo					
Florida Seminoles					
The First Mexican Americans					
California History					
Mr. Jefferson's Expedition					
Westward Bound					
Going West with Lewis and Clark					
Sacagawea: Intrepid Interpreter and Guide					
York: Brave Explorer					
Westward Stop and Go					
Paving the Way to California					
Joe Meek: Mountain Man					
Heading West					
A Different Story					
Forced Removal					
Remember the Alamo					
Eyewitness at the Alamo					
The Hero of San Jacinto					
Santa Anna: Napoleon					
Settling the West					
A Day on the Trail					
A Rocky Ride					
What's for Dinner?					
Women's Voices from the Trail					
Tabitha Brown's letters and excerpt from *Adventures on Horseback*					
Interview with Frances Jenner: History as Adventure					
Quilts: Stitching Stories					
Work and Play					

chart continues on page xx

Article	History	Culture	Economics	Geography	Government
Settlers in the West *(continued)*					
Mormon Migration					
Rough and Tumble: Growing Up in a Mining Town					
Into the Mine					
Baby Doe, The Silver Queen					
Go for the Gold!					
First Transcontinental Railroad					
The Celestials' Railroad					
Placing Out					
Exodusters					
Benjamin 'Pap' Singleton: Father of the Black Exodus					
Nicodemus Stakes a Claim in History					
Following the Herd					
It's Knot Easy					
Swing Your Partner: Frontier Fun					
Bandit Heroes					
Bass Reeves, Deputy U.S. Marshall					
Riding with the Pony Express					
Conflict Between Settlers and Native Americans					
Andrew Jackson: Hero or Not?					
The War's Western Roots					
Caught in the Crossfire					
Into the West					
On the Little Bighorn					
Destroying a Culture					
A Time of Troubles					
Message of Hope					
Ending a Way of Life: Wounded Knee					
Capturing a Vanishing World					
Current Day Issues in the West					
Sand Creek's Story					
Ranch of the Swallows					
Facing the Future					
Reclaiming the West					

HOW TO ACCESS THE DIGITAL COMPANION RESOURCE

The Digital Companion Resource provides all of the reproducible texts, plus primary source documents, and a bank of more than sixty additional historical images in a full-color digital format that is ideal for projecting and group analysis. We've also included the professional journal article, "Teaching for Historical Literacy."

To access the Digital Companion Resource:

1. Go to www.heinemann.com.

2. Click on "login" to open or create your account. Enter your email address and password or click "register" to set up an account.

3. Enter keycode TTSNFWE and click register.

4. You will receive a link to download *The Westward Expansion* Digital Companion.

You can print and project articles and images from the Digital Companion. Please note, however, that they are for personal and classroom use only, and by downloading, you are agreeing not to share the content.

These buttons are available at the top of each article for your convenience:

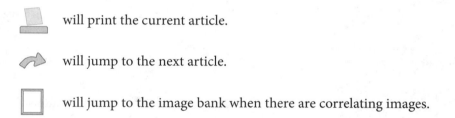

will print the current article.

will jump to the next article.

will jump to the image bank when there are correlating images.

For best results, use Adobe Reader for Windows PC or Mac. Adobe Reader is also available as an app for iPad and Android tablets. However, the Print function will not work on tablets.

HOW MIGHT I USE THIS RESOURCE?

In the first column we summarize foundational comprehension strategies that foster student engagement and understanding across content areas, but particularly in content literacy. As students build their own repertoire of reading and thinking strategies, these become tools they use 24/7. The second column describes how students use these strategies to acquire knowledge and deepen their understanding of history.

Comprehension strategies for content literacy	Students use these in history when they:
Monitor understanding.	Stop, think, and react during reading.
	Learn new information and leave tracks of thinking by annotating the text.
	Respond to and discuss the text by asking questions, connecting to prior knowledge and experiences, drawing inferences, and considering the big ideas.
Activate and build background knowledge.	Connect the new to the known; use background knowledge to inform reading.
	Recognize misconceptions and be prepared to revise thinking in light of new evidence.
	Consider text and visual features.
	Pay attention to text structures and different genres.
Ask and answer questions.	Ask and answer questions to:
	▪ Acquire information.
	▪ Investigate and do research.
	▪ Interpret and analyze information and ideas.
	▪ Read with a critical eye and a skeptical stance.
	▪ Explore lingering and essential questions.
Draw inferences and conclusions.	Infer ideas, themes, and issues based on text evidence.
	Analyze and interpret different perspectives and points of view.
Determine importance.	Sort and sift important information from interesting but less important details.
	Construct main ideas from supporting details.
	Evaluate the information and ideas in a text.
	Distinguish between what the reader thinks versus what the author wants the reader to understand.
Summarize and synthesize.	Analyze, compare, and contrast information across sources to build content knowledge and understanding.
	Evaluate claims and supporting evidence.
	Generate new knowledge and insights.

Adapted from Anne Goudvis and Stephanie Harvey, 2012. "Teaching for Historical Literacy." *Educational Leadership* March 2012: 52–57.

TEN CONTENT LITERACY LESSONS FOR CLOSE READING IN HISTORY

"The most obvious way to enhance students' world knowledge is to provide knowledge-enriching experiences in school; yet literacy programs have long missed the opportunity to use reading, writing, and speaking as tools for developing knowledge" (Cervetti et al. 2009).

This is especially true for history. We believe strongly that kids should be reading, writing, thinking, and doing in history. But far too often, conventional history instruction has focused on memorizing facts and dates without learning about the time period, the people themselves, and the challenges they faced. Students too often experience social studies and history as a passive slog through the textbook. This dumbed-down approach to history is a sure way to put students to sleep and guarantee they never come to understand the discipline, much less engage in it.

In this resource, we have designed ten lessons that merge effective, foundational content-literacy practices with thoughtful approaches to reading historical articles, viewing images, and reasoning through documents. These lessons encourage thoughtful reading and discussion that go far beyond answering the questions at the end of the chapter. By teaching these ten lessons, teachers will guide students to use reading and thinking strategies as tools to acquire and actively use knowledge in history.

Lesson	Title	Page
1	Read and Annotate: Stop, think, and react using a variety of strategies to understand	L-1
2	Annotate Images: Expand understanding and learning from visuals	L-3
3	Build Background to Understand a Primary Source: Read and paraphrase secondary sources to create a context for a topic	L-6
4	Read and Analyze a Primary Source: Focus on what you know and ask questions to clarify and explain	L-9
5	Compare Perspectives: Explore the different life experiences of historical figures	L-12
6	Read Critically: Consider point of view and bias	L-15
7	Organize Historical Thinking: Create a question web	L-18
8	Read with a Question in Mind: Focus on central ideas	L-21
9	Surface Common Themes: Infer the big ideas across several texts	L-24
10	Synthesize Information to Argue a Point: Use claim, evidence, and reasoning	L-27

Bibliography

Our passion for historic reading goes way beyond this book. Here is a list of terrific, engaging books and resources to keep history alive in your classroom.

BOOKS ABOUT WESTWARD EXPANSION

Blaisdell, Bob, ed. *Great Speeches by Native Americans.* Mineola, NY: Dover Publications. 2000.

Bowes, John. *The Trail of Tears: Removal in the South.* New York, NY: Chelsea House. 2007. From the Landmark Events in Native American History series, including *Little Bighorn, The Long Walk: The Forced Navajo Exile, Red Power: The Native American Civil Rights Movement, The Apache Wars: The Final Resistance, Black Hawk and the War of 1832: Removal in the North.*

Bruchac, Joseph. *A Boy Called Slow: The True Story of Sitting Bull.* New York, NY: Philomel. 1994.

Bruchac, Joseph. *Sacajawea.* New York, NY: HMH Books for Young Readers. 2000.

Bunting, Eve. *Train to Somewhere.* New York, NY: Clarion Books. 1996.

Caduto, Michael, and Joseph Bruchac. *Keepers of Life: Discovering Plants through Native American Stories and Earth Activities for Children.* Golden, CO: Fulcrum Publishing. 1997. From the Keepers of Earth series, including *Keepers of the Animals, Keepers of the Night,* and *Native American Gardening.*

Charleyboy, L. and M. B. Leatherdale, eds. *Dreaming in Indian: Contemporary Native American Voices.* Buffalo, NY: Annick Press. 2014.

Chu, Daniel, and Bill Shaw. *Going Home to Nicodemus: The Story of an African American Frontier Town and the Pioneers Who Settled It.* Morristown, NJ: Julian Messner. 1994.

Dwyer, Helen, and D. L. Birchfield. *Sioux: History and Culture.* New York, NY: Gareth Stevens. 2012. From the Native American Library series, including *Apache, Cheyenne, Mohawk, Navajo,* and *Nez Perce.*

Erdrich, Louise. *The Birchbark House.* New York, NY: Hyperion Books for Children. 1999.

Erdrich, Louise. *The Porcupine Year.* New York, NY: Harper Collins. 2008.

Freedman, Russell. *Children of the Wild West.* New York, NY: Clarion Books. 1983.

Furbee, Mary Rodd. *Outrageous Women of the American Frontier.* San Francisco, CA: Jossey-Bass. 2005.

Gifford, Eli, Michael Cook, and Warren Jefferson, eds. *How Can One Sell the Air? Chief Seattle's Vision.* Summertown, TN: Native Voices/Book Publishing Co. 2005.

Glatzer, Jenna. *Native American Festivals and Ceremonies*. Philapdelphia, PA: Mason Crest. 2003. From the Native American Life series.

Grutman, J. H., and Gay Matthaei. *The Ledgerbook of Thomas Blue Eagle*. Watertown, MA: Charlesbridge. 1999.

Hakim, Joy. *History of US: Liberty for All?* Revised Third Edition. New York, NY: Oxford University Press. 2005.

Hakim, Joy. *History of US: The New Nation*. Revised Third Edition. New York, NY: Oxford University Press. 2007.

Jenner, Frances Bonney. *Prairie Journey*. Irie Books. 2012.

Josephson, Judith Pinkerton. *Growing Up in Pioneer America*. Minneapolis, MN: Lerner Publications Company. 2006.

Kalman, Bobbie, ed. *Wagon Train*. New York, NY: Crabtree. 1999. From the Life in the Old West series, including *The Gold Rush, Homes of the West, Women of the West*, and *The Railroad*.

Katz, William Loren. *Black Women of the Old West*. New York, NY: Atheneum Books for Young Readers. 1995.

Mellor, Mike. *The American West, 1840–1895*. Cambridge, UK: Cambridge University Press. 1998.

Neihardt, John. *Black Elk Speaks*. Lincoln, NE: University of Nebraska Press. 1979.

Nelson, S.D. *Black Elk's Vision: A Lakota Story*. New York, NY: Abrams Books. 2010.

Nelson, Vaunda Micheaux. *Bad News for Outlaws*. Minneapolis, MN: Carolrhoda Books. 2009.

Philip, Neil. *A Braid of Lives*. New York, NY: Clarion Books. 2000.

Rappaport, Doreen. *The Flight of Red Bird: The Life of Zitkala-Sa*. New York, NY: Penguin Group. 1997.

Sandler, Martin W. *Pioneers*. New York, NY: Harper Collins. 1994.

Schlissel, Lillian. *Black Frontiers: A History of African American Heroes in the Old West*. New York, NY: Aladdin Paperbacks/Simon and Schuster Children's Publishing Division. 2000.

Secakuku, Susan. *Meet Mindy: A Native Girl from the Southwest*. Hillsboro, OR: Beyond Words Publishing. 2003. From the My World: Young Native Americans Today series, including *Meet Lydia: A Native Girl from Southeast Alaska, Meet Naiche: A Native Boy from the Chesapeake Bay Area*, and *Meet Christopher, an Osage Indian Boy from Oklahoma*.

Simmons, Marc. *Jose's Buffalo Hunt: A Story from History*. Albuquerque, NM: University of New Mexico Press. 2004. From the Children of the West series, including *Friday the Arapaho Boy, Teddy's Cattle Drive*, and *Billy Blackfeet in the Rockies*.

Turner, Ann. *Sitting Bull Remembers*. New York, NY: Harper Collins. 2007.

Wagner, Tricia Martineau. *African American Women of the Old West*. Guilford, CT: The Globe Pequot Press. 2007.

Wadsworth, Ginger. *Words West: Voices of Young Pioneers*. New York: Clarion Books. 2003.

Walker, Paul. *Remember Little Bighorn: Indians, Soldiers and Scouts Tell Their Stories*. Washington, D.C.: National Geographic. 2015. See also *Remember the Alamo*.

Warren, Andrea. *Pioneer Girl: A True Story of Growing Up on the Prairie*. Lincoln, NE: University of Nebraska Press. 1998.

Warren, Andrea. *We Rode the Orphan Trains*. New York, NY: HMH Books for Young Readers. 2001.

Winter, Jonah. *Wild Women of the Wild West*. New York, NY: Holiday House. 2011.

Yin. *Coolies*. New York, NY: Philomel Books. 2001.

DOCUMENTARIES

"New Perspectives on the West." PBS, 2001. DVD.

"We Shall Remain: America Through Native Eyes." PBS American Experience. 2009. DVD collection. Includes *After the Mayflower, Tecumseh's Vision, Trail of Tears, Geronimo, Wounded Knee*.

MAGAZINES

Cobblestone, an American history magazine for grades 5–9

Dig, an archaeology and history magazine for grades 5–9

Kids Discover, a social studies and scientific magazine for grades 3–7

Junior Scholastic, a current events and social studies magazine for grades 5–8

The New York Times Upfront, a current events and social studies magazine (both national and international news) for middle and high school students

Scholastic News, a curriculum-connected current events news weekly online for grades 1–6

US Studies Weekly, a U.S. history newspaper for students in grades K–9

WEBSITES

Library of Congress: http://www.loc.gov

Smithsonian Museum: http://www.si.edu/

Kids Discover: http://www.kidsdiscover.com/

PBS: http://www.pbs.org/

PBS: The New Perspectives on the West: http://www.pbs.org/weta/thewest /program/With background information and other resources for the documentary series

Brooklyn Museum's Art of the Americas Collection, including photos of historic Native American clothing and artifacts: https://www.brooklynmuseum. org/opencollection/arts_of_the_americas

History Colorado website, with links to museums and historical sites in Colorado, with an online exhibit, and teacher and student resources: http://www.historycolorado.org/educators/online-exhibits-digital-badges

Crazy Horse Memorial website: https://crazyhorsememorial.org/

Native Languages online guide: http://www.native-languages.org/

Little Bighorn Battlefield National Monument website: https://www.nps.gov /libi/index.htm

Sacred Land Film Project: http://www.sacredland.org/

Media and educational materials to deepen public understanding of sacred places, indigenous cultures, and environmental justice

The Wounded Knee Museum website: http://www.woundedkneemuseum.org/

Works Cited

Allington, Richard L., and Peter H. Johnston. 2002. *Reading to Learn: Lessons from Exemplary Fourth-Grade Classrooms.* New York, NY: Guilford Press.

Anderson, Richard C., and P. David Pearson. 1984. "A Schema-Theoretic View of Basic Processes in Reading Comprehension." In *Handbook of Reading Research,* Vol 1. Edited by P. David Pearson, R. Barr, M.L. Kamil, and P. Mosethal, 255–91. White Plains, NY: Longman.

Cervetti, Gina N., Carolyn A. Jaynes, and Elfrieda H. Hiebert. 2009. "Increasing Opportunities to Acquire Knowledge Through Reading." In *Reading More, Reading Better.* Edited by E. H. Hiebert. New York, NY: Guilford Press.

Goudvis, Anne, Stephanie Harvey, Brad Buhrow, and Anne Upczak-Garcia. 2012. *Scaffolding the Comprehension Toolkit for English Language Learners.* Portsmouth, NH: Heinemann.

Goudvis, Anne, and Stephanie Harvey. 2012. "Teaching for Historical Literacy." *Educational Leadership* March 2012: 52–57.

Harvey, Stephanie, and Anne Goudvis. 2005. *The Comprehension Toolkit: Language and Lessons for Active Literacy.* Portsmouth, NH: Heinemann.

Harvey, Stephanie, and Anne Goudvis. 2007. *Toolkit Texts: Short Nonfiction for Guided and Independent Practice* (Grades PreK–1, 2–3, 4–5, 6–7). Portsmouth, NH: Heinemann.

Keene, Ellin Oliver, Susan Zimmermann, Debbie Miller, Samantha Bennett, Leslie Blauman, Chryse Hutchins, Stephanie Harvey, et al. 2011. *Comprehension Going Forward: Where We Are and What's Next.* Portsmouth, NH: Heinemann.

Pearson, P. D., Elizabeth Moje, and Cynthia Greenleaf. 2010. "Literacy and Science, Each in the Service of the Other." *Science* April 23 (328): 459–63.

President and Fellows of Harvard College. 2007. *Interrogating Texts: Six Reading Habits to Develop in Your First Year at Harvard.* Available at: http://hcl.harvard.edu/research/guides/lamont_handouts/interrogatingtexts.html.

Read and Annotate

Stop, think, and react using a variety of strategies to understand

ANNOTATING TEXT WHILE READING can be a powerful thinking tool. The practice of responding to the text—paraphrasing, summarizing, commenting, questioning, making connections, and the like—actively engages the reader in thinking about the main issues and concepts in that text. The purpose of this lesson is to encourage students to leave tracks of their thinking so they better understand and remember content information and important ideas.

RESOURCES & MATERIALS

- enough copies of an article for all students

CONNECT & ENGAGE

■ **Ascertain kids' prior knowledge about the text topic.**

Today we are going to read about [topic]. What do you think you know about this? Turn to someone near you and talk about [topic]. *[If the topic is unfamiliar, we project or post one or two images on the topic and allow all kids to engage in a discussion through observation and questions.]*

MODEL

■ **Show readers how to annotate thinking.**

When we annotate a text, we leave tracks of our thinking in the margins or on Post-its. I'll read a bit of the text out loud and show you my inner conversation, the thinking I do as I read. I'll annotate by taking notes to leave tracks of that thinking. These tracks allow me to look back so I can remember what I read and fully understand it. *[We read the beginning of the text out loud, stopping occasionally to ask kids to turn and talk about their own thinking and to model the following close reading strategies.]*

- Stopping to think about and react to information
- Asking questions to resolve confusion or to consider big ideas or issues
- Paraphrasing the information and jotting our learning in the margin
- Noting the big ideas or issues
- Inferring to fill in gaps in information in the text
- Bringing in prior knowledge that furthers understanding

GUIDE

▪ **Monitor kids' strategy use.**

[After reading a paragraph or two, we turn this over to the kids by asking them to read and annotate in pairs.] Now I want you to take over jotting your thinking on your copy of the article—or on Post-its if you prefer. I'll continue reading the text and stop to let you turn, talk, and jot down your thoughts. *[As we pause in the reading, we circulate among the kids to check to see if and how they are using the strategies we modeled and if they are coming up with their own thoughts and annotations.]*

COLLABORATE/PRACTICE INDEPENDENTLY

▪ **Invite kids to finish the article.**

Now I'll stop reading. Continue to read and annotate the article, either with a partner or on your own.

SHARE THE LEARNING

▪ **Invite kids to share, first in small groups and then as a class.**

When you have finished the article, find two or three others who have finished. Form a group to share out your reactions to the article. Think about the important ideas in the article as well as any issues, questions, or thoughts you have. *[After groups have had time to discuss, ask kids to share out their thinking with the whole class, especially important ideas and questions.]*

FOLLOW UP

▪ Kids might read related articles independently or investigate questions or gaps in information on this topic, continuing to annotate to leave tracks of their thinking.

▪ Inspire kids to assume the role of historians in search of information on a particular topic, locating information online or in print, annotating their thinking as they research, and summarizing what they learned for their cohistorians.

Annotate Images
Expand understanding and learning from visuals

POSSIBLE TEXTS

We select a variety of images on a particular topic that spur purposeful, interesting questions and discussion. The following images can be found with captions in the historical images pages in the book, as well as full size in the image bank. Some possibilities include:

- "Historical Image: Native American Ledger Book Art"
- "Historical image: George Catlin"
- "Historical Image: Annie Oakley"
- "Historical Images: The Cutting of My Long Hair"

VISUAL LITERACY IS CRITICAL TO LEARNING because graphic and pictorial elements often carry or enhance the message in print and digital media. In this lesson, we encourage close viewing and reading using a variety of entry points and aspects of visual images to gain historical information and to further understanding.

RESOURCES & MATERIALS

- a copy of an image for each student (Use the images in the text to be read as well as those from the image bank or other sources.)
- Anchor Chart with three columns headed What We Think We Know, What We Wonder, and What We Infer
- Anchor Chart: Questions to Consider When Viewing an Image

ENGAGE

▪ **Invite students to study and respond to a shared image.**

[We choose one image and provide students with copies of that image or project the image for class discussion.] Look carefully at the detail in this image and really think about what you notice, infer, and wonder about it. Be sure to think about what you already know about this topic to help you understand.

▪ **Chart students' thinking.**

Now turn and talk about what you know, wonder, and infer from the image. Also discuss questions and inferences that the image prompts you to think about. Keep in mind that we are always learning new information, and what we already know may be limited or even inaccurate, so be prepared to change your mind in light of new evidence. After talking, we'll come back together and share out our observations, inferences, and questions. *[We jot kids' thinking on a chart as we share out.]*

What We Think We Know	What We Wonder	What We Infer

MODEL

- Show students how to annotate the image with reactions, inferences, questions, and connections to prior knowledge.

[We use kids' responses to guide our think-aloud and annotate the image with some of the important information we want them to know.] Watch me as I jot down my inner conversation about this image—those are the thoughts that go through my head as I view it. Notice the language I use to jot my thinking—and how I annotate my thoughts right on the copy of the image. I might choose a small part of the image and view it more closely.

As I look at the image, I notice . . . and have a strong reaction to it. I think this is about. . . . When I read the caption here, it tells me more about what this is. Additional text will certainly add more important information. But I respond to the image first, to get a sense of what it's all about. And I ask myself some questions: What is the purpose of this document? What's the purpose of this image? Who created it and why? I can infer the answers to these questions, and I may get them answered when I read on, but I may even need to do further research when I am finished to get a more complete understanding.

GUIDE/COLLABORATE

- Encourage kids to work in pairs to annotate their copies of the image.

Now it's your turn. Choose from among the remaining images and work with a partner to discuss and record your thoughts. Annotate your copies of the image with your own ideas: what you notice, questions you have, connections to your background knowledge. You might want to look back at our original thinking about the image that we recorded on our chart. I'll come around and listen in on your conversations and post some questions you might consider as you annotate your image.

Questions to Consider When Viewing an Image

Who created this and why?

When I looked at this part of the image, I wondered. . . .

What can we infer from this image and other features?

What can we infer from other information we viewed or read?

How do images such as this help us better understand the topic?

SHARE THE LEARNING

■ **Record kids' thinking as they share ideas and questions about the images.**

Come back together now and let's discuss our background knowledge, questions, and inferences. *[We call kids' attention to the* What We Think We Know, What We Wonder, *and* What We Infer *chart we began earlier.]* Do we understand who created these images? Do we now understand some different perspectives on this topic? Turn and talk about how images such as these enhance our understanding of the topic. Did your thinking change after closely viewing these images and talking about them?

FOLLOW UP

■ Find more images for students to choose from that are related to the topic under study. (See the table of contents for the image bank for some possibilities.) Encourage kids to work in pairs or independently to study the images closely, guided by the *Questions to Consider When Viewing an Image* chart. As kids share out what they learned from each of the images, the whole class learns from multiple images.

■ What images or artifacts of today will historians of the future study to learn about us? Invite students to create a time capsule of images—personal photographs, print images, artifacts—and imagine what future historians will infer about our times.

Build Background to Understand a Primary Source
Read and paraphrase secondary sources to create a context for a topic

POSSIBLE TEXTS

Secondary sources that provide background for the upcoming study of a primary source are appropriate for this lesson.

- Background for Dolls Never Appealed to Me, "Growing Up Native American"
- Background for The Trail of Tears, "Forced Removal"
- Background for Colonel Travis' Appeal for Help and Davy Crockett's Journal, "Remember the Alamo"
- Background for Orphan Train Newspaper Accounts and Personal Accounts, "Placing Out"

PRIMARY SOURCES can only be read in historical context. Just like working historians, students with background knowledge about the events, people, and ideas behind a primary source are far better able to interpret and understand it. Historians read secondary sources extensively to get a better understanding of historic events and ideas. Then they use the knowledge they have built to interpret and understand the primary source, ultimately using all sources to arrive at a more robust understanding. This lesson is preparation for Lesson 4; here, students build background knowledge by paraphrasing and getting the gist of secondary sources to prepare for study of a primary source document in Lesson 4.

RESOURCES & MATERIALS

- a copy of a primary source document or artifact to project or show
- several secondary sources related to the time period in which the primary source was created, enough copies for all students
- chart paper

ENGAGE

■ **Define primary source and surface background knowledge.**

[We briefly project a copy of a primary source document.] What you see here is a copy of what is called a *primary source*. A primary source is an original document or artifact that is created at a specific point in history by someone who lived at that time. When we read or study a primary source, it's important to have some context for it—who wrote or said or created it, why was it written or created, and what historical events surrounded it.

This primary source was created by [creator] in [time period]. Turn and talk about what you know about this time period, this person, and what was happening at the time. *[Kids share background knowledge with a partner.]* Let's come back together and share out some of your prior knowledge about this. *[We list some of the ideas and information that kids come up with on a chart for all to see.]*

MODEL

- Demonstrate how to paraphrase and annotate secondary sources to build knowledge about a topic.

To prepare for studying this primary source, we'll be reading two articles about this person/this time period/these events. The articles are known as *secondary sources*; they are nonfiction articles written to inform us about a historical time. We'll use what we learn from reading them to inform our reading of this primary source.

As I read, I'm going to read for the essence of what's happening during this time period, with these people. My purpose is to get the gist—to capture the important events and big ideas to add to my store of knowledge. So I'm going to read a small section of the text, stop and think about it, and then write in my own words what is going on or what I learned from this section.

[We read the beginning of the text aloud.] After reading this part, I'm going to paraphrase, or put into my own words, what happened. I'll write a short phrase or two in the margin about this. Notice how I bracket this section of the text and jot down the gist as I read. From this section, I learned … and I'm thinking this will help me understand our primary source because I now have some historical context for it.

GUIDE

- Continue reading as kids paraphrase information and annotate in the margins of the text.

Now it's your turn. I'll keep reading aloud, but I'll stop to let you turn and talk, annotate your thinking, and write down the gist of this next section of the text. Remember to focus on the most important information and ideas that you think relate to the primary source we're going to read. *[We listen in to partner talk and glance at marginal annotations to make sure kids are getting the point. We then ask kids to share out what they have learned from the reading so far.]*

COLLABORATE/PRACTICE INDEPENDENTLY

- Invite kids to continue reading secondary sources to build background about the time period under study.

[We let students continue independently with the same article or—for more experienced classes—encourage them to choose among additional related secondary sources.] Keep reading about . . . , and continue to paraphrase and annotate in the margins as you read. Note that we don't always have to read sources word by word, but can skim and scan to find the parts that are most helpful to our purpose.

SHARE

■ **Chart students' learning.**

Let's come together and discuss the information we found. We'll write down some of what you discovered as you read to get the gist. Remember, share out what you think will help us most with reading our primary source. I'll add to our list so we can keep this information and these ideas in mind as we read.

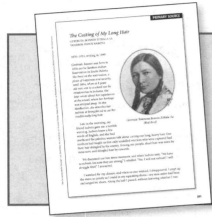

FOLLOW UP

■ Read a primary source that relates to the information that students learned in this lesson. Use Lesson 4 to further support primary source reading.

■ Challenge kids in pairs or teams to summarize—as historians might—the key information behind the topic under study and present their findings to the rest of the class in a creative, memorable format (e.g., art, diorama, poster).

Read and Analyze a Primary Source
Focus on what you know and ask questions to clarify and explain

POSSIBLE TEXTS

Any primary source document related to a time period or topic under study is suitable for this lesson. Some of the primary sources included in this collection are:

- "George Catlin's Account"
- "Land Cannot Be Sold"
- "Trail Dairies of Amelia Knight"
- "This I Believe" and "I Will Fight No More Forever"

PRIMARY SOURCE DOCUMENTS can offer unique insights into the time period students are studying, but they often present significant reading challenges. Created in different time periods and for a variety of purposes, these documents are often characterized by unfamiliar formats, arcane language—both archaic or unusual vocabulary and unfamiliar or difficult sentence structures—and content beyond the experience of today's reader. This lesson offers a strategy for approaching the reading of primary source documents. It is important to do Lesson 3 to build a historical context before we ask kids to analyze a primary source, because students need a great deal of background knowledge about the topic at hand. We would not consider having them read a primary source cold without any knowledge of the historical context.

RESOURCES & MATERIALS

- a primary source document, enough copies for every student
- Anchor Chart: Reading Primary Source Documents

CONNECT & ENGAGE

■ Review the definition of primary source.

For a while we've been studying about [time period], right? So we already know a bit about it. One way to understand even more about that time is to read *primary source documents*. Who can remind us what a primary source is? [*We let students share their background knowledge and define primary source as "information—an original document or artifact—created at a specific point in history." They should know this from the previous lesson.*]

It's important to have a good deal of background knowledge about the people and events of the time period before tackling a complex primary source because these documents often have words and expressions that we don't use today. We call this arcane language. It's common for readers to come to an unfamiliar word or an idea and get stuck. Even if we read on to clarify understanding, reading on in a primary source sometime leads to even more confusion because there are so many unfamiliar words and concepts.

MODEL

■ **Explain a strategy for reading a primary source containing arcane language.**

Let's take a look at this example of a primary source document. I'll read aloud the first couple of sentences. *[We read aloud enough to give kids a taste of the language.]* Wow. Pretty hard to understand, isn't it? That's why when we read primary sources we usually need to read it several times to make sense of it and get the right idea. However, just reading it over and over doesn't help. We need to read it closely and use strategies to understand what we don't know. We particularly need to think about any background knowledge we already have.

Have you ever come to a word or an idea you didn't understand when you were reading? Turn and talk about a time you remember that happening and what you did to understand what you were reading. *[Kids turn and talk and share out a few examples of ways they figured out difficult words and language.]*

One of the best ways to understand a primary source with a lot of unfamiliar words and ideas is to focus on what we *do* understand the first time we read it, perhaps think about what we have already learned about the content. Too often we get stuck on an unfamiliar word and that's it. So we focus on what we *do* understand the first time we read it and get a general idea of what the source is mostly about. Then when we reread it, we think about our questions and address those.

■ **Model how to write notes on what you know and questions you wonder about.**

OK, so let's try it. *[We read a paragraph of the document.]* As I read this part of the document the first time, I don't have a clue what this word means, so I am not going to try to read it over and over. But I do understand this one, because I have some background knowledge about it. I can tell that the writer must have meant . . . when writing this. Thinking about what I know helps me get through this difficult text. So although there are quite a few words here that I do not understand, I can at least begin to get an idea of what this is mainly about by focusing on what I know. I'll also jot down any questions I have. We will get more information when we read this again.

So here is an Anchor Chart with some guidelines to help as we read primary sources. *[We review the process for each of the readings outlined on the Anchor Chart and then use the beginning of our document to model the first step. As we model, we make clear that any annotations focus on what we understand and on questioning difficult parts.]*

Reading Primary Source Documents

Reading #1: Focus on what you know. Annotate the text with what you do understand and ask questions about what you don't.

Reading #2: Use what you have come to understand to figure out the answers to your questions and infer the meaning of puzzling parts.

Successive Readings: Fill in the gaps by noting previous annotations, asking and answering questions, and making inferences for a more robust understanding.

GUIDE/PRACTICE INDEPENDENTLY

■ Monitor kids' primary source strategy use as they continue on their own.

Now work in pairs to think through this primary source document. Continue reading it with a partner, thinking about what you already know to understand new information. Annotate any important ideas you understand and write questions about the parts you need to come back to figure out. *[We circulate to make sure students can actually annotate and make progress with the text, pulling them back together to tackle it as a group if not.]*

SHARE THE LEARNING

■ Call kids together to pool their knowledge and questions.

Let's get together and share our learning and our questions. *[We go back through as much of the document as students have read, noting our understandings, answering each other's questions, and making a chart of the questions we want to figure out in the next reading.]*

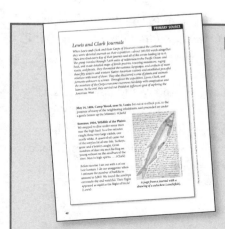

FOLLOW UP

■ The first reading of primary sources that contain particularly arcane language might take more than one session to finish. Give kids plenty of time to discuss things they understand. On subsequent readings, go back and model the process of reading for answers to questions and using known information to make inferences about the time period and the document's meaning.

■ Involve kids in a reenactment—either dramatizing or creating a tableau— of the creation of the primary source.

Compare Perspectives

Explore the different life experiences of historical figures

POSSIBLE TEXTS

This lesson requires texts that reflect varying perspectives on the same event or time period. The following articles and primary source text deal with the experiences of different women on the trail.

- "Women's Voices from the Trail"
- "Primary source: Trail Diaries of Amelia Knight"
- "Tabitha Brown: Determined to Go West"
- "Quilts: Stitching Stories"

WHEN WE LEARN ABOUT HISTORICAL EVENTS or a time period, it is important to understand that historical time from a variety of different perspectives. History is very much about the "untold stories" of people whose perspectives and experiences may not get top billing in the history books and that too often go unrecognized. But history is about all of us, so an important goal of this resource is to include voices, people, and perspectives that can provide kids with a fuller understanding of historical times and the people who lived in those times. The purpose of this lesson is to provide students with opportunities to compare and contrast life experiences of people living in this period so as to better understand their perspectives.

RESOURCES & MATERIALS

- images of different people within a particular time period
- chart paper
- a three-column chart and matching Thinksheets for each student: Person/Experiences & Perspective/My Thinking
- articles reflecting different experiences of several people

CONNECT & ENGAGE

▬ Introduce the idea of different perspectives.

[We post images of different people of the times—children, women, and men, for example.] Let's take a look at these different people. Turn and talk about what you notice about these pictures. Who do you see? What do you think you know about some of these people? Who is not here?

Even though all these people lived at the same time, let's consider how they might have experienced life in these times. Who has some background knowledge or some ideas about this? *[We record kids' background knowledge and thoughts on a chart, guiding them to understand that each person pictured experiences life in a different way.]*

We're going to read a variety of different articles today and compare and contrast the lives of different people who lived in this time period. We'll consider what might be similar about peoples' lives and what might be very different. Let's read part of one account together and then you'll read another account with a different perspective with a small group.

MODEL

■ **Record text evidence reflecting a person's experiences and perspective in a historical time.**

[To prepare kids to compare and contrast different perspectives later in the lesson, we model how to think about a historical figure's experiences.]
I'm going to read this article that is written from the perspective of [person or people]. The authentic information here shows us what these people's lives were like.

I'll begin by identifying who this is about and then read this account aloud. I'll read to find out what important experiences he or she had and how these shaped the person's perspective, or point of view. Using evidence from the text and perhaps the historical record, I'll also jot down my thinking about their experiences and point of view. I can organize my thinking on this chart:

Person	Experiences & Perspective	My Thinking

GUIDE

■ **Guide pairs to jot down text evidence for important aspects of a person's experience.**

[We hand out a three-column Thinksheet—Person/Experiences & Perspective/ My Thinking—to each student.] Now I'll keep reading and ask you to work with someone sitting near you to ferret out more of these peoples' experiences as well as their perspectives on the times. You and your partner can discuss this and also record your thinking. Remember, the thinking column includes your interpretations and inferences as well as your questions from your reading.

COLLABORATE/PRACTICE INDEPENDENTLY

■ **Ask kids to work in small groups to study other historical people.**

Now choose another article about a different person living in this same time period. Get together with three or four friends who are interested in the same article and record your thinking on your Thinksheets. As you read, think about how your historical characters' experiences affected their points of view, their perspectives on the times. Be sure to tie their experiences and perspectives to the text and also include your thinking.

SHARE THE LEARNING

■ Invite students to talk about and compare historical people and compare them to others.

[Once students have surfaced a variety of perspectives, we reconvene the group to compare and contrast the different lives of the people they read about.] Now let's talk about the historical people in your articles. We consider how their experiences influenced their view of the world, and how people differ based on these life experiences. *[Kids love to work big, and large posters can be very helpful for sharing out the experiences/evidence information that kids have gathered.]*

Questions to guide sharing:

• What experiences did your person have?
• How did this person's experiences shape his or her perspective?
• How are his or her experiences like or different from other people we read about?
• Do you think this person's life experiences and perspective might have been, to some extent, "unrecognized" in general historical accounts of these times?
• Discuss why his or her perspective and life experiences are important to an understanding of people of this time period.
• Why do you think it might be important to consider a lot of different experiences and perspectives when studying history?

FOLLOW UP

■ Provide additional groups of articles organized to highlight different viewpoints and perspectives on the same time period and engage students in comparing and contrasting different views.

■ Ask students each to assume the role of a historical character they have read about. Put two or three different characters together and prompt them to discuss an event or condition of their time from the perspective of their character: What do you think about . . . ?

■ Encourage students to conduct independent research on a lesser-known historical figure and craft a biography and portrait.

Read Critically
Consider point of view and bias

As we read historical sources, it is important to read with a critical eye and a skeptical stance. Some articles provide balanced, "objective" information on a topic or issue. Several different perspectives and points of view are represented. Other articles may be written from a specific point of view with a definite perspective or even bias. Many articles fall somewhere in between. One way to support kids to become questioning readers is to show them how to discern the purpose of the sources they read. In this lesson, we help kids surface the author's intent and discuss why the article was written.

POSSIBLE TEXTS

This lesson is best taught with articles or primary source texts that have specific and clearly different points of view.

- "Battle of Little Bighorn Newspaper Account"
- "I Will Fight No More Forever"
- "A White Man's Name"

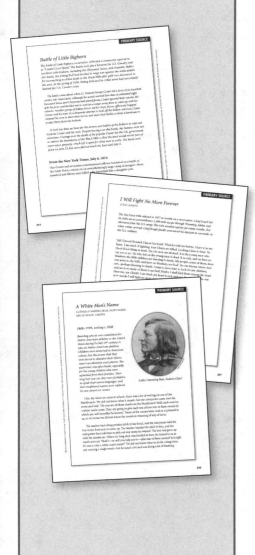

RESOURCES & MATERIALS

- Anchor Chart: Considering Point of View and Bias
- copies of two articles and historical images representing different perspectives on the same person, event, or time

CONNECT & ENGAGE

■ **Introduce questions that explore purpose, point of view, and bias.**

[We project or share a copy of an article and discuss the title and its author. We pose questions to prompt kids to think about the point of view.] Before we read an article, it is helpful to discern whether the intent of the article is to be objective and offer information from several points of view or if it is written from a particular perspective. We ask ourselves questions like these.

Considering Point of View and Bias

- What is the author's purpose for writing the article? Is it written to inform us about a topic? To persuade us to have a particular opinion or view? For some other reason?

- Are several points of view or perspectives on the topic expressed? Or is there just one?

- What is the source of the information in the article or image?

- Can we detect any bias given the ideas in the article and the sources the author used to write the article?

Turn and talk about some of these questions. *[Kids do.]* This last question asks about bias. Who can tell me what *bias* is? *[We discuss the term* bias *and define it as "a preference or prejudice," noting that it usually refers to a point of view that doesn't recognize opposing or balanced views.]*

MODEL
■ **Read and think aloud to uncover the author's point of view.**

[We hand out copies of an article to each student and read the beginning aloud, keeping in mind the questions posed on the chart. We think out loud about both the information and the point of view to begin to uncover the author's purpose for writing the article.] The author of this article is writing about [historical events]. Based on what's happening here, it sounds like the author has some strong feelings and a definite perspective. Now that I read on, I learn that the information we have about these events comes from [source of information]. The actual words make me think. . . .

From the information the author includes and the sources he or she references, I'm thinking the author may be biased. That's what I think so far.

GUIDE
■ **Guide students to read with a critical eye and a skeptical stance.**

Now I'll keep reading. While I do, keep our questions in mind *[We reference the* Considering Point of View and Bias *Anchor Chart.]* and jot notes in the margins of your copy. What's the point of view? Can you detect any bias? What does text evidence tell you about the article's purpose?

PRACTICE INDEPENDENTLY
■ **Invite students to finish the article independently and/or read a second article with a different point of view.**

Go ahead and read the rest of the article, jotting your notes in the margins. Keep our list of questions from the chart in mind.

SHARE THE LEARNING
■ **Listen in on small-group sharing.**

Join together with two other people and share out your thinking about the questions on the *Considering Point of View and Bias* Anchor Chart. Did you all come to the same conclusions? What are some different points of view that you noticed? Why do you think people believed the way they did? How did their personal experiences affect their point of view?

FOLLOW UP

- Provide kids with pairs or groups of articles, images, or combinations of both that depict the same event. Encourage them to compare these, focusing on the perspectives of their creators.

- Create a dramatic interpretation of a scene from the life of a particular person. Keep in mind the point of view of each character as you write the scene.

Organize Thinking
Create a question web

KIDS' HISTORICAL THINKING often begins with their authentic questions. We encourage kids' curiosity and engagement in history by keeping a list of their questions as we find out more about a topic or time period. We add to our knowledge of the topic as we find answers and create a list of lingering questions for research and investigation. This lesson suggests ways that students can organize questions for further study.

RESOURCES & MATERIALS

- an article containing illustrations, photographs, or other images as well as text that will stimulate students' questions
- a board or chart on which to create and display a question web
- a collection of articles on a variety of related topics

ENGAGE

■ **Let kids know that their own questions are the most important ones.**

Sometimes when I read about an unfamiliar topic or learn new information, I find myself asking a lot of questions. Sometimes I ask questions to help me fill in gaps in my knowledge or explain something I don't understand. Other times I wonder what might have happened if circumstances were different, so I might ask, "What if . . . ?" or "What might have happened if . . . ?" Sometimes my questions go unanswered and require further investigation; we call those *lingering questions*. What I do know is that our own questions really help us dig deeper into a topic and further our understanding.

MODEL

■ **Demonstrate how viewing and reading can prompt questions.**

We're going to do some viewing and reading—and pay special attention to our questions while we do. First, let's take a look at the image in this article. What questions does it raise for you? Next, go ahead and look over the article to see what it's about. Turn and talk about your thinking. Maybe you have some background knowledge or some thoughts about this. *[Kids share out briefly.]*

I'm going to begin viewing and reading. I'm going to stop right here because I already have a question. I'm wondering. . . . I'll jot that down *[I write the question on one of the stems of the question web.]* and keep going. This section of the article leads me to wonder something else. *[Again the question is written on the web.]* As I think about these questions a bigger question comes to mind. I'm going to put that in the middle of what we'll call our *question web*—it's a visual map of our questions. My bigger question goes right in the middle here:

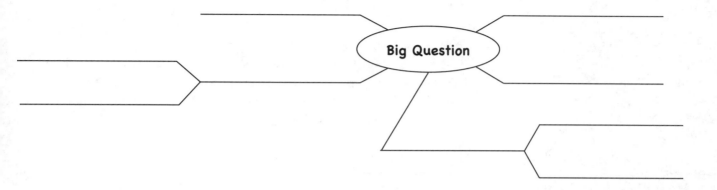

And then as I view and read, I'll add my other questions on stems around it—they are related to the big question—and put related questions near each other.

GUIDE/SHARE THE LEARNING

■ **Read and view together, adding kids' questions to the web.**

[We read on, asking kids to turn and talk to surface their questions.] Let's keep reading and viewing together . . . . Let's stop here. Go ahead and turn and talk about your questions. Jot them on a Post-it so we can share them and add them to our web. *[Kids generate questions and jot these on Post-its. As they share, we have them put the questions on our group question web, guiding them to place related questions near each other.]* These are related to our big question, so we'll place them around our bigger question.

I noticed that as we kept reading, we were able to answer a couple of these questions. I can jot a short answer or response right on the web. It's just a brief thought to capture our thinking.

■ **Share out questions that were answered as well as lingering questions.**

Now that we've finished the article, let's add any final questions to the web. Now go ahead and turn and talk with your partner and discuss if we've discovered some information that provides some insight into our big question. *[We discuss what we've learned about our big question, wrapping up the conversation by identifying lingering questions that remain.]*

COLLABORATE/PRACTICE INDEPENDENTLY

■ Give kids a choice of investigations.

You're going to have a choice for continuing this work. Some of you seem quite intrigued by a couple of these lingering questions—questions that remain after our reading. If you'd like, go online and see if you can find a source or two that might give you some information about your question.

Another option is to read an additional source on a topic you choose. I have a whole bunch of articles right here, so if you'd like to tackle a different article or topic, come on up and peruse these. You can work with a partner, a small group, or on your own, but be sure to pay special attention to your questions. Try organizing them on your own web.

FOLLOW UP

■ Question webs are great investigation starters. Kids often gravitate to questions and topics that matter to them, and researching answers provides the perfect opportunity for students to use their developing repertoire of reading and thinking strategies.

■ Kids love to make their thinking visible. They can create many kinds of visuals—on posters, on the computer, with a collage of images and illustrations—to share the new information they are learning.

Read with a Question in Mind
Focus on central ideas

OFTEN WHEN WE READ to understand big ideas and important information, we read with a question in mind. When we keep one or two focus questions in mind as we read, we can more easily zero in on the information and ideas that are most important to understand and remember.

RESOURCES & MATERIALS

- images related to the topic currently under study, some with labels or captions, others without
- Post-it notes
- copies of an article on the topic for every student
- Anchor Chart, Reading with a Focus Question in Mind, and matching Thinksheets for every student
- a selection of additional articles on the topic

CONNECT & ENGAGE

■ **Engage students in a gallery walk.**

[We post images at different points around the room.] We have placed a variety of images around the room, all of which relate to the article we will be reading. Move around the room, look at the images, and discuss what you notice or wonder with others gathered around each image. After talking, jot down on Post-its any inferences or ideas you have about the image as well as any questions that come to mind. Stick these right on the image. You might put your initials on the Post-its you write so you can keep track of your own thinking.

MODEL

■ **Relate the kids' thoughts about the images they just observed to the topic of the article to be read. Show kids how to read with a question in mind and use a Notes/Thinking scaffold to take notes that will address the focus question(s).**

Did you guess from the pictures in your gallery walk what topic we're going to begin studying today? *[Students name the topic.]* Right! Now, let's take a quick look at this article, its title and features. What is it mostly about? Are there one or two important ideas that stand out? Turn and talk about what you were thinking and wondering about as you looked at the images in our gallery walk. How do your questions and inferences relate to the topic of the article?

■ **Demonstrate how to turn the big idea of the article into a question—one that gets at the big ideas in the article.**

So, from the images and a quick look at the text, I'd guess that one of the big ideas that is important to understanding this time in history is. . . . I can turn this big idea into a focus question and ask. . . . Keeping a focus question like this one in mind will guide us to find out important information about the topic.

[We hand out the Thinksheets and call attention to the matching Anchor Chart.] To keep my thoughts organized, I'm going to write our question(s) at the top of my *Reading with a Focus Question in Mind* page. It has two columns, *Notes* and *Thinking*, because both the information from the article and our thinking about it are important!

Listen and watch as I read and take notes on the article. I'll make sure the information I record relates to the focus question. So in the *Notes* column, I'll write facts and information about our question(s); in the *Thinking* column, I'll jot down what I think about the information—my reactions and responses. Maybe I'll have some additional questions or some background knowledge, all of which I can jot in the *Thinking* column. *[We read the beginning of the article, picking out information that relates to our question, writing it on the chart, and recording our responses.]*

Reading with a Focus Question in Mind

Focus Question: _____

_____

Title: _____

Notes	Thinking

GUIDE

■ **Continue to read the article aloud as kids take notes.**

Now I'll keep reading this article while you take notes. Be sure to keep the focus question(s) in mind, jotting down only information that will help you understand the answers. Remember, including our thinking as we take notes means we'll process and understand the information more thoroughly. *[We continue reading, stopping occasionally to give kids time to turn and talk about the focus question before recording their ideas on the Thinksheet.]*

COLLABORATE/PRACTICE INDEPENDENTLY

- Give kids an opportunity to study related sources, taking notes on and responding to the focus question.

On your own or with a partner, finish reading this article and writing down your notes and thinking about this article. Next, choose one of these other articles or images and continue to think about our focus question. *[We call attention to the images posted for our gallery walk as well as a collection of related articles.]* Does this new source add to your knowledge on this topic? Read it with the focus question in mind and take notes on it.

SHARE THE LEARNING

- Ask kids to discuss the focus question in small groups, summarizing their learning.

[We help kids form groups of three or four, making sure that among the members of the group, they have read several of the articles so they can discuss each knowledgeably.] Let's get into groups to discuss what we have learned about our focus question. Get together with two or three other people; make sure that together you have read and taken notes on several articles and images. Share with your group your learning and thinking about the articles you have read.

After you discuss the focus question using each article, take a look at the questions and inferences you jotted on the images at the beginning of the lesson. How has your thinking changed? What do you know now that you didn't when you first viewed the images? What questions that you asked still linger?

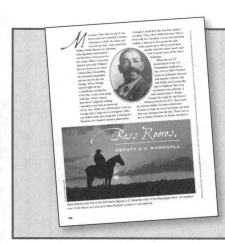

FOLLOW UP

- In small groups, have students do follow-up research to try to resolve any lingering questions. There are many websites rich with historical information; check out the recommended resource list on page xxiv to get started. If their queries are still unanswered, students might try contacting historical museums or other institutions. Researchers are often willing to answer questions, especially those of engaged, curious students.
- Kids love to share their new findings. They can give presentations or create short movies to share the new information they are learning.

Surface Common Themes
Infer the big ideas across several texts

IN REAL-WORLD READING, we rarely read simply one text on a topic. Generally, we read a wide range of texts on a common theme to learn more about it and to understand a variety of perspectives. We infer the big ideas across these various texts to learn more about the overall topic or issue. The purpose of this lesson is to guide students to use evidence from several texts to infer broad historical themes.

RESOURCES & MATERIALS

- two-column Anchor Chart—Evidence from the Text/Big Ideas—and matching Thinksheets for each student
- a set of resources (e.g., an expository article, a piece of historical fiction, and an image) on the same historical topic for each group of three students

CONNECT & ENGAGE

■ **Engage the kids and review what it means to infer.**

Today we're going to interact with several texts on a single topic to get more information. The more texts we read and the more images we view, the more we learn. To better understand the issues and information, we're going to infer the big ideas across several of these texts. Does anyone remember what it means to infer? Turn and talk about that. *[Kids turn and talk and share out some thoughts.]*

Inferring is the strategy we use to figure out information that is not explicitly stated in the text. To infer the big ideas, we need to think about what we already know and then merge our background knowledge with clues in the text to make a reasonable inference and surface some big ideas or themes about the topic or issue. If our inference doesn't seem reasonable, we can gather more clues and information from the text. If we ignore text clues and rely solely on our background knowledge, our inferences could be off the mark. So we're constantly looking for clues, text evidence, and more information to make reasonable inferences and come up with big ideas. Reading a number of articles gives us more background knowledge, which gives us more information upon which to base our inferences.

MODEL

■ **Model how to use text evidence to infer big ideas.**

[We display a two-column chart on which to record evidence and big ideas.] While I'm reading this article, I'll closely read the words, and I'll pay attention to the images and features, searching for clues to help me infer the big ideas. When I find some evidence that supports a big idea, I'll write it on the chart. We can find evidence for big ideas in words, pictures, features, actions, and details that are included in the text. Usually, there are several big ideas that bubble to the surface in an article.

[We read the article aloud, stopping when a big idea or theme is apparent.] I think these words are good evidence for the big idea of. . . . So I'll write the words from the text in the *Evidence* column and the big ideas that I infer in the *Big Ideas* column. Here, these images help me to infer the big idea of . . . , so I'll record information about the images in the *Evidence* column, too. Sometimes I look closely at the character's actions in historical fiction to infer the big ideas. My background knowledge may be helpful here. All of these clues are evidence for the theme of. . . .

Evidence from the Text (words, pictures, features, actions, details)	Big Ideas

GUIDE

■ **Invite kids to come up with text evidence for some big ideas.**

OK, now it's your turn. Let's read a bit together before you go off and try this in a small group. *[We read through a page of text.]* Now that I have read a page, turn and talk about what you think are some of the big ideas here. Look for clues and cite that as evidence for your big ideas. *[Kids share their ideas with a partner.]*

Who has a big idea they would like to share? What is the evidence for that idea?

Let's add to our chart. Sometimes the evidence came from words quoted directly from the text, and other times from pictures and features in the text.

COLLABORATE

▪ **Support kids as they infer big ideas across several texts.**

Now you can get together in groups of three. I have three pieces of text; they are all different, but they focus on the same topic. Since they are grouped around a common topic, they are likely to have some similar big ideas, and all will likely include evidence for those big ideas. As you read through these articles, they will add to your background knowledge, increasing the likelihood that you will make reasonable inferences when you are inferring the big ideas. Share your thinking with each other; note the text clues and the big ideas that occur to you based on your reading and viewing and jot them on your Thinksheets. *[We distribute three related resources to each group and* Evidence from the Text/Big Ideas *Thinksheets to each student.]*

SHARE

▪ **Record kids' evidence and big ideas.**

[We gather kids in a sharing session to talk about their group's big ideas and evidence.] What are some of the big ideas you inferred as you read and viewed? As you share them, I'll add them to the class' *Evidence from the Text/Big Ideas* Anchor Chart.

Did you find some similar ideas across all of the articles and images?

Great thinking about using text evidence to infer the big ideas. We can continue to make inferences beyond the book, especially if there is some good evidence to support them.

FOLLOW UP

▪ Add related resources to the original three and have kids continue to look for corroboration of their big ideas—or for new ones.
▪ Students might create dramatic tableaux to support their inferred themes: a series of frozen scenes carefully crafted to represent evidence of the big ideas.

Synthesize Information to Argue a Point
Use claim, evidence, and reasoning

A GOOD ARGUMENT expresses a point of view, uses information as evidence to support that view, and applies the information to persuade others. To make a good argument, the learner must turn information into knowledge, gathering evidence about the ideas in the text and synthesizing that information to make a claim that will convince others of the validity of the argument. To make a valid claim, however, the arguer must have some background about the issue; before making a claim and sharing the evidence, the claimant needs to have viewed or read several sources on the topic so that he or she knows enough to make a reasonable claim about it. As a result, this lesson on synthesizing information to argue a point is best taught near the end of a unit of study.

RESOURCES & MATERIALS

- several articles on the same topics or with similar themes (some read beforehand)
- three-column Anchor Chart with columns headed Claim, Evidence, and Reasoning and matching Thinksheets for each student
- Anchor Chart: Questions to Guide Effective Arguments

CONNECT & ENGAGE

■ **Invite students to share what they already know about argument.**

How many of you have ever heard the word *argument*? Turn to each other and talk about what you know about arguing. [*Kids turn and talk, then share out, mostly about personal disagreements they have had with others.*] Today we're going to talk about a more formal kind of argument.

■ **Define the term *argument*.**

Have you ever believed in something so much that you have wanted to convince others to agree with you? It is common to feel that way. Sometimes it happens outside when we want to make rules for a new game. Sometimes it happens at home when we are trying to get one more dessert out of Mom. And sometimes it gets a little unpleasant, with people getting mad at each other. Well, the type of argument we are talking about today is about convincing others to see the issue from your point of view. But rather than getting mad and fighting about it, in this kind of argument we gather evidence to make a point and try to convince the other side based on valid information.

So writers make arguments all the time, and they do it without fighting. They share evidence that helps them make their case. They might argue that we should eat healthier foods and support their argument with statistics showing the health risks of eating junk food. Or they might argue that soccer is a safer game than football, and to make their case share information about the danger of concussions that come from getting tackled in football. This kind of argument is based on a claim—that we should eat healthier food or that soccer is a safer game, for example. Turn to each other and talk about something you believe and would like to make a case for or a claim about. Share evidence that would back up your case. *[Kids turn and talk and then share out.]*

MODEL

■ **Read through a piece of text and show students how to use text evidence and reasoning to make and support a claim.**

When we make a claim, we need to provide evidence in support of the claim, valid evidence from a text or other source. And to make a decent argument, we need to know quite a bit about our topic. So we read about the issue or topic a bit and form an opinion. Then we merge the evidence in the text with what we already know to convince others of our claim. So let me show you how it works as I read through this article on. . . . I have an Anchor Chart here with columns headed *Claim, Evidence,* and *Reasoning.* As I read through the article, I'll collect evidence for the claim I'm making and add it to the first column.

Claim	Evidence	Reasoning

I have read a bit on this topic over the past week or so, and I already have a belief or opinion about it that I can turn into a claim. I'll state my claim—that is, the argument that I am going to try to make about the issue—in the first column. *[We write a claim in the first column and continue reading.]*

Here is some evidence for my claim. . . . supports my claim because. . . . I'll jot this in the second column.

Now in the third column, I'm going to show my reasoning—how I interpret the evidence to support my claim. I believe . . . because the evidence shows me that. . . .

It helps that I have learned about this topic beforehand. I already knew . . . from previous readings, so I can reasonably make this claim based on the evidence from this article as well as from my background knowledge.

Reasoning is an important part of this process because if my goal is to make a case for my point of view and convince others, I need to be able to reason through this issue or topic myself in order to understand it well enough to persuade others. And always remember, an argument is not just our opinion, but our point of view supported by evidence.

GUIDE/COLLABORATE

■ **Encourage students to work in pairs to read through an article, make a claim, and support it with evidence and reasoning.**

So it's time for you to give it a whirl. With partners, choose one of these articles on [*the same topic or issue*]. Talk about what you already know about the topic based on the article we just read together as well as other things you've learned. Think about an argument, or claim, you would like to make. Write your claim on your Thinksheet. As you read this additional article, look for evidence that supports your claim and jot that down as well. And talk with your partner about your reasoning.

Think about some of these questions as you reason through the text. [*We display guiding questions and read them aloud.*]

Go ahead and get started. I'll come around and check in with your partnerships as you reason through the text, thinking about your claim and the evidence you find to support it. Remember, if you can't find evidence to fit your claim, you might need to revise your claim to fit the evidence!

Questions to Guide Effective Arguments

- What is my point?
- Who is my audience?
- What might the audience already think about this argument?
- Does the evidence back up my claim? If so, how?
- Which evidence will most likely convince my audience of my claim?
- What would be a good counterargument? Is there evidence to support the other side? If so, what is it?

SHARE

■ **Bring kids back together to share their claims, evidence, and reasoning.**

[*Kids share their forms and we discuss their claims as well as possible counterarguments.*] Whenever we make an argument, we need to be prepared for a counterargument—a claim that contradicts our own. When faced with an opposite opinion, we need to address it with more evidence in support of our own claim or with evidence that disproves the opposite claim.

- This is an introductory lesson on synthesizing information to present an argument. Since making an effective case is a complex process, it requires repeated discussions and practice. So teaching this lesson with a wide variety of issues and articles comprises the next steps.

- Teaching kids to write a paper with a strong argument is an eventual goal. A good resource to support that process is available at the University of North Carolina Writing Center http://writingcenter.unc.edu/handouts/argument. This site will support you as you engage kids in claim-and-evidence writing, although it needs to be adapted for kids younger than college age.

"Sand Creek Memorial"
A Project Created by Karen Halverson

I realized how important it is that we, as educators of history, teach students to question, to strive to understand the past in order to better understand ourselves and the world around us, and thereby empower them to take wise action for the future."

Fourth-grade teacher Karen Halverson describes how she guided her students to connect the past to the present by delving into one of the darkest moments in Colorado history. The Sand Creek Massacre occurred on November 29, 1864, when Colorado Volunteer Cavalry (federal soldiers) attacked Cheyenne and Arapaho who were peacefully camped by Sand Creek in eastern Colorado. Today, the land where these events occurred is a national historic site, the only one in the United States with the word "massacre" in its official name. (See the article, "Sand Creek's Story" on page 236.)

Karen's class had spent weeks immersed in the history of their state. She used a number of the history lessons summarized in this volume as kids read, discussed, and wrote about a variety of nonfiction, historical fiction, and primary sources. This work was foundational and created a more complete historical context that prepared kids to tackle the difficult issues that the Sand Creek Massacre raises even today.

Karen then introduced current speeches, radio broadcasts, and articles that brought the drama, mysteries, complexities, and tragedy of these historic events alive for kids. Too often historical events can seem "far away and long ago." But not this time: the students in Karen's classroom raised their voices about what had happened to people in the past to take action in the here and now.

For a recent article from *Smithsonian Magazine* on the Sand Creek national historic site, see http://www.smithsonianmag.com/history/horrific-sand-creek-massacre-will-be-forgotten-no-more-180953403/?no-ist.

For weeks, we were immersed in our study of Westward Expansion and Colorado history. Students had been reading a variety of texts, viewing images, jotting notes and thinking, discussing events and issues, and writing historical fiction pieces. Our mission was to look at history through a variety of perspectives, consider how these different perspectives affected encounters between native nations, settlers and others, and to continually question, "How do we know what really happened in history?" Alongside all of this, we had been reading aloud *Hard Face Moon* by Nancy Oswald. As they experienced life as a young boy in Black Kettle's tribe, students gained an intimate glimpse into the struggle between Native Americans hoping for peace on the land and soldiers from the Colorado Volunteer Cavalry committed to paving the path of manifest destiny.

On this day, we had reached a pivotal point in Hard Face Moon: the moment of the Sand Creek Massacre. The anticipation was high and the timing was impeccable. As I read, students were riveted, gasping at the horror and injustice, saddened by the bloodshed and loss. It was hard for students to believe that this had happened to innocent Cheyenne and Arapaho people, mainly women, children, and the elderly: "But the white flag of peace flew high alongside the American flag over their camps.... How could they...?" Rich discussion followed and students shared their confusion, questions, and devastation. And then the deep questions were posed: How does this event in history affect us now? What is its relevance now? How does this change how we view the world and choose to be now?

Inviting the native voice into our contemplation of this tragic event, we viewed a video from PBS-Colorado Experience entitled, "Sand Creek Massacre." Descendants of the Arapaho and Cheyenne families who had been at Sand Creek spoke powerfully, reflecting sadly on the past and their hope for healing in the future. As students jotted notes about the gist of what happened and their thinking, these native words lingered and the image of a peace flag waving above tipis was etched into most notebooks and all student minds.

Bringing all of this forward, we watched and listened to Colorado Governor Hickenlooper's 2014 apology to the descendants of Sand Creek, followed by an NPR news segment announcing a proposal for a Sand Creek Memorial to be built in Denver. To better understand the details of this proposal and the arguments for and against it, students read and annotated two NPR news articles and then charted the pros and cons as we understood them. Discussion ignited. "This memorial must be built!" Voices grew

STUDENT PROJECT

Dear Legislators,

I have found that people forget what happened in history, like the Sand Creek Massacre. But people can't forget what happened to the Cheyenne and Arapahoe. After so much suffering from the shock and crisis of the Sand Creek Massacre, a memorial would start to right our wrong, help Native American descendants heal and remind us never to make such a big mistake again.

...The Sand Creek Massacre is remembered in history as "the Battle of Sand Creek". A battle is when both sides are ready to fight. A massacre is when one side is ready and attacks without warning. Colorado needs to remember history more accurately. Also the governor of the time, John Evans, made no attempt to apologize for the Sand Creek Massacre. . . . It was wrong! [Current] Governor John Hickenlooper started us on the path of righting a wrong when he apologized in his 2014 speech to Native Americans for the treachery of the Sand Creek Massacre. A memorial would begin to right our wrong.

...A memorial would remind everyone of the horror of the Sand Creek Massacre but it would also honor Native Americans and show that we care. Other people should care about this because the Native people were almost wiped out. Please reconsider building a memorial so that the next generations recognize the symbol of peace between everyone. Please support going forward with a Sand Creek Memorial.

Sincerely,
Dale

fervent. "Native Americans deserve a stronger apology and the opportunity to heal from this tragedy!" Students wanted to be heard.

In the following days, we prepared to write letters to our legislators. Given topics such as "Sand Creek," "Healing," and "Apology," students fleshed out their thinking and feelings through freewriting. Learning about the structure and craft of a persuasive letter, students drafted heartfelt writing determined to convince others to move this Sand Creek Memorial project forward. Revisions, edits, printed final letters...The excitement grew as students anticipated their voices making an impact on legislators' hearts and minds.

SAND CREEK LETTERS

In these letters, the students provide evidence from history that backs up their advocacy for a memorial for the Sand Creek Massacre by using information and ideas from both historical sources and recent articles and speeches. In a democracy, nothing is more important than kids learning to participate in a public conversation, finding out about something that matters to them, and then synthesizing their thoughts and opinions to take action.

STUDENT PROJECT

Dear Legislators,

I am writing on behalf of building a Sand Creek Massacre Memorial near the Denver State capitol.

What people need to know is that relatives from Native Americans involved in the Sand Creek Massacre still grieve and cry over what happened. I don't think it is right that the whites killed that many Native Americans. So I think that a Sand Creek Memorial should be built. It would help stop the grieving and injustice.

It would help right the wrong, and it would apologize in a proper way....The U.S. government needs to apologize for the Sand Creek Massacre, a descendant from the Cheyenne says. "The tragedy still lives among us."

People should care about the Sand Creek Massacre because a memorial would help end all the grieving that the Native American descendants are having. Please build a Sand Creek Memorial.

Sincerely,
Damian

Dear Legislators,

I am writing to ask you to consider building a memorial for the Sand Creek Massacre. We need a memorial to heal the trauma of this horrible event in history. ....Native Americans taught the pioneers useful things and traded very helpful tools, we couldn't have survived in America without them. A memorial would recognize their helpfulness. It wasn't right for soldiers to come into the peaceful Cheyenne and Arapaho camps and almost kill all of their people. We need to make it right by apologizing and healing ourselves and present day Native Americans. Native Americans in Colorado have said "It seems as if the blood is still spilled on the ground."

Some people in Denver say the memorial is too big, it costs too much and it doesn't match the design of the capitol building. It is not impossible to fix problems about these things. Does the design matter when we almost wiped out a race of people?

If a memorial for the Sand Creek Massacre is built anyone who visits it will feel a sadness for those died and the descendants of those who survived. They will be touched and carry a deep kindness and thoughtfulness about how their words and actions affect others. Everyone, not just Native Americans, will be healed by this memorial. Fighting will stop and a sense of calmness will sweep over everyone like a gust of wind.

Right before the Sand Creek Massacre an American flag and a peace flag were gently waving in the breeze about Black Kettle's tipi as a sign of peace with the white men. Later that day with peace agreements signed and peace flags floating in the breeze, white soldiers still came and attacked the Cheyenne and Arapaho camps. This was wrong and the healing brought by this memorial will bring serenity to all.

Sincerely,

Anna

As we came to the end of our study, I realized how important it is that we, as educators of history, teach students to question what has been accepted as fact, to search for the truth, and to strive to understand the past in order to better understand ourselves and the world around us. When we do all this, we empower children to take wise action for the future.

Library of Congress

PROMISES AND DESTINIES
Westward Expansion

Westward Expansion describes a time of great growth and excitement in the United States. President Thomas Jefferson authorized the Louisiana Purchase in 1803 because he believed that a healthy country depended on the independence and virtue of its citizens, which could best be acquired through owning land and farming. And farmers needed more land than was available in the increasingly crowded Northeast. However, this period of excitement for some was also a time of great conflict, pitting those who felt it was the United States' destiny to expand against those who had lived in North America for thousands of years.

The female figure in the print above portrays America pursuing its manifest destiny, but the native people and the bison seem to be fleeing in the face of what America brings with her.

Since the end of the Revolutionary War (1775–1783), Americans had looked to their future growth. The Northwest Ordinance of 1787 established a process for how territories could become states. It also called for the United States to practice "utmost good faith . . . towards the Indians" who already resided in those areas. But far too often, the U.S. government broke promises and violated treaties in pursuit of its manifest destiny: the belief that the United States had a right and a duty to expand throughout the North American continent.

Many people left their homes in the east and moved west in search of economic opportunities. It was a chance to better themselves and improve their lives. But as eager settlers pushed westward across the Appalachian Mountains, some native groups tried to resist them. They desperately tried to hold on to their traditional territories and ways of life. Shawnee leader Tecumseh led a native confederation to fight against settlements in the Midwest from 1809 to 1813. Others, such as the Cherokee in the Southeast, tried to coexist. But most settlers wanted the best place for themselves. This conflict would increase and become more violent as more tribes found themselves struggling against the huge tide of settlers seeking better lives for themselves and their families.

Soon the government was enacting treaties and acts designed to protect settlers and yet still appease native tribes. The 1830 Indian Removal Act gave President Andrew Jackson authority to move eastern tribes to areas west of the Mississippi River. Five years later, the U.S. government and a faction of the Cherokee people signed the Treaty of New Echota, in which a small group of Cherokees exchanged all the Cherokees' traditional land in the Southeast for land west of the Mississippi River. From 1838 to 1839, the army rounded up about 13,000 Cherokees and forced them to relocate to present-day Oklahoma, about 1,000 miles away. Thousands of Cherokees died on the forced march, which became known as the Trail of Tears.

Moving West

In the mid-1800s, the first wave of emigrants began heading to Oregon and California. The Mexican-American War of 1846–1848 gave the United States the areas of Texas and California, and a treaty with Great Britain gained the territory of Oregon. Settlers heading west saw the Great Plains mostly as something to be crossed, not somewhere in which to settle. Yet pioneer wagon trains involved large numbers of wagons, families, and livestock. They took a toll on the land as they passed through it. And the discovery of gold in California in 1848, Oregon in 1850, and Washington in 1853

May be reproduced for classroom use. *Toolkit Texts: Short Nonfiction for American History, Westward Expansion*, by Stephanie Harvey and Anne Goudvis, ©2016 (Portsmouth, NH: Heinemann).

Fort Laramie was an important trading post in the 1800s and became a primary stopping point on the Oregon Trail. In 1851, chiefs of the main Great Plains tribes met U.S. government agents there and signed a treaty which separated each tribe onto its own reservation.

Passengers and crew shoot buffalo from a train on the transcontinental railroad in the 1870s.
Bison were killed to clear land for the tracks and for sport.

brought more travelers. When native groups began defending their territory, the U.S. government signed the 1851 Treaty of Fort Laramie. It promised to provide money to Native Americans and to restrict the settlement of nonnative people.

But Congress cut the promised aid, and settlers came anyway. The U.S. Army began to build forts along the routes traveled by settlers to offer them aid and protection. This led to a clash of cultures. Native Americans didn't believe land could be owned. Native groups and the animals they depended on roamed freely, and the increasing numbers of farms and ranches limited this ability to wander naturally.

Claiming Land

The Homestead Act of 1862 allowed U.S. citizens to claim 160 acres of unoccupied land west of the Mississippi and east of the Rocky Mountains and ultimately own it for free, providing that they lived on it and made improvements to it for five years. This was especially beneficial for groups like immigrants to the U.S., former slaves, and single women. As settlers arrived and began to claim and

sometimes clear large tracts of land for farming, native people were excluded from their traditional spaces and once-plentiful big-game populations, such as bison, were hard to find.

The Sioux, Northern Cheyenne, and other native groups on the Great Plains grew concerned about the shrinking herds of bison. They relied on these creatures for food, shelter, and clothing. But railroad companies hired men to kill the animals to clear room for the tracks and for sport. They slaughtered millions of animals, taking only the hides and leaving the rest to rot.

Establishing Reservations

With their most important food source disappearing, some native leaders worried about their bands' ability to survive. They moved near forts and signed treaties with the U.S. government. Others fought back and attacked settlers and soldiers. Settlers, on the other hand, wanted safety and protection as they created homes in the new west. In 1868, a government commission sent to address the growing violence in the West recommended that native people be restricted to

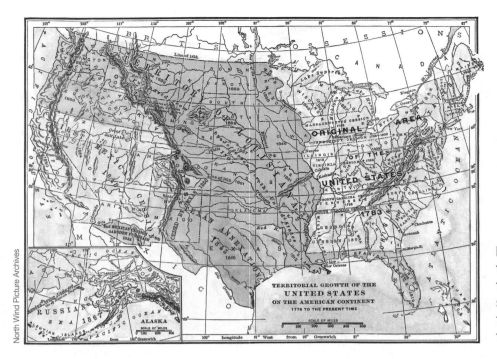

From 1776 to 1899, the United States grew from the original thirteen states, stretching from the Atlantic to the Pacific with each new territory acquired.

May be reproduced for classroom use. *Toolkit Texts: Short Nonfiction for American History, Westward Expansion*, by Stephanie Harvey and Anne Goudvis, ©2016 (Portsmouth, NH: Heinemann).

large reservations, which were tracts of land set aside for Native American groups. In this way, native people could be contained and kept from interacting with emigrants.

In a meeting at Fort Laramie in 1868, the Great Sioux Reservation was set aside for the Sioux. It included all the land in present-day South Dakota west of the Missouri River. The treaty of Fort Laramie also allowed the Sioux to continue to hunt in areas outside the reservation as long as big game was available. And the U.S. government agreed to provide food and other supplies to the Sioux who accepted this arrangement.

But life on the reservation was difficult. The nomadic Sioux, used to roaming freely instead of having permanent homes, were now told to be farmers. However, poor soil, drought, and inadequate resources from the government made farming a losing enterprise. The agents sent to represent the government and distribute food and other supplies were often corrupt and frequently unconcerned about the interests of the native people. The experiences of the Sioux tribe were echoed by other native tribes as they too were pushed off their lands and onto reservations.

Breaking Promises

The U.S. government often failed to uphold its end of agreements with native tribes, such as payments for the land. At times, it decreased or cut back on the promised supplies. And the government never stopped trying to acquire additional portions of native land. By the late 1800s, most Native American groups were living on reservations that represented a fraction of their original territory.

By 1890, the government announced that all of the wilderness of the West had now been explored. Only Utah, Arizona, New Mexico, and Oklahoma were not yet admitted to the union as states. Tribes like the Sioux were struggling to survive in a world that was changing around them. The government's failures to try to understand the native way of life and to keep its promises ultimately led to the Wounded Knee Massacre—the last major act of violence in a century-long effort to push Native Americans out of the way.

Westward expansion helped the United States fulfill what it thought of as its destiny. By 1900, the population of the U.S. had grown from 5 million to 76 million. It was a time that provided opportunities for some U.S. citizens to change their lives, but it was also a time of great conflict. Ultimately, native tribes paid the price of expansion by losing their homes as settlers gained theirs, making it a time of both destinies fulfilled and promises broken.

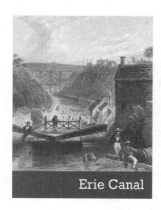

Erie Canal

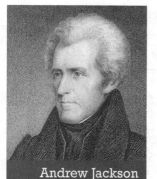

Andrew Jackson

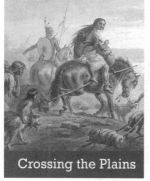

Crossing the Plains

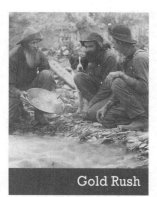

Gold Rush

Erie Canal and Plains: Yale University Art Gallery. Andrew Jackson and Gold Rush: Library of Congress.

1816–1851 U.S. government forces more than 100,000 Native Americans to move from their homelands in the Southeast to an area west of the Mississippi River.

1821 Mexico wins independence from Spain and takes control of the territories of New Mexico and California.

October 26, 1825 The Erie Canal opens, linking New York City to the Great Lakes, and thus the West. This begins a period of rapid canal development in the North and Northwest, revolutionizing domestic trade and transportation.

1828 Andrew Jackson is elected president. He promises to expand the United States westward.

1830 Indian Removal Act becomes law. It gives President Andrew Jackson the power to negotiate with native groups in the South to acquire their lands and move them to territory west of the Mississippi River.

1832 In the case of *Worcester v. Georgia*, Chief Justice John Marshall rules that the Cherokees comprise a "domestic dependent nation" within Georgia and thus deserve protection from harassment. However, the extremely anti-Indian Andrew Jackson refuses to abide by the decision.

November 1835 The Texas rebellion begins when a group of Texan leaders convene to draw up a provisional government and declare independence from Mexico. Shortly after, fighting breaks out.

March 1836 A Mexican force of 4,000 troops lays siege to the town of San Antonio, where 200 Texans resist, retreating to an abandoned mission, the Alamo. After inflicting over 1,500 casualties on Santa Anna's men, the defenders of the Alamo are wiped out on March 6, 1836. The Alamo becomes a symbol of the Texans' determination to win independence.

1838–1839 U.S. government forces Cherokee people to travel 1,000 miles to Indian Territory (present-day Oklahoma) in what becomes known as the Trail of Tears. Around 4,000 of the 16,000 migrating Cherokees died.

February 1845 After James K. Polk becomes President of the United States in January, Congress passes a measure to annex Texas, trusting Polk to oversee Texas' admission more effectively than John Tyler would have.

July 1845 Five months after the United States Congress votes to annex Texas, a Texas convention votes to accept annexation, despite the warning by the Mexican government that any agreement to join the United States will be equivalent to a declaration of war.

December 1845 Texas is officially granted statehood and becomes the 28th state.

January 1848 A carpenter discovers gold at the base of the Sierra Nevada Mountains, sparking a gold rush which brings tens of thousands of new settlers to California, establishing towns and cities.

DID YOU KNOW?
The terms of the treaties between the U.S. government and native groups in the 1800s usually involved the native groups agreeing to give up sections of their traditional land, while the government promised regular payments of money and supplies and access to health and educational services.

By Kathiann M. Kowalski and Marcia Amidon Lusted, *Cobblestone,* © by Carus Publishing Company. Reproduced with permission.

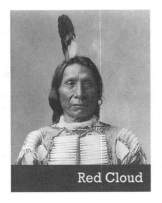

Red Cloud

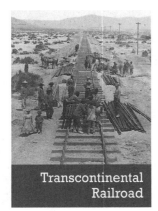

Transcontinental Railroad

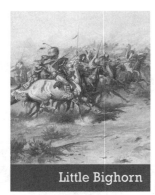

Little Bighorn

Red Cloud and Railroad and Little Bighorn: Library of Congress.

February 1848 At the close of the Mexican War, the Treaty of Guadalupe Hidalgo is signed, ceding Texas, New Mexico, and California to the United States, which now controls land stretching all the way across North America.

September 1850 Under the Compromise of 1850, engineered by Henry Clay, California is admitted to the Union as a free state.

1851 Treaty of Fort Laramie with Sioux, Northern Cheyenne, Arapaho, and other nations promises that permanent settlers will stay out of much of the Great Plains.

1861 Treaty of Fort Wise promises sufficient food if Northern Cheyenne and Arapaho will move to Colorado reservation.

1862 Dakota Sioux chief Little Crow leads uprising in Minnesota. It ends in the mass execution of 38 Dakota men.

1864 Union soldiers attack a peaceful Northern Cheyenne and Arapaho camp in present day Colorado, resulting in the Sand Creek Massacre. About 200 people—mostly women, children, and the elderly—are killed.

1866 Lakota Sioux chief Red Cloud attacks military strongholds that have been built without permission on Sioux land in Wyoming and Montana. Red Cloud's War leads to the defeat of a cavalry force under Captain William J. Fetterman and the abandonment of the Bozeman Trail by the U.S. Army.

1867 Medicine Lodge Treaty moves southern Plains tribes to Oklahoma.

1868 Indian Peace Commission concludes that most of the violence in the West stems from the United States' violations of its own treaties. Treaty of Fort Laramie promises the Sioux permanent control of a large area in the Dakotas, including the Black Hills, as part of the Great Sioux Reservation.

May 1869 The first transcontinental railroad is completed when the Union Pacific and Central Pacific railroads join their tracks at Promontory Point, Utah. The railroad facilitates western settlement, shortening the journey from coast to coast, which took six to eight months by wagon, to a mere one week's trip.

1871 Indian Appropriation Act declares that all native people are wards of the U.S. government. The government no longer recognizes individual tribes as having **sovereign** powers to negotiate treaties.

1874 U.S. military expedition discovers gold in the Black Hills.

1876 Battles of the Rosebud and the Little Bighorn result in the defeat of U.S. Army units by Sioux and Northern Cheyenne forces.

1877 U.S. government seizes the Black Hills and breaks up the Great Sioux Reservation into six smaller areas.

1887 Dawes Act supports native **assimilation** into "American" society.

1889–1890 U.S. government cuts Sioux rations. Sioux people turn to the Ghost Dance movement.

1890 Wounded Knee Massacre results in the death of between 225 and 250 Lakota Sioux men, women, and children.

February 1912 Arizona, the last of the 48 contiguous United States, is admitted to the Union, completing the century-long process of conquering and organizing the American West.

Sovereign means self-governing.

Assimilation is the process of absorbing a group into the prevailing culture.

By Stephanie Harvey and Anne Goudvis, ©2016 (Portsmouth, NH: Heinemann). May be reproduced for classroom use. *Toolkit Texts: Short Nonfiction for American History, Westward Expansion,*

By Marcia Amidon Lusted. May be reproduced for classroom use. *Toolkit Texts: Short Nonfiction for American History, Westward Expansion*, by Stephanie Harvey and Anne Goudvis, ©2016 (Portsmouth, NH: Heinemann).

A Chippewa mother holds her baby in the cradleboard that she uses to carry her safely while she works.

From The New York Public Library

Growing Up
Native American

What was it like to grow up as a Native American? Daily life for children varied depending on where they lived and what tribe they belonged to. Some tribes were nomadic, meaning that they moved from place to place and did not have a permanent settlement. They usually lived in tepees or lodges that could be quickly assembled and disassembled. Others lived in more settled villages. But just as pioneer children had families and communities, Native American children also had their families and extended families, as well as their tribe.

Family Life

Pioneer families at this time might have more than five or six children, but native families tended to have only three or four.

A newborn child was very important to the tribe, and there were often special ceremonies to celebrate births. Children were generally not called by their proper names in everyday life, but instead were referred to by nicknames or relationship names (like "son" or "daughter"). Babies were carried and nursed by their mothers for the first several years of their lives. They were often strapped to cradleboards, which were boards or frames similar to portable cradles, where babies could be fastened in and carried safely. They made it possible for their mothers to do the work they needed to do and still keep their babies close. However, children were also just as likely to be raised by their grandparents as their parents. Extended families lived together, and it made sense for the older members, who might not be able to hunt or look for food anymore, to take care of the children.

Native American children did not attend formal schools. Instead, they were taught by their parents and members of their tribe. They learned not only the everyday skills they needed, such as hunting or cooking, but also the stories, traditions, and histories of their ancestors. Tribal elders told stories that seemed like entertainment but were also a way to pass along this important traditional information. Children learned their everyday skills simply by following their parents around as they performed their daily work. They were also taught to be strong and not to show emotion. They were expected to learn the ways of their tribe and follow them.

Library of Congress

Play and Toys

Even small babies had strings with beads, animal teeth, or rabbit's feet tied above their cradles to give them something to look at and play with. Older children played games that were very similar to blind man's bluff, tug of war, stickball, and hide and seek, as well as holding races. Ball games used balls made of animal skin stuffed with hair or grass, or from an inflated animal bladder. Adults also played games, usually as part of special ceremonies to honor the tribal gods, but sometimes for fun, too. Their games were either games of skill, or games of chance using dice or sticks or that involved guessing. Children also played these games, but boys and girls usually played separately, sometimes with different versions of the rules. Children had toys, too. Girls played with dolls made of animal skin, bone, corn husks, wood, or grass. Creating clothes for their dolls taught girls skills like weaving and bead making. They might have miniature tipis for their dolls. Boys played games that tested their skills and stamina and made them stronger and better warriors. They might also have miniature versions of bows and arrows, fishing equipment, or slingshots.

Rites of Passage

Moving from childhood to adulthood was marked by a ceremony as well. Afterwards, the child was officially an adult and was expected to behave as one. Ceremonies were different for boys and girls, and usually happened at puberty. Some tribes also had a ritual for boys known as the vision quest. Young men would go off into the wilderness alone, without food or drink. They were expected to stay

For this young Cheyenne boy, dressing as a warrior with a small bow and arrow is more than play. The rabbits and other small game he hunts will help feed his family.

By Marcia Amidon Lusted. May be reproduced for classroom use. *Toolkit Texts: Short Nonfiction for American History, Westward Expansion,* by Stephanie Harvey and Anne Goudvis, ©2016 (Portsmouth, NH: Heinemann).

Cheyenne girls played with dolls and tipi dollhouses made by their grandmothers.

there until they had a vision. The vision usually gave them guidance about their new adult life, or provide them with a spirit guide who would be with them from then on. Sometimes they might even foretell the future.

Childhood for Native Americans, just as for other American children, might vary according to where they lived, what climate they had to deal with, and what foods they had to hunt for or harvest. But they shared many common threads: being nurtured by family and community, learning from the adults around them, and being valued and treasured so that they could grow up to be strong and successful adults.

Today, Native American children have educational opportunities similar to other children while still maintaining their culture through powwows and other tribal activities.

Dolls Never Appealed to Me

MOURNING DOVE (CHRISTINE QUINTASKET)
SALISHAN SWHY-AYL-PUB
c. 1885–1936, writing in the 1930s

Native American kids had fun and played like children everywhere. Boys and girls usually played separately. Boys played games that tested their skills and made them stronger and better warriors. Usually, girls played with handmade dolls. But not all girls chose to play with dolls, as this Native American woman remembers from her childhood.

My mother and grandmother made dolls of buckskin stuffed with deer hair, with red seeds for eyes and wisps of horsetail glued on the head for hair, but dolls never appealed to me. I preferred playing with the bows and arrows my father made for me or listening to old men tell stories of warfare and horrible bloodshed. Most of all, I loved my dogs. The village was full of them. They were very ordinary—mongrels, really— but to me they were wonderful, faithful creatures who would follow me everywhere on my play hunts for deer and along imaginary trails.

Portrait of Mourning Dove

For more excitement, we played with calves and horses. Boys would chase a calf that was wild and had never been tied before. They would try to ride it but the back was often wet from sweat, and there was no mane to hold on to. Sometimes they would try to ride a colt. If it became tired and panting, then I could often stay on its back for a short period. When the boys were weary of the animals, they showed off. . . . They would jump paver rails to show off

May be reproduced for classroom use. *Toolkit Texts: Short Nonfiction for American History, Westward Expansion,* by Stephanie Harvey and Anne Goudvis. ©2016 (Portsmouth, NH: Heinemann).

their physical agility. I stood in admiration until the boys began to tease me to join them. I tried to jump the rail but missed and was thrown to the ground, bruising my shins. I choked back tears, afraid my cousins would call me and old woman or crybaby. For many days afterward, however, I practiced until I could briefly ride the colt and calf or beat the boys at the footrace and broad jump. The animals grew accustomed to me, and my muscles were hard and strong by the time I had my own pony.

From an early age, children from Plains Indian tribes grew up on horseback, becoming very skilled riders long before they were teenagers.

The Beliefs of the Plains Indians

Top: Purestock/Getty/HIP. Bottom: The Denver Public Library, Western History Collection, X-31818 (detail).

By Marcia Amidon Lusted. May be reproduced for classroom use. *Toolkit Texts: Short Nonfiction for American History, Westward Expansion*, by Stephanie Harvey and Anne Goudvis, ©2016 (Portsmouth, NH: Heinemann).

The Plains Indian tribes had their own, very complex set of spiritual beliefs, grounded in the world around them: the land, the sky, even the rocks and trees and the animals that they interacted with every day of their lives. Most tribes did not believe in one supreme god or sacred being, except for the Sioux tribe who had *Wakan Tanka*, the "Great Spirit." To the Plains tribes, all the elements of the natural world were connected, and should be respected. Brave Buffalo, a Sioux medicine man, described his childhood experience with discovering his beliefs:

When I was ten years of age I looked at the land and the rivers, the sky above, and the animals around me and could not fail to realize that they were made by some great power. I was so anxious to understand this power that I questioned the trees and the bushes. It seemed as though the flowers were staring at me and I wanted to ask them, "Who made you?"

Sioux medicine man
Brave Buffalo

Nez Perce leader
Chief Joseph

Because the Plains tribes considered all of the land to be sacred, they also did not believe it could be owned by people. Chief Joseph of the Nez Perce tribe said

The Earth was created by the assistance of the sun, and it should be left as it was. The country was made without lines of demarcation, and it was no man's business to divide it.

However, this aspect of their spirituality would be the most difficult one to maintain against the increasing tide of settlers.

Unlike Christianity, which relied on ministers and priests to conduct services, the Plains Indians did not always have a sacred leader. They did sometimes have *wakan* (meaning "blessed"), also called a shaman, who were people whose prayers were thought to have been answered by the Great Spirit. Wakan were thought to possess great powers, especially for healing. They were also the ones to decide when the time was right for hunting.

Plains Indians

Sioux medicine man
Black Elk with his family

Individual tribe members often went on vision quests. They went alone to remote areas to fast and ask for the help of the spirits. If they were successful, they would have a spirit guide to provide help in curing ailments, winning battles, or other important matters of tribal life. A tribe member who was especially respectful and reverent might even gain the future protection of a guardian spirit.

Animals played an important spiritual role as part of the natural world. Among all the animals that these tribes considered to be sacred were the buffalo and the eagle. Buffalo were sacred because they provided everything the tribes needed to survive. Hunting buffalo included religious rituals such as dances, prayers, and other ceremonies that "called" the buffalo to the tribe for hunting. Eagles were considered to be the most sacred of birds, and their feathers were prized, each one symbolizing a good deed by its wearer. Plains tribes also believed in sacred symbols, particularly the circle. Just as the seasons and cycles of life flowed in circles, and the sun itself was a circle, Plains tribes arranged their teepees and villages in circular patterns. Many of their tribal dances and ceremonies took place in circles as well. Black Elk, a member of the Oglala Sioux, described the power of the circle:

> You have noticed that everything an Indian does is in a circle, and that is because the Power of the World always works in circles, and everything tries to be round. The sky is round, and I have heard that the earth is round like a ball, and so are all the stars. The wind, in its greatest power, whirls. Birds make their nests in circles, for theirs is the same religion as ours. The sun comes forth and goes down again in a circle. The moon does the same, and both are round. Even the seasons form a great circle in their changing, and always come back again to where they were. The life of a man is a circle from childhood to childhood, and so it is in everything where power moves.

The Plains Indians drew their spirituality from the patterns of the world around them and the natural resources that once made their lives possible. The coming of settlers to the Plains not only made the traditional ways of life difficult or impossible, but also undermined those natural landscapes and cycles that made up the core of these tribes' most sacred beliefs.

By Marcia Amidon Lusted. May be reproduced for classroom use. *Toolkit Texts: Short Nonfiction for American History, Westward Expansion*, by Stephanie Harvey and Anne Goudvis, ©2016 (Portsmouth, NH: Heinemann).

Native American Ledger Book Art

The Plains Indians recorded their side of the story of the conflict between Native Americans and the U.S. government from the mid-1800s through the early 1900s. They did this in pictures, not words.

Plains ledger art was a continuation of the traditional practice of using images to record important knowledge and events, including successes in hunting and war. These images—pictographs on rock walls and mineral-pigment painting on buffalo hides—also documented oral storytelling. Symbolic narratives painted on tipis, buffalo robes, shields, and other clothing and objects were easily understood by all who viewed them.

Beginning in the mid-1800s, as the buffalo were being slaughtered and new drawing materials were available to Plains warrior-artists for the first time, the pictorial tradition found a new form. Native Americans used storekeepers' ledger and accounting books and other types of paper from traders, settlers, military officers, missionaries, and U.S. government agents instead of buffalo hides. With pencils, crayons, fountain pens, and occasionally watercolors, the traditional imagery was continued with new materials.

(continued on next page)

Native American Ledger Book Art (continued from previous page)

Most early ledger art showed battles and hunting, but as the buffalo disappeared and the Plains tribes were increasingly confined, the drawings began to focus more on personal experiences and daily life. Once only created by warrior-artists, women also began creating ledger art.

Early ledger drawings were collaborative: one artist may have created the first drawings, but the books were often passed around and others added their own depictions of the same event. Sadly, the full record in early ledger drawings was lost as art dealers removed pages from bindings to be sold individually.

Yale University Art Gallery

Attacking the Grizzly Bear (1844) by George Catlin

George Catlin

George Catlin (July 26, 1796–December 23, 1872) was an American painter and author who specialized in portraits of Native Americans. Catlin completed law school and briefly practiced law, but then became a professional artist. After seeing a delegation of Plains Indians in Philadelphia while traveling with his friend, explorer William Clark, Catlin decided to dedicate his life to recording the lives and customs of Native Americans. He traveled extensively throughout North America in the 1830s, visiting fifty tribes between 1830 and 1836. Two years later, he ascended the Missouri River to Fort Union, where he spent time with the eighteen tribes, including the Pawnee, Omaha, and Ponca in the south and the Mandan, Cheyenne, Crow, and Blackfeet in the north. There, at the edge of the frontier, he created the most vivid portraits of his career. After later trips along the Arkansas, Red, and Mississippi Rivers, as well as visits to Florida and the Great Lakes, he created over 500 portraits and collected artifacts. Catlin kept detailed records of his journeys.

(continued on next page)

The Snow-shoe Dance (1844) by George Catlin

George Catlin (continued from previous page)

Catlin returned to the east coast in 1838 and assembled his paintings and numerous artifacts into his Indian Gallery. He began giving public lectures about his observations and recollections of life among the Native Americans. Catlin traveled with his Indian Gallery to major cities, such as Pittsburgh, Cincinnati, and New York.

Catlin hoped to sell his Indian Gallery to the U.S. government so that his collection would be preserved. Unfortunately, he failed to persuade officials in Washington, D.C. He was forced to sell the original Indian Gallery, now 607 paintings, due to personal debts in 1852. Today, nearly all of the original Indian Gallery are housed at the Smithsonian American Art Museum's collection. Another 700 sketches are in the American Museum of Natural history in New York City.

George Catlin's Account

George Catlin was an artist who was determined to record as much of culture of the native peoples as possible. Catlin made several trips to the West and lived with different tribes, recording their lives in paintings, drawings, and in writing. Some of the tribes of the Great Plains had originally lived in the East and were pushed westward by the migration of settlers. Others, like the Sioux and Crow, had lived on the prairie for years. Members of these tribes were expert horsemen who lived by hunting huge herds of bison that roamed the Great Plains. The herds in 1850 were estimated at as many as fifty million animals. In this account, Catlin describes the hunting and fighting skills of the Plains Indians.

c. 1836

Amongst their feats of riding, there is one that has astonished me more than anything of the kind I have ever seen . . . in my life: a stratagem of war, learned and practiced by every young man in the tribe; by which he is able to drop his body upon the side of his horse at the instant he is passing, effectually screened from his enemies' weapons as he flies in a horizontal position behind the body of his horse, with his heel hanging over the horse's back. . . . In this wonderful condition, he will hang whilst his horse is at fullest speed, carrying with him

his bow and his shield, and also his long lance of fourteen feet in length, all or either of which he will wield upon his enemy as he passes; rising and throwing his arrows over the horse's back, or with ease and equal success under fire horse's neck. . . . A Sioux, even firing from horseback can drive an 18 inch arrow completely through the neck of a bison. In warfare, according to U.S. Army Colonel Hastings, an Indian on horseback has no equal in fighting ability. An Army trooper must reload after each shot. During that time his Sioux opponent can fire a total of eight arrows.

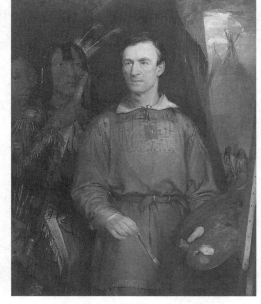

*Portrait of George Catlin
by William Fisk*

The Sacred Buffalo

By Marcia Amidon Lusted. May be reproduced for classroom use. *Toolkit Texts: Short Nonfiction for American History, Westward Expansion*, by Stephanie Harvey and Anne Goudvis, ©2016 (Portsmouth, NH: Heinemann).

Historians estimate that hundreds of thousands of American bison, also known as the American buffalo, lived on the American Plains in the mid-19th century.

AT ONE TIME, hundreds of thousands of buffalo roamed the Plains of North America. And to the Plains Indian tribes, the buffalo was not simply an animal that inhabited their landscape, and which they hunted purely for food. The buffalo was a sacred animal. They were considered to be a gift from the spirits because they provided tribes with everything they needed to survive: food, clothing, shelter, and other basics. The Plains Indians used every part of the buffalo, wasting nothing. Raw buffalo hides were used to make shields, ropes, saddles, moccasins, buckets, and drums. Tanned buffalo hides were used to make tipi covers, robes, and bags. Buffalo stomachs were used as containers for holding water. Bones, horns, and hooves were used to make utensils, cups, and tools. Buffalo dung was used as fuel for fires. Many tribes' movements followed the movement of buffalo herds throughout the seasons.

Because buffalo were so important to them, the Plains tribes developed many methods for hunting them. A hunter might dress up in a buffalo hide or a wolf skin and slowly move close enough to a buffalo to be within range of an arrow. Hunters might also drive the buffalo into a canyon or other enclosure, or onto thick snow or soft ice, to make them easier to kill. Another inventive method was to entice the buffalo onto a high bluff or cliff and then drive them over the edge. The animals that fell and were injured could be quickly killed. This kind of hunt required many members of the tribe to work together. A mature buffalo could yield as much as 400 pounds of meat for the tribe's consumption.

The U.S. government allowed the large scale hunting of bison by white hunters and settlers because it allowed ranchers to graze their cattle on the prairies without competition from the bison. It also deprived the Plains tribes of their food source, slowly forcing them to leave their traditional lands and relocate to—and remain on—reservations. The market for buffalo robes and buffalo hides was also an incentive to hunters to

Artist and writer George Catlin lived and worked among the Plains Indians. This painting, created in 1832, shows how Native Americans disguised themselves as wolves to hunt the buffalo.

Yale University Art Gallery

kill buffalo. The railroads also encouraged hunting, since buffalo stuck on the tracks could damage locomotives. During cold weather, herds also took refuge in the passages cut through steep grades, often blocking trains and causing days of delay. By 1884, the American buffalo was close to extinction, and with it, the traditional Plains Indians way of life.

Karl Bodmer was another artist who captured the American West with his drawings and paintings. These drawings show Native American tools and weapons, many made with buffalo hide.

The Vore Buffalo Jump

In the early 1970s, engineers preparing to build an interstate in Wyoming discovered large quantities of buffalo bones and projectile points buried deep in the ground. The interstate was moved and archaeologists began excavating the site. They determined that the site was massive: bone and cultural artifacts extended throughout the area almost 200 feet in diameter. Historians believe that Native American hunters stampeded bison into the pit, which was deep enough to kill or injure the animals that were driven into it. The Vore site was used as a kill and butchering site from about 1500 to about 1800. About ten tons of bones were removed from the site, whose pit is estimated to contain the remains of 20,000 buffalo.

By Marcia Amidon Lusted. May be reproduced for classroom use. *Toolkit Texts: Short Nonfiction for American History, Westward Expansion*, by Stephanie Harvey and Anne Goudvis, ©2016 (Portsmouth, NH: Heinemann).

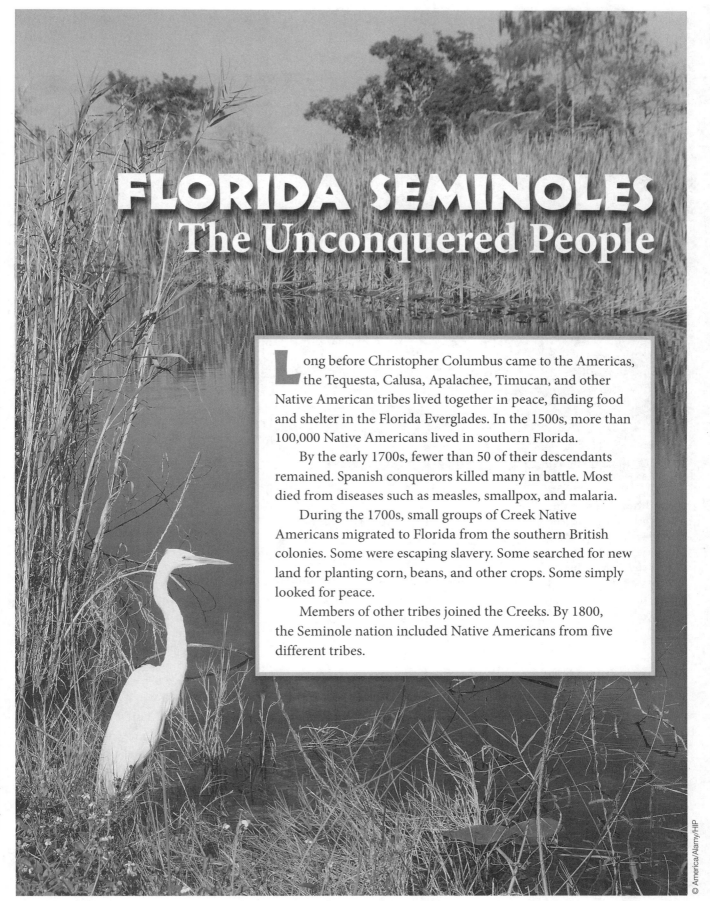

FLORIDA SEMINOLES
The Unconquered People

Long before Christopher Columbus came to the Americas, the Tequesta, Calusa, Apalachee, Timucan, and other Native American tribes lived together in peace, finding food and shelter in the Florida Everglades. In the 1500s, more than 100,000 Native Americans lived in southern Florida.

By the early 1700s, fewer than 50 of their descendants remained. Spanish conquerors killed many in battle. Most died from diseases such as measles, smallpox, and malaria.

During the 1700s, small groups of Creek Native Americans migrated to Florida from the southern British colonies. Some were escaping slavery. Some searched for new land for planting corn, beans, and other crops. Some simply looked for peace.

Members of other tribes joined the Creeks. By 1800, the Seminole nation included Native Americans from five different tribes.

Traditional Seminole cultural, religious, and recreational activities are dependent on a healthy Everglades ecosystem.

May be reproduced for classroom use. *Toolkit Texts: Short Nonfiction for American History, Westward Expansion,* by Stephanie Harvey and Anne Goudvis, ©2016 (Portsmouth, NH: Heinemann).

Soon enslaved Africans began escaping from their owners to the safety of Seminole territory. They knew that the Spanish government would not allow the slave owners to enter Florida and recapture them. (Florida was not yet part of the United States.)

The Seminoles welcomed the African newcomers, teaching them the skills they needed for survival in the Everglades. Close friendships grew among the Africans and Seminoles. Within a few decades, these "Black Seminoles" were part of the Seminole nation.

Seminole hunters now used muskets to hunt deer, turkeys, alligators, and other game. Men also fished and trapped. Women grew corn, sugar cane, guava, and bananas on small, well-tended fields. Older children watched small herds of horses and cattle. Young children and the elders who cared for them spent their days gathering wild fruits, nuts, and berries.

As the population of the young United States grew, pressure to take over the Native Americans' land became stronger. Thousands of Seminoles were forced to leave

WHO NAMED THE SEMINOLES?

Some scholars think that the term came from the Spanish word *cimarron*, meaning "wild." Another story traces the origin back to the first inhabitants of the Everglades. Descendents of the ancient Tequesta tribe merged with members of the Creek tribes who fled to Florida during the Creek War of 1813–14. These *yat'siminoli*, or "free people," fought Spanish and English attempts to take their land and destroy the tribe.

their homes during the three Seminole wars of the early 1800s. By 1842, only a few hundred Seminole men, women, and children remained in Florida. They stayed hidden deep in the swamplands of the Everglades.

For several decades, these "Unconquered People" lived off the land. Their only contact with the outside world came from rare visits to trading posts. There they exchanged egret plumes, alligator hides, patchwork clothing, and beaded jewelry for flour, sugar, cotton cloth, ammunition, and other supplies. The 20th century brought many changes to the Seminole nation. As Florida's population grew, they had more contact with people of different cultures. Seminoles changed their lives to live peacefully with their new neighbors.

Today, more than 2,000 descendents of the original "Unconquered People" live on six reservations in Florida. Tourism, cattle, and citrus groves have replaced their early 20th-century trade in animal hides and crafts. Museums and stores around the world display the rich patterns of Seminole patchwork and jewelry.

Today's 21st-century Seminoles work to preserve their Everglades homeland as well as the ways of their ancestors. Some still live in **chickees** and wear clothing adapted from traditional styles. Ancient tribal ceremonies, dance, and music celebrate the passing of the seasons. The heritage of an unconquered people living free and proud within their Everglades home remains within the spirit of every Seminole alive today.

> To **conquer** means to "win a battle or war."
>
> **Unconquered** means "unbeaten."
>
> A **chickee** is a shelter supported with posts with a raised floor and thatched roof.

A Seminole village with several chickees, traditional houses made of thatched palmetto and a cypress frame.

North Wind Picture Archives

May be reproduced for classroom use. *Toolkit Texts: Short Nonfiction for American History, Westward Expansion*, by Stephanie Harvey and Anne Goudvis, ©2016 (Portsmouth, NH: Heinemann).

Native Americans Across North America

In the 1800s, Native Americans lived in all regions of the United States. Their ways of life differed throughout the country, usually based on the geography of their homelands. One way to group Native American tribes is by the languages they speak. The map above, created by explorer John Wesley Powell in 1890, shows the linguistic stocks, or groups of related languages, spoken by different Native American peoples.

North Wind Picture Archives

The First Mexican Americans

As a result of war and conflict, the borders of the United States changed. Lands that were originally Mexican homelands became part of the U.S., and the people of Mexico became Mexican-Americans.

Priests, Spanish soldiers, and Native Americans all had roles to play at a California mission (above).

EXPLORING THE "NEW WORLD"

These early Mexican Americans mostly lived in what is now the southwestern United States, especially the present-day states of California, Arizona, New Mexico, and Texas. (Some also lived in Louisiana, Florida, and Colorado.) Prior to the 1500s, only Native Americans resided in this region. This changed in the early part of the sixteenth century when Spanish explorers from Mexico and Cuba began to travel through the Southwest.

May be reproduced for classroom use. *Toolkit Texts: Short Nonfiction for American History, Westward Expansion*, by Stephanie Harvey and Anne Goudvis, ©2016 (Portsmouth, NH: Heinemann).

Artist Frederic Remington painted this scene of Spanish explorer Francisco Vasquez de Coronado traveling across New Mexico.

DID YOU KNOW?

The Treaty of Guadalupe-Hidalgo was signed in 1848, ending the U.S.–Mexican War. The United States gained all of present-day California, Nevada, and Utah, and parts of New Mexico, Arizona, Colorado, and Wyoming. The United States paid Mexico $15 million for this land, called the Mexican Cessation. The land area of the United States grew by nearly a third in one day!

At first, the explorers were interested mainly in finding gold. But as Spanish leaders learned more about the area, they realized it made sense to build forts, missions, and villages there. In 1598, Spanish settlers founded the town of San Juan de los Caballeros in present-day New Mexico. Soon, this community was home to more than one hundred families. Spain's colonization had begun.

The Spanish influence quickly spread elsewhere in the Southwest. By the 1800s, the Spanish had built cities such as Santa Fe (New Mexico), San Antonio (Texas), and Los Angeles (California). This region was the northernmost part of the Spanish colony known as New Spain. But the geographic distance between Spain and the Americas was great. The Spanish became distracted by wars and quarrels in Spain. As a result, Spain's power in the New World started to fade and Mexico began to take more control of its own affairs. When Mexico won its independence from Spain in 1821, the Southwest came under Mexican authority.

BLENDING TRADITIONS, CREATING A NEW CULTURE

By that time, the people of the Southwest, or northern Mexico, had established a rich and vibrant culture. In some ways, this culture originated in Spain. After all, Spanish was the official language. And the dominant religion, Roman Catholicism, also came from Spain. The Spanish influence made sense: Many northern Mexicans were descended from the original settlers of San Jaun de los Caballeros and other early Spanish communities.

But in other ways, the people of northern Mexico were not Spanish at all. Years of living in the area's deserts and mountains had changed their lifestyles. The people of the Southwest ate corn, peppers, and other foods not widely known in Spain. They told stories about North American animals that Europeans had never heard of, much less seen. After a while, the Mexicans of the Far North even pronounced certain words differently from the Spanish pronunciations.

The Native Americans of the region played an important role in this change. While at times hostile toward the Indians, the Spanish nonetheless recognized the tribes' extensive hands-on experience with the land. So instead of relying on European methods, the Spanish adopted Indian ways of watering crops and hunting animals. These new routines kept them alive while changing their culture.

Unlike in the British colonies, the Spanish recognized marriages between Europeans and Native Americans. As a result, the people of northern Mexico began to reflect various ethnic groups. By the time Mexico won its independence, combined Spanish and Indian traditions made for one uniquely Mexican culture.

SHIFTING BORDERS, CHANGING CITIZENSHIP

The people of northern Mexico thought of themselves as Mexican. In the 1830s and 1840s, though, the U.S. government decided that it wanted northern Mexico. By 1850, through a combination of war (U.S.-Mexican War, 1846–1848) and negotiation (Treaty of Guadalupe Hidalgo), nearly all of Mexico's Far North was under U.S. **jurisdiction**. Without moving, the people of northern Mexico became immigrants. Culturally, they were still Mexican; politically, however, they had become the first Mexican Americans.

Jurisdiction means territorial range of authority or control.

Commander of U.S. forces in the American Southwest, General Stephen Kearny captured present-day New Mexico in 1846 at the beginning of the U.S.-Mexican War.

North Wind Picture Archives

California History

A STORY OF PEOPLE AND PROGRESS

It was March 28, 1776, and Father Pedro Font stood on a hill overlooking the sea. Father Font and two hundred forty Spanish settlers had just completed a five-month march across 1,700 miles of mountains and desert. They had left Spain's settlements in Mexico to start a fort and a religious mission in the Spanish colony of California. They would name the mission and fort after a Catholic saint, Saint (San) Francisco.

A Beautiful Site

Father Font praised the site the settlers had chosen for the mission. In his diary, he wrote, "Although in my travels I saw very good sites and beautiful country, I saw none which pleased me so much as this. And I think if it could be well settled like Europe there would not be anything more beautiful in all the world."

Indeed, the Spanish were just beginning to discover the beauty of California. The first Spanish explorer had set foot in California in 1540, but at the time, Spain had not thought the area worth settling. Spain's headquarters in the New World were in central Mexico, and California seemed too far away.

In 1578, the English sea captain Francis Drake landed in California. Drake claimed the land for England, but no English settlers came there. During the 1600s, the English were busy building colonies on the East Coast of North America. Once again, California seemed too far away.

Father Pedro Font and 240 Spanish settlers started the mission of San Francisco in 1776, shown above as it looked in the 1830s.

Spanish Roots

When Spain sent settlers to California in 1769, the only people living there were the Native Americans whose ancestors had settled there thousands of years before. One reason Spain sent its settlers was to make sure the area became a Spanish colony, and not an English or Russian one. (Russian fur traders had been exploring the region in hopes of advancing their own fur trade.) The Spanish decided to start a series of missions all along the California coast. In these missions, priests would teach the original inhabitants, Native Americans, about the Catholic religion, and show them how Europeans lived. By 1804, there were 21 Spanish missions in California.

In addition to the missions, the Spanish built presidios, or forts, and pueblos, or towns. In 1781, forty-four men, women, and children left the San Gabriel mission to found a pueblo where they could grow food for the mission's priests. The settlers started their community on a site not far from the mission, and gave the town a 14-word name which was eventually abbreviated to just two words—Los Angeles, meaning "the angels."

Despite new pueblos like Los Angeles, California grew slowly. By 1845, there were only 7,000 non-native people living in the colony. But California had become a popular stopping place for trading ships from the United States and other nations. American sailors who visited California wrote exciting letters and stories about the area. For the first time, people in the United States became interested in the mysterious land across the continent.

Los Angeles was founded by a small group of settlers in 1781.
This illustration shows Los Angeles in its early years, as well as
the nearby farmland that provided food for the growing community.

From The New York Public Library

By Sue Macy, *Cobblestone,* © by Carus Publishing Company. Reproduced with permission.

This lithograph of San Francisco, created around the time of the Gold Rush, shows the crowded harbor and the diverse population of the young city.

Shifting Borders

California had come under Mexico's rule in 1821. Mexico had won its independence from Spain in 1821, and had also won control of Spain's other territories in North America. In 1846, the United States went to war with Mexico. The United States won the war in 1848, and took over the California territory as part of its victory.

Glittery Dreams

Just one week before California became part of the United States, a carpenter from New Jersey made a tremendous discovery. The carpenter, James Marshall, was building a sawmill in Sutterville, California, when he noticed some shiny pebbles at his feet. Marshall brought the pebbles to his employer, John Sutter, who proved that they were nuggets of gold. News of this discovery spread east, and the Gold Rush was on. Historians believe that between 100,000 and 200,000 people migrated west after learning of Marshall's discovery.

California entered the Union as the 31st state on September 9, 1850, at the height of the Gold Rush. At the time, it took weeks to travel to this state from the rest of the nation. In the 1860s, two railroad companies decided to do something about that. They hired thousands of Chinese and Irish workers to build a transcontinental railroad, one that would join the East and West coasts of the United States. On May 10, 1869, the railroad was completed.

East Meets West

With the transcontinental railroad to make transportation easier, California grew quickly. The state's population jumped form 546,000 in 1870 to 1,480,000 in 1900. In the meantime, California became a leading grower of oranges, grapes, and other farm products. It became a leading oil producer too, after Californians struck oil in the 1860s.

California has long been the home for newcomers to the United States. Beginning in the 1850s, thousands of Chinese immigrants fled war and hard times in China to work on the railroad, look for gold, and start their own businesses in California. Newcomers from Japan started arriving in the late 19th century, and once in California, they became some of the state's most successful farmers. Yet life in California was not always easy for these and other groups of immigrants. Their different habits and customs caused some Californians to treat them cruelly. Only recently have Chinese and Japanese Americans started to receive credit for their important contributions to California's history.

These Chinese children walk along the sidewalk in San Francisco's Chinatown in the early 1900s. Chinatown continues to be a vibrant community in San Francisco today.

Meeting Native Americans

Mr. Jefferson's Expedition
The Journey of Lewis and Clark

"OCIAN IN VIEW! O! THE JOY."
In November of 1805, a small group of explorers reached the Pacific Ocean after a grueling trip of more than 4,000 miles. They were the first Americans ever to travel overland from the Mississippi River to the Pacific Coast.

There were 23 army privates and three sergeants in the group—all experienced frontiersmen. These men were the Corps of Discovery. They were led by two captains, Meriwether Lewis and William Clark. Clark brought along his servant, an enslaved man named York. There were also two interpreters, one a French Canadian fur trapper and the other a half-French, half-Shawnee Indian scout. With the French Canadian was his 16-year-old Shoshone Indian wife, Sacagawea, who carried their newborn baby. Captain Lewis's dog, Seaman, completed the group. These were the members of the Lewis and Clark expedition.

Their trip was the fulfillment of a 20-year dream—not the explorers' dream but Thomas Jefferson's. Shortly after the Revolutionary War ended, Jefferson had begun making plans to explore the West. At that time, the "far frontier" meant the area that is now Kentucky and Ohio. But Jefferson was already dreaming of the land beyond the Mississippi River.

In 1783, Jefferson wrote to George Rogers Clark. Clark was a famous frontiersman and a military hero of the Revolution. Jefferson asked Clark if he would lead an exploring party to the Pacific Ocean. General Clark thought the expedition was a good idea but said he would not go himself.

Jefferson refused to give up. In 1785, he helped the American explorer John Ledyard plan a one-man exploration of the West. In 1793, he planned an expedition to be led by the French scientist Andre Michaux. Unfortunately, neither expedition became more than a dream.

When he was elected president of the United States, Jefferson tried again. In 1803, the United States made a huge purchase: the Louisiana Territory, 800,000 square miles of land west of the Mississippi. Now it was time to find out just what the nation had bought. This time, Jefferson asked his secretary, Meriwether Lewis, to lead the expedition. Lewis then asked Jefferson to make William Clark a co-leader of the group. William Clark was the youngest brother of George Rogers Clark, the man Jefferson had asked to lead the same expedition 20 years earlier.

The expedition spent the first winter in present-day North Dakota with the Mandan Indians, who lived in lodges like this one.

President Jefferson made almost all the plans for the trip. He decided on the route the expedition would follow and what its goals would be. He decided that Lewis and Clark should make friends with the Native American tribes and study their languages and customs. He asked them to find out if a fur trade could be started between these Native Americans and the United States. He asked them to discover if they could travel most of the way from the Mississippi to the Pacific by water. (This would make an easy trade route possible.) They were also asked to make maps and bring back drawings and descriptions of new animals and plants.

It was now up to Lewis and Clark to turn these plans into reality. They left the Mississippi River on May 14, 1804, reached the Pacific Ocean in November 1805, and returned to the Mississippi on September 23, 1806. They had spent two years, four months, and nine days traveling 8,000 miles through wilderness unknown to most Americans. They had met with angry grizzly bears and struggled through flash floods, deep snows, and high mountains. They had also fulfilled almost all of Jefferson's hopes.

There were some disappointments. The most important was that no water route existed that would allow easy trade between the Mississippi and the Pacific. However, so much had been learned about the native peoples, the plants, the animals, and the geography of the new land that the expedition had been an amazing success.

Lewis and Clark had fulfilled Jefferson's dream. They also started many other Americans dreaming—of moving farther west.

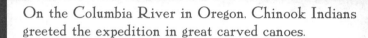

On the Columbia River in Oregon, Chinook Indians greeted the expedition in great carved canoes.

WESTWARD BOUND

O n May 14, 1804, Meriwether Lewis, William Clark, and the Corps of Discovery set out across America. On the journey west, the expedition met almost 50 different Native American groups, or tribes. For the first time, Americans living in the east began to realize how many native people lived in this vast land west of the Mississippi. All along the way, Native Americans helped make Lewis and Clark's incredible journey possible. Read about some of the people Lewis and Clark met.

A Mandan Village

May be reproduced for classroom use. *Toolkit Texts: Short Nonfiction for American History, Westward Expansion,* by Stephanie Harvey and Anne Goudvis, ©2016 (Portsmouth, NH: Heinemann).

The Oto and Missouri people were hunters and farmers along the Missouri River. These were the first native peoples with whom Lewis and Clark held a ceremonial meeting, or council. Lewis and Clark gave away presents and showed off the latest technology: compasses, magnets, and telescopes. They spoke about the natives' new "Great Father" in the East: President Thomas Jefferson. Lewis and Clark repeated this ceremony each time they met a new Native American tribe.

The Mandan people farmed along the Missouri, too. During the winter that Lewis and Clark spent at Fort Mandan, the adventurers traded with the Native Americans for food and other supplies. While there, Lewis and Clark met the Shoshone woman Sacagawea and her husband, who guided them for the rest of the journey.

The Shoshone people lived east of the Rockies and moved from place to place hunting and gathering food. The Shoshone knew the land on both sides of the Rocky Mountains, and they had horses, which the expedition needed for crossing the mountains.

The Nez Perce people lived in villages on the plains west of the Rocky Mountains, where they fished in clear streams and gathered plants in the mountain fields. They also had the largest herd of horses in the land. After the terrible 11-day crossing of the Bitterroot Mountains, the starving explorers stuffed themselves on the delicious salmon and other food the Nez Perce gave them.

The Clatsop people lived on the south side of the great Columbia River. They had plenty of food; they also had fur for clothes and trading. One of the village chiefs, Coboway, helped the explorers decide where to build their home for the winter of 1805–06.

Mato-Tope,
A Mandan Warrior

Library of Congress

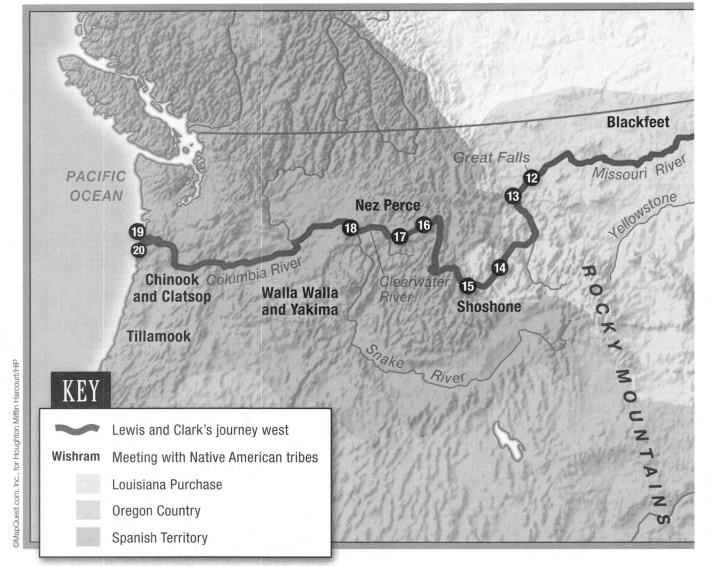

KEY

Lewis and Clark's journey west

Wishram Meeting with Native American tribes

Louisiana Purchase

Oregon Country

Spanish Territory

PACIFIC OCEAN

Blackfeet

Great Falls

Missouri River

Yellowstone

Nez Perce

Chinook and Clatsop

Columbia River

Walla Walla and Yakima

Clearwater River

Shoshone

ROCKY MOUNTAINS

Tillamook

Snake River

Going West with Lewis and Clark

1804

❶ **May 13** Expedition departs St. Louis. Clark wonders whether supplies will be sufficient for trading with the Indians they expect to meet.

❷ **July 4** The Corps names Independence Creek in celebration.

❸ **August 3** With the Oto and Missouri tribes, Lewis and Clark hold their first American Indian council.

❹ **August 20** Sergeant Charles Floyd dies, probably of a burst appendix— the only Corps member to die on the journey.

❺ **September** Lewis and Clark hold council with the Teton Sioux.

❻ **November** Sacagawea and her husband join the explorers.

❼ **December** The explorers build Fort Mandan, where they spend the winter.

May be reproduced for classroom use. *Toolkit Texts: Short Nonfiction for American History, Westward Expansion,* by Stephanie Harvey and Anne Goudvis, ©2016 (Portsmouth, NH: Heinemann).

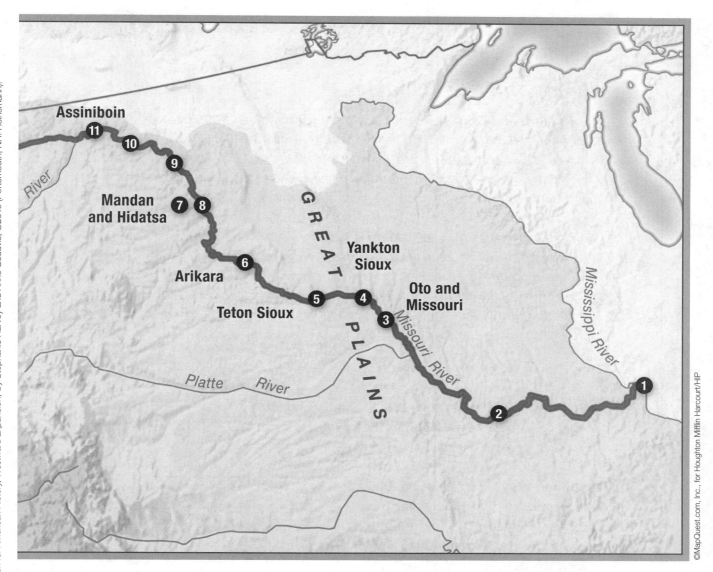

©MapQuest.com, Inc., for Houghton Mifflin Harcourt/HIP

1805

⑧ January Mandans hold a buffalo-calling ceremony; several days later, buffalo arrive.

⑨ February 11 Sacagawea's son is born.

⑩ April Part of the Corps returns to President Jefferson with notes, plants, and animals.

⑪ May 20 Lewis and Clark name a stream Sah-ca-ger-we-ah after their guide.

⑫ June At the Great Falls of the Missouri, the Corps has to carry their boats for 18 miles.

⑬ June 14 A grizzly bear attacks Lewis.

⑭ July 4 Corps celebrates their second 4th of July.

⑮ August Expedition meets the Shoshones, Sacagawea's people.

⑯ September During the 11-day crossing of the Bitterroot Range, the men almost starve to death.

⑰ September The explorers meet the Nez Perce and get sick stuffing themselves with salmon and other food.

⑱ October The group reaches the Columbia River.

⑲ November 7 The Corps of Discovery reaches the Pacific Ocean.

⑳ December The expedition builds Fort Clatsop and celebrates Christmas.

Lewis and Clark Journals

When Lewis and Clark and their Corps of Discovery crossed the continent, they wrote detailed journals on their expedition—about 140,000 words altogether. They described every day of their journey and all of the events leading up to it. The group traveled through 7,689 miles of wilderness to the Pacific Ocean and back, and made detailed maps of fertile prairies, towering mountains, raging rivers, and forests. They chronicled the customs, languages, and artifacts of more than fifty eastern and western Native American nations and established peaceful relations with most of them. They also discovered scores of plants and animals formerly unknown to science. Throughout the expedition, Lewis, Clark, and the members of the Corps overcame enormous hardship with imagination and humor. In the end, they carried out President Jefferson's goal of exploring the American West.

May 14, 1804, Camp Wood, near St. Louis: Set out at 4 o'clock p.m. in the presence of many of the neighboring inhabitants, and proceeded on under a gentle breeze up the Missouri. (Clark)

Summer, 1804, Wildlife of the Plains: We stopped to dine under some trees near the high land. In a few minutes caught three very large catfish, one nearly white. A quart of oil came out of the surplus fat of one fish. Turkeys, geese and a beaver caught. Great numbers of deer are seen feeding on young willows on the sandbars of the river. Men in high spirits. . . . (Clark)

Before sunrise I set out with 6 of my best hunters. I do not exaggerate when I estimate the number of buffalo to amount to 3,000. We found the antelope extremely shy and watchful. Their flight appeared as rapid as the flight of birds! (Lewis)

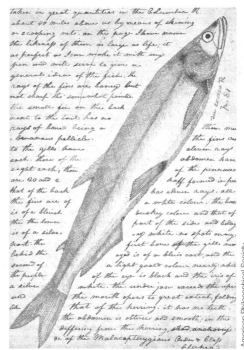

A page from a journal with a drawing of a eulachon (candlefish).

May be reproduced for classroom use. *Toolkit Texts: Short Nonfiction for American History, Westward Expansion*, by Stephanie Harvey and Anne Goudvis, ©2016 (Portsmouth, NH: Heinemann).

Among the Indians: At sunset a part of the Oto and Missouri nations came to camp. Among those Indians, six were chiefs. We sent them some roasted meat. In return they sent us watermelons. . . . To the Grand Chief of the Yankton Sioux we gave a flag and wampum with a hat and chief coat. After dinner we made a large fire and all the young men prepared themselves for a war dance. The Sioux live by the box and arrow, some making a vow never to retreat, let the danger be what it may. The warriors are very much decorated with paint, porcupine quills, and feathers. (Clark)

October 9, 1804: Many Arikaras came to view us all day, much astonished at my black servant. This nation never saw a black man before; all flocked around him and examined him from top to toe. By way of amusement he told them that he had once been a wild animal and to convince them, he showed them feats of strength. The children would follow him, and when he turned toward them and roared, they would run from him and holler and pretend to be terrified and afraid. The Arikanas are the best-looking and cleanest Indians I have ever seen on the voyage. They raise great quantities of corn, beans, simmons (squash), and also tobacco. (Clark)

December 7, 1804, A Winter of Excessive Cold: Captain Lewis took 15 men and joined the Indians, who were killing buffalo on horseback. Three men frostbit badly today. (Clark)

January 10, 1805: The mercury this morning stood at 40 degrees below 0. An Indian man came in who had stayed out all night without fire, and very thinly clothed. This man was not the least injured. Those people bear more cold than I thought possible. (Clark)

May 14, 1805, A Narrow Escape: A sudden squall hit the white pirogue and Charbonneau—who is perhaps the most timid waterman in the world—dropped the rudder, crying to his god for mercy and almost turning the boat topsy-turvey. In this piroque was every article necessary to insure the success of our journey. Repeated

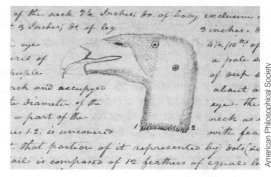

A page from a journal with a drawing of a vulture.

orders could not bring him to do his duty until the bowsman, Cruzatte, threatened to shoot him instantly. The boat righted but was filled with water. The waves were running high. Cruzette ordered two of the men to throw out water with some kettles while he and two other men rowed her ashore. Sacagewea, whose fortitude was equal to any person on board, caught and saved most of the light articles which were washed overboard. (Lewis)

June 13, 1805, The Great Falls of Missouri: My ears were saluted with the sound of a tremendous roaring and I saw spray rise above the plain like a column of smoke. I hurried to gaze on the grandest sight I ever beheld, an enormous cascading fall of water, beating with great fury. (Lewis)

August 17, 1805, We Meet the Shoshonis: A fair cold morning. I saw Indians on horseback coming toward me. Sacagawea danced for the joyful sight and made signs to me that they were her nation. The Great Chief Cameahwait of this nation proved to be the brother of Sacagawea! He is a man of influence, good sense, and easy manners. We spoke to the Indians about our want of

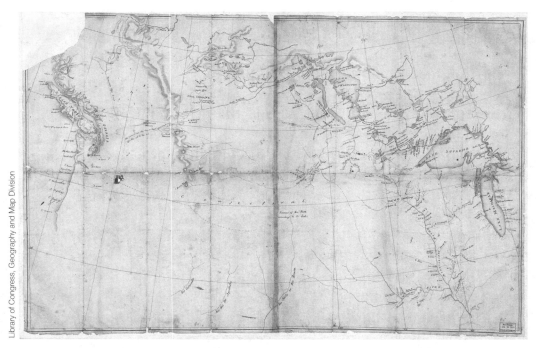

Library of Congress, Geography and Map Division

Map used by Lewis and Clark with notes by Meriwether Lewis showing the Mississippi and Missouri Rivers, Lake Michigan, Lake Superior, Lake Winnipeg, and the country onwards to the Pacific.

May be reproduced for classroom use. *Toolkit Texts: Short Nonfiction for American History, Westward Expansion,* by Stephanie Harvey and Anne Goudvis, ©2016 (Portsmouth, NH: Heinemann).

horses to cross the mountains. They said the route was unfavorable, with immense waterfalls and steep cliffs, and that there were no deer, elk, or game to eat. (Clark)

Late summer, 1805, Crossing the Bitterroot Mountains: On August 30, we set out on our route. Traversed some of the worst roads that a horse ever passed on the sides of steep and stony mountains, some covered with snow. (Clark)

Several horses fell, some crippled. Frazier's horse fell near a hundred yards into the creek, but to our astonishment, he arose to his feet but little injured. (Lewis)

Several times compelled to kill a colt for our men and selves to eat for want of meat. Encamped one night at a bold running creek I called Hungry Creek as we had nothing to eat. (Clark)

To our inexpressible joy, saw a prairie 60 miles distant. We should reach its borders tomorrow. Spirits of the party much revived, as they are weak for want of food. (Lewis)

October 1805, Onward to Oregon: I went on shore and found the Indians much frightened in their lodges. They thought we were not men but birds that fell from the clouds. As soon as they saw Sacagawea, they understood our friendly intentions, as no woman ever accompanies a war party. (Clark)

The river widens and becomes a beautiful gentle stream of about a half mile wide. Great numbers of harbor seals about. Salmon trout which we had fried in a little bear's oil, I thought one of the most delicious fish I have ever tasted. (Lewis)

November 7, 1805, Closer to the Great Pacific: We were encamped under a high hill when the morning fog cleared off. Ocean in View! Oh! The joy. This great Pacific Ocean which we have been so long anxious to see, and the roaring noise made by waves breaking on rocky shores may be heard distinctly. (Clark)

November 18, 1805, Our Goal is Reached at Last!: We behold with astonishment the waves dashing against the rocks & this immense Ocean!

SACAGAWEA
INTREPID INTERPRETER AND GUIDE

Sacagawea was 16 years old and the mother of a tiny baby when she set out with the Lewis and Clark expedition. Sacagawea and her husband acted as interpreters to help the expedition communicate with the Native Americans they met. She was the only woman in the group of more than 30 men.

Sacagawea was a Shoshone from the western mountains, but she had been captured and brought to the plains when she was about 12 years old. The skills Sacagawea learned as a young Shoshone made her a valuable addition to the expedition. She knew which plants were

American painter N.C. Wyeth captured Sacagawea with Lewis and Clark (above) during their expedition.

By Ann Jordan (article) and Laurie A. Cavanaugh (sidebar), *Appleseeds,* © by Carus Publishing Company. Reproduced with permission.

safe to eat. When cactus thorns ripped the men's moccasins, and branches tore their clothing, Sacagawea tanned animal skins and used the leather to make new moccasins and to patch shirts and breeches. The native peoples they encountered knew they were peaceful because war parties did not travel with women and children.

Upon reaching Shoshone lands, Sacagawea was reunited with her brother, now a Shoshone chief. Because of Sacagawea, he was willing to sell horses to the explorers for carrying their supplies across the Rocky Mountains.

Sacagawea's strength and courage helped her survive the hardships of the trip. She faced grizzly bears and rattlesnakes. At times, she was near starvation from lack of food. Once a storm turned over a boat in which she was riding. Some of the men panicked, but Sacagawea stayed calm. Sitting in water up to her waist with her baby strapped to her back, she grabbed the bundles of journals, medicines, and supplies that were floating away and hauled them back into the boat.

Sacagawea's great adventure lasted for 16 months. When it was over, she had traveled across approximately one-third of what is now the United States—not once, but twice.

Sacagewea and her baby Jean Baptiste on the dollar coin

BORN EXPLORER

Sacagawea's baby was only two months old when his Shoshone mother and French Canadian father brought him on the Lewis and Clark expedition. Nicknamed "Pompey" in Clark's journal, Jean Baptiste Charbonneau was probably the youngest explorer ever!

After the two-year journey, Captain Clark kept his promise to give his "little dancing boy" a good education. Speaking two native languages already, Baptiste quickly learned English, French, and Spanish.

When Baptiste grew up, he went west to become a mountain man and trap beaver. Later, he helped travelers cross the dangerous western wilderness. At 41, Baptiste walked 2,000 miles in 104 days, guiding soldiers to the Pacific Ocean. He stayed in California for about 20 years, panning for gold and working at various jobs. In 1866, this born explorer died on the way to Montana, where he was seeking gold.

"Lewis and Clark at Three Forks" by Edgar S. Paxson, 1912, Mural in the Montana State Capitol, courtesy of the Montana Historical Society, Don Beatty, photographer.

YORK
Brave Explorer

The painting above by Edgar S. Paxson shows the Corps of Discovery at a critical point of their journey: the headwaters of the Missouri where three rivers converge to form the mighty Missouri River. Left to right are John Colter, York, Meriwether Lewis, William Clark, Sacajawea, and Charbonneau.

TREKKING TO THE PACIFIC in the first exploration of the American West was an explorer named York. As a member of the Corps of Discovery, York crossed the continent from the Mississippi River to the Pacific Ocean and back. But York was a member with a difference: he was an enslaved African American who had served William Clark since both men were children.

As a member of the expedition, York was given equal status with the other members of the expedition. This was quite different from the position of most enslaved people at this time. York carried a gun, rode a horse, and voted on decisions affecting the group. York had many responsibilities on the expedition, including hunting, fishing, cooking, scouting, and caring for those who fell ill. York exhibited bravery when he risked his own life to save Clark during a flash flood on the Missouri River. He made his contributions and was a valued part of the team.

York's presence may have also had an unexpected benefit. The native peoples along the way had never seen anyone of African descent. According to historians, the color of York's skin made him fascinating to the Native Americans he encountered. The Native Americans came to respect him, and native children and women often followed him around because of his powerful build and uniqueness. Some believe that getting to know York may have made the native peoples more willing to allow the expedition to travel safely through native lands.

Unfortunately, the freedom and equality held by York during the expedition ended when the journey ended. He was the only member of the expedition to receive no pay or land. York was Clark's slave for ten more years before he was finally granted freedom. Some records indicate that York died of cholera in Tennessee, and others suggest that he went back to live with the Native American tribes he met on his great journey. But no one can deny the bravery of this unique explorer who played a meaningful role in the first exploration of the American West.

Toolkit Texts: Short Nonfiction for American History, Westward Expansion, by Stephanie Harvey and Anne Goudvis, ©2016 (Portsmouth, NH: Heinemann).

By Heather Anderson. May be reproduced for classroom use.

WESTWARD STOP AND GO

North Wind Picture Archives

Pioneers from the thirteen original colonies packed up their belongings in horse-drawn wagons and traveled west to settle the Northwest Territory.

THE DESIRE TO MOVE WEST and settle open territory was a driving force in the growth of the United States. Rapid expansion in the western territories raised many questions about governing and statehood. The Ordinance of 1784 and the Land Ordinance of 1785 helped sort out some of the answers and became the foundation for the Northwest Ordinance of 1787.

Establishing Settlements

By the 1740s, English settlements had pushed to the foothills of the Appalachian Mountains in Pennsylvania, Virginia, parts of North and South Carolina, and Georgia. Virginia took the lead in crossing the mountains by attempting to purchase land from the Native Americans.

Pioneers left behind the thirteen original colonies and traveled westward across the Mississippi Valley. They gradually began to settle along rivers in what is now eastern Tennessee and on Native American hunting grounds in the Bluegrass Region of Kentucky. Small settlements also emerged along the Ohio River and in the Illinois area and the Great Lakes region. By the 1780s, it was thought that America's population would surpass England's.

The enormous western territory was placed under the **jurisdiction** of Congress in the first plan of the Union, the Articles of Confederation. The creation of this new government, however, was delayed by the fact that four of the original colonies—Virginia, Massachusetts, New York, and Connecticut—held claims to land in the Northwest Territory. Virginia, the state with claims to most of the territory, objected to giving the new government its land. Provisions for the **cession** of lands, therefore, were removed from the Articles of Confederation in 1777. Maryland, however, a state without western land claims, refused to ratify the Articles of Confederation until the western territory was ceded to Congress.

> **Jurisdiction** means authority or control.
>
> **Cession** is the giving up or surrendering of a possession, such as a territory.

Defining the West?

On March 1, 1784, Virginia agreed to cede its land to the government. On that same day, Thomas Jefferson, the man who would become the third president of the United States, submitted a proposal to Congress for a temporary government in the Northwest Territory. The Ordinance of 1784 was the first major attempt by the national government to organize its vast western region.

In the Ordinance of 1784, Jefferson and his committee drew on principles outlined in the Declaration of Independence. They wrote of equality, stating that "the territory ceded or to be ceded by individual states to the United States . . . shall be divided into distinct states. . . ." Jefferson proposed the creation of sixteen states that eventually would govern their own affairs and be incorporated into the Union on an equal status with the original thirteen states. When the population of an individual western territory reached twenty thousand, citizens could draft their own constitution. When the population equaled that of Delaware, the smallest existing state (fifty-nine thousand, at that time), it could then be admitted to the Union as a state. (Jefferson also included a statement prohibiting slavery in the territory, but this ban was stricken from the final document by one vote.)

Library of Congress

Thomas Jefferson was the chief author of the Ordinance of 1784—the first major attempt to organize a temporary government in the Northwest Territory.

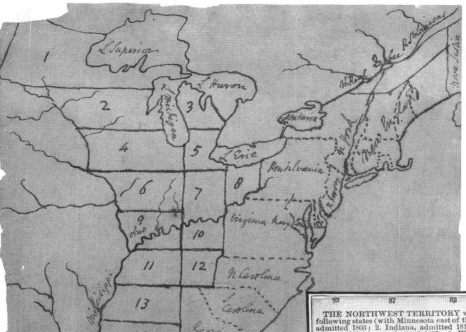

The map at left outlines Jefferson's proposal for the Northwest Territory. The map below shows the location of the Northwest Territory in the United States in 1787.

Creating a Patchwork

The Ordinance of 1784 never went into effect, primarily because Congress delayed setting up a survey of the territory so that the lands could be "offered for sale." The Land Ordinance of 1785 aimed to correct that problem. It called for the division of western land into a **geometric grid**. Land was broken up into **townships** of six miles square with lines running north and south and east and west at right angles. The Land Ordinance of 1785 allowed settlers to survey and establish clear title to their land, but progress enacting it was stalled by the presence of Native Americans in the territory. The survey of the first area, in eastern Ohio, was only half complete by the time the Northwest Ordinance of 1787 was passed.

A **geometric grid** is a pattern or arrangement with fixed points or lines.

Townships are subdivisions of counties, which are subdivisions of states.

THE NORTHWEST TERRITORY was divided into the five following states (with Minnesota east of the Mississippi): 1. Ohio, admitted 1803 ; 2. Indiana, admitted 1816 ; 3. Illinois, admitted 1818 ; 4. Michigan, admitted 1837 ; 5. Wisconsin, admitted 1848. (See note on map of U. S. 1783.)

THE
NORTHWEST TERRITORY, 1787
South Carolina ceded her western
territory to the U. S. in 1787

SCALE OF MILES
0 50 100   200   300   400

Longitude   West   from   82   Greenwich

The vision of a rapidly populated western territory motivated American leaders to focus on issues involved in settlement. George Washington thought the West would "settle faster than any other [territory] did," but no one anticipated the problems involved in governing unsettled territory. Although replaced by the Northwest Ordinance of 1787, the earlier ordinances established the foundation upon which new states could be admitted to the Union.

This contemporary aerial view of the American Midwest shows the patchwork of fields that resulted from the Land Ordinance of 1785.

May be reproduced for classroom use. *Toolkit Texts: Short Nonfiction for American History, Westward Expansion*, by Stephanie Harvey and Anne Goudvis, ©2016 (Portsmouth, NH: Heinemann).

Facts to Remember

✳ The original federal constitution of the United States was the **Articles of Confederation**, ratified in 1781. The **Constitution of the United States**, ratified in 1788, replaced the Articles of Confederation.

✳ The **Continental Congress** was the federal legislature of the thirteen original colonies under the Articles of Confederation. The first Continental Congress met in 1774 and the second met in 1775. **Congress** is the legislative branch of the federal government established in 1789 by Article I of the Constitution of the United States.

✳ A **settlement** is the establishment of people in a new region. A **colony** is formed by a group of emigrants who settle in a nonself-governing region and are controlled by a distant country.

✳ A **territory** is a portion of a country's land that is given limited self-government while preparing for statehood. A **state** is an internal, independent portion of land that is self-governing and part of a union.

✳ The **Ordinance of 1784**, drafted by Thomas Jefferson and his committee, provided a plan for a temporary government and the admission of states in the Northwest Territory. This ordinance never went into effect.

✳ The **Land Ordinance of 1785** provided for use of a square grid system to divide the land. This effect still is visible today: From the air, you can see a lined patchwork of fields below. The **Northwest Ordinance of 1787** created a plan for governing the Northwest Territory and for creating new states.

Land Can Not be Sold

BLACK HAWK MAKATAIMESBEKIAKIAK
SAUK

Black Hawk, Chief of the Sauk and Fox Indians, led a resistance movement in the Northwest Territory that became known as the Black Hawk War of 1832. He dictated an account of his life the following year, through the interpreter Antoine Leclair.

Library of Congress

Black Hawk

My reason teaches me that Land cannot be sold. The Great Spirit gave it to his children to live upon, and cultivate as far as is necessary for their subsistence, and so long as they occupy and cultivate it, they have the right to the soil—but if they voluntarily leave it, then any other people have a right to settle upon it. Nothing can be sold but such things as can be carried away.

Paving The Way
TO CALIFORNIA

Artist W.H. Jackson captured this scene of a trapper train blazing a trail to the Rocky Mountains in 1830.

A **province** is a territory governed as a political unit of a country or empire.

American trappers, drawn by the promise of fresh sources of fur, were the first to open overland trails to California.

By 1825, trapping parties had found many passes through the Rocky Mountains and had managed to get as far west as the valley of the Great Salt Lake (in present-day Utah). The California coast, on the other hand, had been visited only by ships sailing the Pacific Ocean or by those traveling north from the Spanish lands to the south. The land between America's westernmost coastline and the Great Salt Lake was home to various Native American tribes. But it remained a vast, unknown area of mountains and deserts that no white man had ever crossed.

Blazing Trails

In the spring of 1826, the newly formed Rocky Mountain Fur Company decided to send the first overland trapping expedition to the California coast, which at that time was a **province** of Mexico. The group hoped to find new hunting grounds for beaver, as well as establish a post from which to ship furs to China and the East Coast of the United States. Jedediah Smith, a seasoned mountain man, led the journey. Setting out from the Great Salt Lake, Smith blazed the first of the key east-west trails that would open the way for pioneers from the Missouri frontier.

Starting out in mid-August 1826, Smith's party of eighteen men and fifty horses, guided by two Indians, reached the San Gabriel mission (a part of present-day Los Angeles) at the end of November. The Franciscan missionaries at San Gabriel welcomed the travelers, but the Mexican governor would not allow them to remain in the area. So the expedition traveled north to the San Joaquin Valley, where they found hunting grounds. Untrapped beaver streams were flowing out of the Sierra Nevada Mountains, and deer and elk were plentiful. Leaving most of his party camped in California, Smith took two men with him and crossed back over the snow-covered Sierra Nevada range. They returned to the fur traders' **rendezvous** north of the Great Salt Lake.

A second party was organized, again led by Smith, who followed his original southern route through the Mojave Desert. This time, however, Indians attacked and killed more than half of the group. But Smith and seven survivors again reached the San Gabriel mission. The governor, who rightly feared that Smith was paving the way for American settlers to follow into California, briefly imprisoned Smith. Undaunted, Smith led his men north along the San Joaquin Valley, joined the members of his

> A **rendezvous** is a meeting at a prearranged time and place.

Mountain man and explorer Jedediah Smith was one of the first white men to cross the Sierra Nevada Mountains.

first party, and traveled by way of the Sacramento Valley to Oregon.

Routes Established

In the years that followed these expeditions, scores of trappers came to California—some to find their fortunes and some to settle down. In the early 1830s, a second southern trail—the Gila Trail from Santa Fe (in present-day New Mexico) to California—was established. In 1833, a party of explorers led by Joseph Walker left Salt Lake. The group made a grueling crossing of the Sierras and became the first white men to reach California's Yosemite Valley. They finally reached the coastal settlement of Yerba Buena (later renamed San Francisco) in December 1833. Returning by a different route the following February, the travelers found Walker Pass (named for Joseph Walker) at the southern end of the Sierra Nevada Mountains. This completed the route for settlers that became known as the California Trail.

Tales Lure Many

Shortly after 1840, American settlers began to follow the paths of the fur traders to the California coast. The first **emigrants** were lured by travelers' tales and newspaper and magazine stories that featured California as the territory with the best harbors, the richest soil, and the healthiest climate in the world. Even more

© Zack Frank/Shutterstock

In some places, well-worn portions of the westward trail are still visible today.

May be reproduced for classroom use. *Toolkit Texts: Short Nonfiction for American History, Westward Expansion*, by Stephanie Harvey and Anne Goudvis, ©2016 (Portsmouth, NH: Heinemann).

Mountain Camp - Sierra g Nevada.

inviting to many newcomers was the report that the Mexican government charged only a small fee for a generous grant of fertile land for farming or pasture to those who would become Mexican citizens. These tales had a tremendous impact on would-be pioneers.

The first overland emigrant party to head for California left the Kansas Territory in the spring of 1841. Led by John Bidwell, the thirty-three settlers included gentlemen, frontiersmen, missionaries, and schoolteachers—a cross section of American society at the time. The Bidwell-Bartleson party abandoned its wagons west of the Great Salt Lake. After many hardships, they reached the base of the Sierras, struggling across on foot and horseback before the first heavy snows could trap them. About the same time, a second company of settlers reached the southern part of California by way of New Mexico. In 1843, Walker led the Chiles-Walker group through Walker Pass. But they, too, had to leave their wagons east of the Sierra Nevada Mountains in order to cross.

Finally, in 1844, Elisha Stephens led the first covered wagons from Council Bluffs, Iowa Territory, to California. Hardships—even the tragedy of the Donner-Reed party in 1846–1847—could not slow the swelling streams of settlers that traveled overland seeking their piece of the California dream.

Daniel A. Jenks was a gold prospector who made the overland journey from his home in Rhode Island to California twice. Along the way, he captured his experiences on the trail in drawings and journal entries. This drawing shows a camp in the heart of a forest of tall pines. Covered wagons rest, their wheels nearly hidden by tall grass in the clearing. Men and women cook over a large open fire near a stream in the Sierra Nevada Mountains in 1859.

Joe Meek
MOUNTAIN MAN

May be reproduced for classroom use. *Toolkit Texts: Short Nonfiction for American History, Westward Expansion*, by Stephanie Harvey and Anne Goudvis, ©2016 (Portsmouth, NH: Heinemann).

I t all started when early explorers to the West brought back beaver pelts they had received in trade with Indians. The luxuriant fur became a popular fashion, and in the early 1800s, the fur trade took off. A great demand for men who were willing to find and trap beaver followed.

Joseph Meek was one such man. He lacked any experience as an explorer, a diplomat, or a trapper—but he was to fill all these roles in his search for adventure and riches in America's wilderness.

Before he was 20 years old, Meek was hard at work as a trapper in the Rocky Mountains. He saw how the potential to make a good living outweighed the risks: A season's worth of 300 to 400 furs could mean $1,000 to $2,000 at a time when skilled workers, such as carpenters, made only about $1.50 a day.

Meek liked living by his own rules, and like most mountain men, he did not mind traveling to remote, unknown parts of the country. Mountain men were among the first white people to see natural wonders such as the geysers and boiling springs of the Yellowstone region, the Teton Mountains, the Great Salt Lake, and the Mojave Desert. They were the first to have contact with certain Native American groups. Meek's travels led him to become one of the first mountain men to travel overland to California in 1833.

A typical mountain man usually lacked a formal education, but he possessed many skills. To make his time in the wilderness worthwhile, he learned to be an

It was a lonely existence, but men such as Joe Meek enjoyed the freedom and adventure of exploring the frontier.

expert trapper. He developed survival and hunting skills, which included finding food and shelter in every season. He found ways to communicate with the different Indians he met, as well as with French-speaking traders from Canada and Spanish-speaking people from the Southwest.

Some people romanticized the independent lives of the mountain men, but in reality they faced constant danger and discomfort. Months could pass without seeing another person. They had to rely on their ability to sense danger and live by their wits. Meek survived a grizzly bear attack and the loss of his Native American wife in an Indian raid.

Mountain men such as Meek provided important links between the East and the unknown country beyond the Mississippi River. At the annual rendezvous, or fur gathering, mountain men exchanged news and socialized. Descriptions of what they had seen and where they had traveled in the West made their way back East.

In time, the shrinking demand for furs and felt hats, combined with the near extinction of the beaver, brought an end to this unique way of life. By the middle of the 19th century, groups of settlers, often guided by mountain men, were crossing the frontier regularly. Mountain men may have been the first and the last white men to experience America's true wilderness and the native peoples who lived there freely.

As for Meek, he married twice more. His third wife was the daughter of a Nez Perce chief, and together they settled in the Oregon country. The man who had devoted years to living in the untouched wilderness later became an outspoken supporter of the movement to make Oregon a federal territory of the United States.

Indians and fur traders met and exchanged goods at an annual rendezvous. Hundreds of mountain men and several thousand Indians attended gatherings like this one.

May be reproduced for classroom use. *Toolkit Texts: Short Nonfiction for American History, Westward Expansion,* by Stephanie Harvey and Anne Goudvis, ©2016 (Portsmouth, NH: Heinemann).

HEADING WEST

What made America's early pioneers want to pull up stakes and embark on a perilous journey into the unknown West?
Why did they sell their property, load their belongings onto wagons, say good-bye to their friends, and head for California?

Entire families often traveled together, but sometimes the decision to head West meant parting from loved ones.

THE GREAT MIGRATION

Most of the first travelers to the West were simply farmers and families looking for land and opportunity. Later, during the gold rush of the mid-nineteenth century, many went west hoping to get rich. Whatever the reasons, all of the early settlers of the American West were willing to take risks to find a better life for themselves and their families.

ACROSS THE PLAINS AND OVER THE MOUNTAINS

Ever since the Revolutionary War, the American frontier had pushed steadily westward. That movement came to a halt, however, by about 1840, along what is today the western border of Missouri. There, the lay of the land changed. It no longer was covered with forests. Settlers could not simply chop down a few trees, build a house, and start a farm. The frontier landscape turned into sweeping **prairie** lands known today as the Great Plains (in those days, however, it was called

The **prairie** is an extensive area of flat, treeless land.

the Great American Desert). It was Indian Territory, which meant that the land was beyond the safety or control of the U.S. government.

To the west of the plains were the Rocky Mountains. Somewhere beyond the Rocky Mountains was the Oregon Territory. News of fertile land there stirred excitement among the restless frontier settlers of the mid-1800s. To the south of the Oregon Territory was a land called California. Word of these abundant lands was carried east by missionaries and fur trappers.

AN UNCERTAIN FATE

Times were tough in the United States around 1840. Westward growth seemed to be held up at the Missouri border, **malaria**-carrying mosquitoes were thick along the rivers there, and the country was in a **recession**. People were ready for opportunities that would improve their lives. Although wagon parties headed for California set out from the frontier in the early 1840s, back on the frontier, those planning new wagon train expeditions had no way of knowing the fate of these groups.

Pioneers to California realized they had a limited amount of time to make their long journey. They could not leave before May, when the grass on the prairie would be tall enough to feed the cattle. And they had to cross the western mountains before the winter snows. If all went well, the travelers had six months to reach their destination—more than two thousand miles from frontier to coastline. During the trip, they would have to **ford** rivers and streams, hunt buffalo and antelope for food (while carrying enough provisions to feed themselves when game was scarce), deal with stoppages for illness or broken wagons, accommodate bad weather and other hazards, and remain near rivers so they could provide food and water for their animals.

A wood engraving, "Caravan of Emigrants for California"

Library of Congress

Malaria is an infectious disease characterized by chills, fever, and sweating.

A **recession** is an extended decline in general business activity.

Ford means to cross a body of water at a shallow spot.

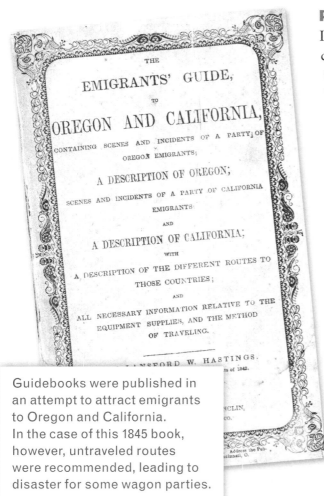

Guidebooks were published in an attempt to attract emigrants to Oregon and California. In the case of this 1845 book, however, untraveled routes were recommended, leading to disaster for some wagon parties.

PIONEERING THE WAY

In the spring of 1844, two wagon train parties combined and prepared to set out for the West Coast. The travelers planned to follow the Oregon Trail together, moving along the Platte River to the Rockies and across the mountains at South Pass as far as Fort Hall on the Snake River (in present-day Idaho). From there, one of the parties, the Stephens-Townsend-Murphy group, would head southwest instead of northwest.

Beyond Fort Hall, though, there was no road—not even tracks—to California.

Despite the hardships, the Stephens-Townsend-Murphy party proved that it was possible to get wagons over the Sierra Nevada mountain range. The route those pioneers took was used later not only by tens of thousands of western settlers, but also by the first railroad across the United States and even today's Interstate 80. Their first, exploring steps eventually became the tracks that other travelers followed, and their story embodies the American pioneer spirit.

As descriptions of the remarkable lands in the West trickled back East, it was with great hope that families joined wagon trains and journeyed across the prairie.

Top: Beinecke Rare Book and Manuscript Library, Yale University. Bottom: Library of Congress.

May be reproduced for classroom use. *Toolkit Texts: Short Nonfiction for American History, Westward Expansion,* by Stephanie Harvey and Anne Goudvis, ©2016 (Portsmouth, NH: Heinemann).

From The Homestead Act, 1862

(U.S. STATUTES AT LARGE, VOL. XII, P.392 FF)

Under the Homestead Act, the government offered plots of 160 acres of land to anyone who settled and improved the land for five years.

Be it enacted, That any person who is the head of a family, or who had arrived at the age of twenty-one years, and is a citizen of the United States, or who shall have filed his declaration of intention to become such, as required by the naturalization laws of the United States, and who has never borne arms against the United States Government or given aid and comfort to its enemies, shall, from and after the first of January, eighteen hundred and sixty-three, be entitled to enter one quarter section or a less quantity of unappropriated public lands, upon which said which may, at the time application is made, be subject to pre-emption claim, or which may, at the time application is made, be subject to pre-emption at one dollar and twenty five cents, or less, per acre; or eighty acres or less of such unappropriated lands, at two dollars and fifty cents per acre, to be located in a body, in conformity to the legal subdivisions of the public lands, and after the same shall have been surveyed: Provided, That any person owning or residing on land may, under the provisions of this act, enter other land lying contiguous to his or her said land, which shall not, with the land so already owned and occupied, exceed in the aggregate one hundred and sixty acres.

This photograph taken in 1904 shows a man standing in front of the Daniel Freeman homestead in Gage County, Nebraska, the first homestead claim under the 1862 Homestead Act.

A Different Story

A Recent Interview with Don Robidoux

Plains Indians hunted and used buffalo for food, clothing, and shelter.

May be reproduced for classroom use. *Toolkit Texts: Short Nonfiction for American History, Westward Expansion*, by Stephanie Harvey and Anne Goudvis, ©2016 (Portsmouth, NH: Heinemann).

Experts in Action

Don Robidoux writes: I was born ten miles north of the Iowa tribe of Kansas and Nebraska Reservation in Fall City, Nebraska. We have about 2,500 tribal members today. I grew up and went to school in Omaha. I joined the Air Force, and after my service, I became a job counselor for the Bureau of Indian Affairs. I have served my tribe as a tribal council member and in the recovery of sacred objects from museums. The tribe has a lot of industry now, but we have gotten away from our old, traditional ways of life.

On the road west, Oregon Trail pioneers met native peoples from different tribes. Sometimes the Native Americans were friendly. Sometimes they were angry about the wagons passing across their land. Don Robidoux of the Iowa tribe answers some questions about Native Americans and the Oregon Trail.

When we study the Oregon Trail, it's important to think about more than the hardships of the pioneers. We should think, too, about how the trail changed the lives of Native Americans. How did the Iowa people come to be involved with the trail?
Originally my people lived on lands between the Missouri and Mississippi Rivers. We ranged from St. Louis to Minnesota. We lived on the land, but we didn't own it. We hunted and fished and lived there. But then we lost the rights to the land. We signed the rights away to the

The Plains people were skilled horseback riders.

May be reproduced for classroom use. *Toolkit Texts: Short Nonfiction for American History, Westward Expansion*, by Stephanie Harvey and Anne Goudvis, ©2016 (Portsmouth, NH: Heinemann).

non-Indians, even when we didn't always know we were signing them away. And soon we were put onto a reservation in Kansas and Nebraska. In the beginning, people probably thought that no one would be interested in those reservation lands. But then the pioneers started coming through with wagons in the 1840s.

So your people were put onto lands near the area where the Oregon Trail began?
That's right. The door to the West was opened, and we accepted the travelers. We didn't just let them pass through. There were many river crossings, and we charged them to ride the ferries we built. River crossings were dangerous, and many people drowned. Families paid to have us ferry them across, so they would be safe.

We also helped transport buffalo hides. That was a money-making business. We didn't know that almost all the buffalo would be killed.

Crossing the Platte River

Was there ever violence with the pioneers?
No, not with us, because we were pretty used to the non-Native Americans by then. We had mixed with the Spanish, French, and British (whom we called the Long Rifles). Originally there were many thousands in the Iowa tribe. But by the time of the Oregon Trail, we had only 234 people. We had to become part of the non-native society, become part of both worlds, and we did. We went to school. We fought in the Civil War and every war since for the United States. But we were too small and too used to the non-native people to fight the pioneers. The bigger tribes further west—the Sioux, Cheyenne, and others—had the real trouble with the pioneers. The pioneers wanted to settle in the middle of their tribal lands.

A family on the move

May be reproduced for classroom use. *Toolkit Texts: Short Nonfiction for American History, Westward Expansion*, by Stephanie Harvey and Anne Goudvis, ©2016 (Portsmouth, NH: Heinemann).

FORCED REMOVAL

For many, the West represented a chance for a wonderful new life. But for America's native people, the push westward resulted in quite the opposite experience. The story of the Cherokee Indians, the single largest Native American group in the Southeast, is just one example of the mistreatment of Indians during this time.

Before the arrival of the first Europeans, Cherokee country included most of present-day Kentucky and Tennessee, as well as parts of western Virginia, North Carolina, South Carolina, and northern Georgia and Alabama. By the 1800s, settlers had taken most of this land.

Forced from their homes (above), the Cherokee Indians suffered on the Trail of Tears, which took its name from the Cherokee phrase *Nunna daul Tsuny*, meaning "The Trail Where They Cried."

The Cherokees were left with only a small section of northwestern Georgia. When gold was discovered there in 1828, the U.S. government wanted this land, too. Under a law passed by Congress called the Indian Removal Act of 1830, President Andrew Jackson ordered the Cherokees to leave.

Centuries of contact with white settlers already had decimated many native populations. Tens of thousands of Indians had died after exposure to diseases against which they had no immunity. In addition, as the number of settlers had increased in the 1700s, American Indian tribes had been pushed from their lands east of the Mississippi River. Now the Indian Removal Act decreed that all native people be resettled on land west of the river, which was seen as the American desert.

In May 1838, army troops began rounding up the Cherokees, removing them from their homes and imprisoning them in stockaded forts. In the fall, the Indians began a forced walk of almost 1,200 miles from Georgia to Oklahoma. The sick, the young, and the elderly rode in wagons, while the others trudged on foot through difficult weather. At night, exhausted, they slept on the frozen ground, covered only by thin blankets.

Hunger, exposure, and disease took their toll. At each stopping point, at least 15 shallow graves were dug in the frozen earth. This terrible forced migration became known as the "Trail of Tears." Four thousand Cherokees, about one quarter of the population, died as a result.

The Trail of Tears would not be the last time that broken promises and treaties resulted in the U.S. government pushing a Native American

group from its lands. By the late 1800s, even those Indians who lived west of the Mississippi came into conflict with the growing presence of permanent settlers. In many parts of the West, traditional Indian hunting and farming lands were taken. Most of the bison that the Indians had relied on for food (meat), tools (bones), and shelter and clothing (hides) were killed.

Some, such as the Sioux and the Apaches, fought back and resisted efforts by the U.S. government to keep them on reservations. But they ultimately were no match for the U.S. Army. Unable to save their land or their way of life through either peaceful or violent methods, most Native Americans found themselves forced to live on reservations by the end of the 1800s.

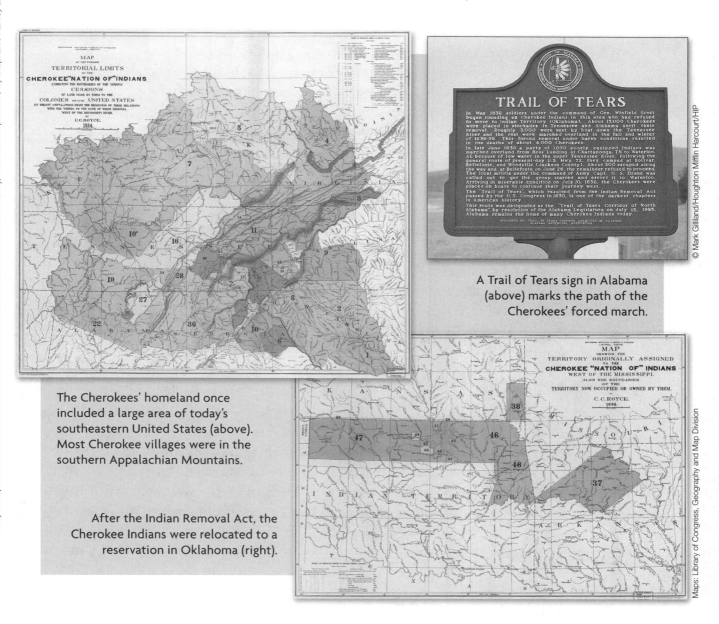

A Trail of Tears sign in Alabama (above) marks the path of the Cherokees' forced march.

The Cherokees' homeland once included a large area of today's southeastern United States (above). Most Cherokee villages were in the southern Appalachian Mountains.

After the Indian Removal Act, the Cherokee Indians were relocated to a reservation in Oklahoma (right).

The Trail of Tears: A Native of Maine

At the beginning of the 1830s, nearly 125,000 Native Americans lived on millions of acres of land in Georgia, Tennessee, Alabama, North Carolina and Florida, the land their ancestors had lived on for generations. Sadly, as part of Andrew Jackson's Indian removal policy, the federal government forced them to leave their homelands and walk thousands of miles to a specially designated "Indian Territory" across the Mississippi River. The Cherokee people faced hunger and disease on this difficult journey, known as the "Trail of Tears." About 4,000 of the 16,000 Cherokee people died on this forced march. A Maine newspaper correspondent wrote the following account after watching the Cherokee people pass through Kentucky in 1838.

On Tuesday evening we fell in with a detachment of the poor Cherokee Indians. . . . That poor despised people are now on their long and tedious march to their place of destination beyond the Mississippi River. In the first detachment which we met, were about eleven hundred Indians—sixty wagons—six hundred horses, and perhaps forty pairs of oxen. We found them in the forest camped for the night by the road side, comfortable—if comfortable they might be in a December night, and under a severe fall of rain accompanied with heavy wind. With their canvass for a shield from the inclemency of the weather, and the cold wet ground for a resting place, after the fatigue of the day, they spent the night with probably as little of the reality as the appearance of comfort. We learned from the officers and overseers of the detachment in the morning, that many of the aged Indians were suffering extremely from the fatigue of the journey, and the ill health consequent upon it. Several were then quite ill, and one aged man we were informed was then in the last struggles of death. There were about ten officers and overseers in each detachment whose business it was to provide supplies for the journey, and attend to the general wants of the company. The cost of the journey is paid by the American Government as one of the conditions of the pretended treaty which many of the Indians still call fraudulent.

The officers informed us that the Indians were very unwilling to go—so much so that some two hundred had escaped, in collecting them together, and secreted themselves in the mountains in Georgia and the eastern part of Tennessee, and those who were on the way were so unwilling to pursue their journey, that it was some days quite late in the evening before they could get them under way—and even then they went reluctantly. I know it is said that "only a few were unwilling to go"—"the most go willingly and think the remove on the whole, an advantage to the nation." The testimony of the officers and observation have both tended to confirm the belief, however, in my mind that the great majority of the nation feel that they are wronged—grievously wronged, and nothing but arbitrary power compels them to remove . . .

The last detachment which we passed on the 7th, embraced rising two thousand Indians with horses and mules in proportion. The forward part of the train we found just pitching their tents for the night, and notwithstanding some thirty or forty wagons were already stationed, we found the road literally filled with the procession for about three miles in length. The sick and feeble were carried in wagons—about as comfortable for travelling as a New England ox cart with a covering over it—a great many ride on horseback and multitudes go on foot—even aged females, apparently, nearly ready to drop into the grave— were travelling with heavy burdens attached to the back—on the sometimes frozen ground, and sometimes muddy streets, with no covering for the feet except what nature had given them. We were some hours making our way through the crowd, which brought us in close contact with the wagons and the multitude, so much that we felt fortunate to find ourselves freed from the crowd without leaving any part of our carriage. We learned from the inhabitants on the road where the Indians passed that they buried fourteen to fifteen at every stopping place—and they make a journey of ten miles per day only on an average. . . . One aged Indian, who was commander of the friendly Creeks and Seminoles in a very important engagement in company with General Jackson, was accosted on arriving in a little village in Kentucky by an aged man residing there, and who was one of Jackson's men in the engagement referred to, and asked if he (the Indian) recollected him? The aged Chieftain looked him in the face and recognised him, and with a down-cast look and heavy sigh, referring to the engagement, he said, "Ah! My life and the lives of my people were then at stake for you and your country. I then thought Jackson my best friend. But, ah! Jackson no serve me right. Your country no do me justice now."

Remember the Alamo!

March 6, 1836

Prints and Photographs Collection, Archives and Information Services Division, Texas State Library and Archives Commission

Henry McArdle's "Dawn at the Alamo" (above) was completed around 1905 after careful research. William Travis is seen on the wall at the right, with Davy Crockett just below him, using his rifle as a club.

THE MISSION OF SAN ANTONIO DE VALERO, later known as the Alamo, was one of was one of the many missions that Spain set up in the Americas to help bring Christianity to the Native Americans. In 1718, the Spanish, who were governing Mexico and colonizing what is now the southwestern portion of the United States, established the settlement of San Antonio de Bejar at the site of present-day San Antonio, Texas. Built on the San Antonio River, the settlement had its own *presidio*, or fort, to protect the settlers from unfriendly Native Americans. The Mission of San Antonio de Valero, a large, strong-walled structure that included the mission church, was built on the other side of the river.

By 1793, the mission had been abandoned. It was occasionally used as a fort, but the *presidio* across the river was a much better fort and still served the people of San Antonio de Bejar. In fact, until the massacre that took place on March 6, 1836, the Alamo was not a place anyone would choose to remember. How did "Remember the Alamo" become such a famous battle cry?

May be reproduced for classroom use. *Toolkit Texts: Short Nonfiction for American History, Westward Expansion*, by Stephanie Harvey and Anne Goudvis, ©2016 (Portsmouth, NH: Heinemann).

An Invitation from Mexico

To answer that question, we will have to consider what was going on in Texas in the years before 1836. In 1821, a man named Stephen Austin led a large group of American settlers into Texas, which was then governed by Mexico. Stephen's father had been promised 66,000 acres by the Mexican government, which wanted him to bring 200 families into the region to help develop the land and defend it from hostile Native Americans. But Stephen's father had died before he could do this, so Stephen took over. He led a group of more than 200 families into the land his father had been promised, and for the next two years, he worked with the Mexican government to establish his claim to the land. Finally, in 1823, the Mexican government agreed that if the settlers would pledge allegiance to Mexico and adopt the Roman Catholic religion, they could remain on the land and consider it theirs.

These new settlers were willing to leave the United States for several reasons. Many of them were slaveholders and saw in Texas a chance to farm and grown cotton on very large plantations. Others owned large amounts of money to people back in the States, and the Mexican government had promised to protect them from the people to whom they owed money. Still others thought that Texas was a new frontier where they could start over again on better land and begin a new life. Whatever their reasons, historians believe that approximately 30,000 settlers had moved to Texas in the ten years following Stephen Austin's first colony.

Mexico Grows Concerned

The Mexican government grew concerned over this fact because such a large number of settlers could be difficult to control. In 1830, the Mexican congress passed laws restricting further immigration. The border was officially closed. But the area was too large to be patrolled, and new settlers continued to arrive.

Stephen Austin, known as the Father of Texas, brought 200 families to the area in 1825.

The Mexican government resented the fact that it couldn't control the flood of immigrants. Many border skirmishes took place, and the hostility grew between the settlers and the government that was issuing orders from Mexico City.

Antonio Lopez de Santa Anna, who had elected president of Mexico in 1833, seized absolute power in 1834. In the fall of 1835, he sent his brother-in-law, General Martin Cos, into Texas to patrol the border and enforce the immigration laws. He believed the Texians* were about to rebel against his rule, and he felt it was time to overpower them by force. Under General Cos, Mexican soldiers moved into settlements and occupied towns, perhaps hoping that a show of force would ward off revolution. But this was not to be.

Library of Congress

Martin del Castillo y Cos

Texians Revolt

The Texians responded by arming themselves, and defied the soldiers openly. On October 2, 1835, in a little town east of San Antonio, called Gonzales, the Mexicans demanded the surrender of a cannon. The Texians fired the cannon in response, and the Mexicans were forced to retreat. It was a very short battle, but it has since come to be known as "the Lexington of the Texas Revolution" because, like the battle of Lexington in our War for Independence, it marked the beginning of open revolt.

The Texas settlers now set against the vast forces of Santa Anna's army. The United States government would send no official aid because at that time, it did not want to interfere in Mexican affairs. Some southern states secretly sent aid because they wanted to help their slaveholding neighbors, but their help was not enough to change the odds. Even though the Texians won a decisive victory at San Antonio

*The word Texian was used until after Texas became a republic in 1836. At that time, it was changed to Texan.

May be reproduced for classroom use. *Toolkit Texts: Short Nonfiction for American History, Westward Expansion,* by Stephanie Harvey and Anne Goudvis, ©2016 (Portsmouth, NH: Heinemann).

in December of 1835, (General Cos surrendered at the Alamo, promising never to fight against Texians again!), the worst battle lay only a few months away.

A Devastating Defeat

Many different versions have been told describing what took place at the Alamo that following March. It has been difficult for historians to piece together exactly how many defenders and how many Mexicans fought and died. But according to at least one source, 188 defenders, including Davy Crockett, William Travis, and James Bowie, lost their lives in the ninety-minute battle. The same source estimates that anywhere from 1,800 to 2,400 Mexican soldiers attacked the Alamo under Santa Anna's command.

One survivor, Susanna Dickinson, was sent by Santa Anna to be his "messenger of defeat." She carried the news of the massacre to Sam Houston and presented him with a letter from Santa Anna, who requested that the Texians return to their homes and submit to his rule.

The legend of the Alamo is one of heroism and glory. It is a story of brave men who died so that others could be free. But it is important to remember that legends are popular versions of stories that are handed down from earlier times.

As historians, we should look beyond the legend. The battle at the Alamo and the Texas Revolution were fought for several reasons. Some wanted Texas to be a self-governing state. Some wanted it to be an independent republic, and some hoped that it would soon become a part of the United States. Many Texas settlers were cotton growers and slaveholders who hoped to profit from the rich Texas soil. The Mexicans under Santa Anna wanted to retain control and develop the land for Mexico. Because it is both legend and history, the story of the battle at the Alamo offers us two interesting views of an important moment from our past.

Prints and Photographs Collection, Texas State Library and Archives Commission

Susanna Dickinson
(1814–1883)
was sent by Santa Anna to Sam Houston bearing news of the massacre at the Alamo.

From Colonel Travis' Appeal for Help, 1836

In the 1820s, thousands of Americans moved to Mexico for the opportunity to settled on fertile land. Conflict between these settlers and the government of Mexico arose and by the mid-1830s, Texans were fighting for their independence from Mexico. The battle at the Alamo became the most famous event in that revolution. Sam Houston, commander of the Texas army, did not think that the old mission called the Alamo could be held against the Mexican army. But Colonel W. Barret Travis, commander of the Texas defenders, was sure they could hold the Alamo until additional help arrived. No reinforcements arrived because of delays in getting messages through to other Texans. The selection below is the appeal of Colonel Travis to "all Americans" to help.

February 24, 1836

To the People in Texas and All Americans in the World

Fellow Citizens and Compatriots:

I am besieged by a thousand or more of the Mexicans under Santa Anna. I have sustained a continual bombardment and cannonade for twenty-four hours and have not lost a man. The enemy have demanded a surrender. Otherwise the garrison is to be put to the sword if the fort is taken. I have answered the summons with a cannon shot. Our flag still waves proudly from our walls. *I shall never surrender or retreat.*

I call on you, in the name of Liberty, of Patriotism, and of everything dear to the American character, to come to our aid. The enemy are receiving reinforcements daily. I am determined to sustain myself as long as possible and die like a soldier who never forgets what is due to his own honor and that of his country. *Victory or death!*

W. Barret Travis
Lieutenant Colonel, Commanding

A portrait of W. B. Travis

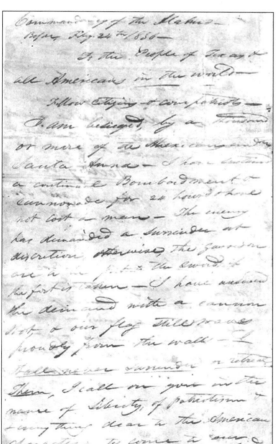
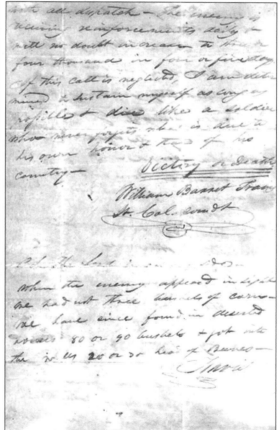

Colonel Travis' letter

From Davy Crockett's Journal, 1836

Born in 1786 to a Tennessee pioneer family, Davy Crockett joined the Tennessee militia as a young man and fought in the War of 1812. He was also a politician, serving first as a justice of the peace and then in Congress, before moving to Texas in 1835. He was at the Alamo in 1836 during the battle between the Texas army and Santa Anna's Mexican army, and he died on March 6, 1836, when the Alamo fell to the Mexican forces.

February 23, 1836

Early this morning the enemy came in sight, marching in regular order, and displaying their strength to the greatest advantage, in order to strike us with terror. But that was no go; they'll find that they have to do with men who will never lay down their arms as long as they can stand on their legs. . . .

We have held a short council of war, and, finding that we should soon be completely surrounded, and overwhelmed by numbers, if we remained in the town, we concluded to withdraw to the fortress of Alamo, and defend it to the last extremity. We accordingly filed off, in good order, having some days before stored all the surplus provisions, arms, and ammunition in the fortress. We have had a large national flag made; it is composed of thirteen stripes, red and white, alternately, on a blue ground with a large white star of five points in the center, and between the points the letters. As soon as all our band . . . had entered and secured the fortress in the best possible manner, we set about raising our flag on the battlements.

March 3

We have given over all hopes of receiving assistance from Goliad or Refugio. Colonel Travis **harrangued** the **garrison**, and concluded by **exhorting** them, in case the enemy should carry the fort, to fight to the last gasp, and render their victory even more serious to them than to us. This was followed by three cheers.

harrangued: argued strongly
garrison: the men in an army post
exhorting: urging with a strong argument

Davy Crockett: Legendary Hero

Davy Crockett was both a real person and a larger-than-life Western legend. While Crockett was an expert frontiersman as well as a politician, he would most likely not be widely remembered except for a series of dime novels and articles written about him. They told wild tall tales about his frontier life. Some of earlier stories were cultivated by Crockett as a way to win votes during political elections. But soon stories about Davy Crockett were part of the folklore of the Wild West. He became a frontier superhero who could leap across rivers, wrestle bears, and fight wildcats, as well as being a hero of the Alamo. These stories did not always reflect his true personality and character as an excellent frontiersman, a good family man, and a fair politician and leader. The legends, and the later movies and television shows that continued them, would overshadow the real man, who was patriotic, courageous, and kind.

The title page from Davy Crockett's Almanack *(1836), shows Crockett wading the Mississippi River on stilts.*

*American artist John Gadsby Chapman painted this portrait of frontiersman
Davy Crockett after his death defending the Alamo.*

Eyewitness at the Alamo

When Mexican soldiers massacred the defenders of the Alamo, they spared the lives of a few people. One of those pople was Enrique Esparza, a 12-year-old Mexican boy. Enrique's father had brought his family into the Alamo for protection at the start of the siege, and had died alongside the Texians opposing General Santa Anna.

In 1907, when he was 84 years old, Enrique's eyewitness account appeared in the San Antonio Express newspaper. The facts in his story were the same as those in the story told right after the battle in 1836 by Susanna Dickinson, another Alamo survivor. The account given below is based on the story that appeared in the Express. Some of the facts differ from those found elsewhere because Enrique Esparza was describing what he could remember, and not what historians believe to be true.

General Cos, the Mexican general mentioned in the account, was the brother-in-law of General Santa Anna. He had led Mexican troops in an unsuccessful effort to crush the Texas revolution in 1835.

American artist William H. Booker painted this scene of Mexican troops storming the Alamo on March 6, 1836.

Private Collection/ Bridgeman Images

Enrique Esparza
as he looked when he
gave his eyewitness
account in 1907.

The Esparza family have lived in San Antonio for many generations. In the winter of 1835, my father's brother was drafted to serve in the army of the dictator-general, Santa Anna. He wanted my father, Gregorio, to join him, but Papa had been friends with the Texians living in San Antonio for a long time. He had worked with them and helped them drive out the soldiers led by General Cos. He did not plan to leave his home and family.

We were well aware that Santa Anna would return soon to seek revenge for the defeat of the Mexican forces in the Alamo in December. He was furious at General Cos for surrendering and promising to leave Texas and fight no more. He gathered a huge trained army and forced General Cos to return with him.

Mama was worried about leaving her home, but determined to go with Papa wherever he went. He sent word that a wagon would come for us. He was busy taking our cattle to the Alamo for food for the barracks.

I went across town to see if I could spot the army coming. To my surprise, as I ran across the Main Plaza, I saw a splendid sight. A large army was coming toward me on horseback and on foot. They wore red coast and blue trousers with white bands crossed over their chests. Pennants were flying and swords sparkling in the bright winter sun. Riding in front was Santa Anna, *El Presidente!* This man was every inch a leader. All the officers dismounted, but only the general tossed his reins to an aide with a flourish. I was very impressed.

Slipping away unnoticed, I ran to tell my parents that the army had arrived. No one had expected a forced march to cross the cold, arid plains of South Texas in winter. Santa Anna had done just that at the cost of the lives of a great many men and livestock. He intended to avenge the insult to his pride without a thought of the price.

At home, my family decided not to wait for the wagon. We gathered up a few clothes and bags of food. As dusk fell, we arrived at the gate to find it bolted. Furious, Mama pounded on the gate and

May be reproduced for classroom use. *Toolkit Texts: Short Nonfiction for American History, Westward Expansion*, by Stephanie Harvey and Anne Goudvis, ©2016 (Portsmouth, NH: Heinemann).

demanded that it be opened. When the sentries recognized Papa as being of one of their best Mexican soldiers, they called him to a small side window. The soldiers pulled us up through the little window one by one and Papa handed in our bundles.

We heard that a messenger arrived from Santa Anna shortly after the window was closed behind us. He demanded unconditional surrender from the few men in the big, indefensible compound. Knowing that they could expect no mercy from the cruel general, the men in the Alamo replied with a shot from the cannon on the roof of the building where we had taken refuge. Santa Anna's answer was many cannon balls striking the walls of the church and convent. The exchange of shots, cheers, and jeers from men on both sides went on all night. The siege had begun. The date was February 23, 1836.

We slept little for the next twelve nights. Only 188 men, several slaves, seven women, and nine children had the hopeless task of delaying the Mexican army until Texians everywhere could rally to their aid.

Santa Anna's troops numbered nearly 5,000 and were camped all around the Alamo. The military bands played almost constantly. The bugles sounded the *Deguello*, the hymn of death without mercy.

The chapel of the Alamo Mission is known as the "Shrine of Texas Liberty."

The Lyda Hill Texas Collection of Photographs in Carol M. Highsmith's America Project, Library of Congress, Prints and Photographs Division.

By Dorothy Crawford, *Cobblestone*, © by Carus Publishing Company. Reproduced with permission.

The red flag symbolizing "no quarter" flew from the belfry of the church in the Military Plaza. It meant death to every man within the Alamo who had so defied Santa Anna.

The Mexican soldiers had been drafted to fight, forced to march in freezing winds for four hundred miles. They needed a foe on whom to vent their anger and frustration.

Cannon balls pounded the fort for days with little effect. Texian sharp-shooters were picking off Mexican soldiers with disconcerting regularity.

At last came a night of quiet and the exhausted men fell into a deep sleep. At dawn, the Mexican forces attacked. The infantry were forced to advance over the bodies of their own dead and wounded by the swords of the mounted cavalry at their backs. They found weak places and poured over the walls like sheep, regardless of the horrendous losses.

> **The last I saw of my father** was when a lantern was held over his body and the bodies of the dead all about the cannon he had tended.

The noise and confusion prevented men from telling friend from foe. Soldiers swarmed over us in hand-to-hand fighting. After emptying their guns, they used them as clubs or killed with knives and bayonets. Two small boys and an older American boy beside me were killed, although unarmed. My father's body fell from the high cannon he was firing to the ground at my feet. My mother fell to her knees beside him, holding my baby sister in her arms. My brothers and I crowded behind her, clinging to her skirts in fright. Some soldiers grouped the women and children together and herded them to the front of the chapel where there were others.

Gathered at the front, the Mexican soldiers continued firing into the bodies and walls for a long time, until lanterns were brought to check for survivors. The last I saw of my father was when a lantern was held over his body and the bodies of the dead all about the cannon he had tended.

After the dreadful ninety-minute slaughter, the Texians were piled on stacks of wood to be burned. My uncle asked for permission to locate his brother's body. He alone was permitted a Christian burial because the family were "good Mexicans." My mother told me to forget the horror of all that I had seen, but to remember that no one who had been in the battle had had one thing to gain, and only the Texians who died were even remembered.

May be reproduced for classroom use. *Toolkit Texts: Short Nonfiction for American History, Westward Expansion,* by Stephanie Harvey and Anne Goudvis, ©2016 (Portsmouth, NH: Heinemann).

THE HERO OF SAN JACINTO

From The New York Public Library

ENERAL SAM HOUSTON listened in grim silence as Susannah Dickinson described General Santa Anna's gruesome assault on the Alamo. After a siege of almost two weeks, all of the nearly two hundred Texans (including Jim Bowie and Davy Crockett) who had stayed to defend the mission had been brutally killed and their bodies burned by the Mexican army. A survivor of the massacre, Dickinson had been sent to the town of Gonzales, Texas, with a message from the Mexican general: He was on his way to purge Texas of all Americans. As at the Alamo, he would show the rebels no mercy.

Above: Sam Houston,
the hero of Texas
independence

Nine days earlier, on March 2, 1836, Texas had declared its independence from Mexico. As commander in chief of the army, it was up to Houston to train an undisciplined volunteer force to oppose Santa Anna. The task was formidable because Mexico's army was experienced, well equipped, and bolstered by thousands of reinforcements. Houston's men numbered 374.

With Santa Anna only days away, the town of Gonzales was in imminent danger. Realizing that he must delay a confrontation until his troops were prepared for battle, Houston ordered an immediate retreat.

Word of Santa Anna's atrocities spread quickly, causing panic among the citizens. As terrified refugees scrambled to join the retreating army, "houses were standing open, the beds unmade, the breakfast things still on the tables." Burning the prairie grass behind them (the lack of grazing land would slow down Santa Anna's horses), the Texans fled eastward.

Progress was slow. Dirt roads turned to rivers of mud as torrential rain fell day after day. Food was scarce and shelter minimal.

As difficult as these conditions were, Houston faced a more pressing problem. His men wanted to fight, not retreat, and their frustration was mounting. There was talk of ousting Houston as commander, and there were threats of desertion. Houston's response was to dig two fresh graves and post a warning: The first men who tried to desert would be buried there.

The provisional government of Texas also criticized Houston. "Sir, the enemy are laughing you to scorn," declared acting president David G. Burnet in a dispatch. "You must retreat no farther. The country expects you to fight."

Despite these attempts to undermine his military authority, Houston did not back down. In a letter to a trusted friend, Houston wrote, "I consulted none. I held no council of war. . . . If I err, the blame is mine."

For weeks, as Santa Anna pursued Houston's troops through central Texas, the Texas army grew stronger. Houston's force had grown to almost eight hundred men. Although still outnumbered, the Texans had drawn Santa

A portrait of
Santa Anna

Tom Blue,
General Houston's
bodyguard during the
Texas–Mexican War

May be reproduced for classroom use. *Toolkit Texts: Short Nonfiction for American History, Westward Expansion,* by Stephanie Harvey and Anne Goudvis, ©2016 (Portsmouth, NH: Heinemann).

Artist Henry Arthur McArdle painted "The Battle of San Jacinto" in 1895 to commemorate the decisive Texan victory.

Anna far from his base of supplies and effectively isolated him from the bulk of the Mexican army.

After taking command of a gift sent by the people of Cincinnati, Ohio—two six-pound cannon, which the troops dubbed the "Twin Sisters"—Houston was ready to halt the retreat. In a letter, he wrote, "Now is the time for action . . . though the odds are greatly against us. I leave the result in the hands of a wise God."

Santa Anna was headed toward the San Jacinto River. Marching through the night, the Texans arrived just hours before the Mexicans and made camp atop a bluff in a grove of moss-laden oak trees. From this protected vantage point, Houston watched as columns of Mexicans marched in and established their own camp on the grassy plain below.

Santa Anna was in no hurry to attack. With a company of five hundred reinforcements due to join him the next day and confident of victory, he decided to delay attack until his force was at full strength.

The sun rose in a clear sky on the morning of April 21, 1836. Houston's scouts reported that the Mexican reinforcements had crossed nearby Vince's Bridge. Houston ordered the bridge burned to prevent reinforcements from arriving and to destroy any chance of an enemy retreat. The Mexicans, with the river alongside them and swampland to their rear, were trapped.

By Christina Mierau, *Cobblestone,* © by Carus Publishing Company. Reproduced with permission.

Santa Anna left this white kid glove behind when he fled from his headquarters in 1848 during the Texas–Mexican War.

By late afternoon, unaware of their predicament and not anticipating any action that day, Santa Anna and his men were enjoying a siesta (rest) when Houston mounted his white stallion, Saracen, and called his men to arms. "Remember the Alamo!" boomed Houston as the Texans swooped down on the unsuspecting Mexicans.

Within twenty minutes, the Battle of San Jacinto was over. Sam Houston, his right ankle shattered by musket fire, sat astride his third horse (the first two had been shot from under him) and surveyed the battlefield. Six hundred thirty Mexicans lay dead, with two hundred eight wounded. Another seven hundred thirty were taken prisoner. Casualties to his own army were light: Only six Texans had been killed and about twenty-five wounded.

Santa Anna survived the attack and was captured. Houston resisted his men's demands that the Mexican general be hanged. Santa Anna's official surrender and recognition of Texas's independence were necessary to secure a lasting peace.

THE LEGEND OF SAN JACINTO CORN

The Battle of San Jacinto had been fought and won. General Sam Houston, his ankle shattered in battle, lay beneath one of the immense oaks that bordered the battlefield. Before him stood his prisoner, General Antonio Lòpez de Santa Anna.

Taking a half-eaten ear of dried corn from his saddlebag, Houston showed it to his captive. "Sir, did you expect to conquer men who fight for freedom when their general can march four days with one ear of corn for his rations?" Houston's men cheered as their general bit into the dried ear.

One of the bedraggled soldiers stepped forward and requested permission to take a kernel of the corn home to plant.

"I'll call it 'Houston Corn,'" he said. The others shouted approval and asked for kernels of their own.

"Certainly, my brave fellows," Houston said. ". . . take it home to your fields . . . see if you cannot make as good farmers as you have proved yourselves gallant soldiers. But don't honor me with it. Call it 'San Jacinto Corn' to honor your bravery here."

According to legend, the men returned home and planted the cherished kernels. Today thousands of acres of Texas corn fields can be traced back to that San Jacinto ear.

DID YOU KNOW? Surprising facts about the legendary leader who fought for Texan independence

SAM HOUSTON

BIRTH DATE: March 2, 1793 in Virginia
DEATH DATE: July 26, 1863 in Texas

He was an honorary Cherokee.

Houston ran away from his family as a teenager and lived for three years with the Cherokee tribe in Tennessee. Houston learned to speak the Cherokee language, embraced the tribe's customs, and was given the name "Black Raven." After resigning as Tennessee governor in 1929, Houston took refuge with the Cherokee in the Arkansas Territory. There, the tribe formally adopted him, and he married a Cherokee woman in a tribal ceremony. Houston became the tribe's spokesman and advocate with the U.S. government. Later as a U.S. Senator, he worked for Native American rights. He sometimes wore traditional Cherokee clothing to government meetings in Washington, D.C.

Houston was the only American elected governor of two different states.

Houston served for four years in the U.S. House of Representatives and then was elected governor of Tennessee in 1927. When Houston's marriage to Eliza Allen fell apart after just 11 weeks, he resigned as governor in 1829. Three decades later, in 1859, Houston was elected governor of Texas.

Houston was the first elected president of the Republic of Texas.

After Texas gained its independence, Houston was elected as its first president in 1836 in a landslide, giving him 80 percent of the vote against opponents. The Texas constitution prohibited him from running for consecutive terms, so Houston served in the Texas legislature before being elected president of Texas again in 1841. After Texas joined the United States in 1845, Houston was elected as one of the state's two new senators.

A statue of Sam Houston as a young man

The Lyda Hill Texas Collection of Photographs in Carol M. Highsmith's America Project, Library of Congress, Prints and Photographs Division.

SANTA ANNA

NAPOLEON OF THE WEST

General Santa Anna (above) as shown in a print first published in 1837.

May be reproduced for classroom use. *Toolkit Texts: Short Nonfiction for American History, Westward Expansion*, by Stephanie Harvey and Anne Goudvis, ©2016 (Portsmouth, NH: Heinemann).

I N THE PALE LIGHT OF DAWN, on March 6, 1836, Mexican Dictator-General Antonio Lopez de Santa Anna studied his troops carefully. His soldiers had been ordered to divide into four battle columns, and now they waited in silence for his signal to attack the Alamo. Santa Anna was known to his people and to the American settlers in the Mexican province of Texas as a harsh and clever ruler. What circumstances had brought him to this Texas plain?

Santa Anna was born at Jalapa, Mexico, on February 21, 1794, at a time when Mexico was under Spanish control and was known as New Spain. At the age of fifteen, he enlisted in the Royal Spanish Army. In 1813, as a young lieutenant, he was sent to the Spanish territory of Texas where he helped to crush an uprising of rebel Mexicans. At that time, Spain would not allow foreigners into her American provinces, but there were a few American among the rebels. Based on this limited experience with Americans, Santa Anna decided that these "Anglos" were too undisciplined ever to make a successful stand against an army trained in the European military tradition.

> Napoleon was a French military and political leader during the French Revolution. He became Emperor of the French in 1804.

Library of Congress

General D. Antonio Lopez de Santa Anna, President of the Republic of Mexico, in a print by A. Hoffy, from an original likeness take from life at Vera-Cruz.

In March of 1821, Santa Anna was promoted by the Spanish from captain to lieutenant colonel. A short time later, he declared himself a supporter of Mexican independence from Spain. He became a full colonel and then a general in the Mexican army before he was thirty years old.

DICTATORSHIP ESTABLISHED

Throughout the 1820s, Mexico had many governments. Each agreed to grant vast acres of free land in Texas to Americans who swore allegiance to Mexico. By 1830, there were approximately 30,000 American settlers in Texas. Santa Anna and other Mexican officials had long dreamed of a strong Mexican empire running from the Rockies to the Pacific. Now,

though, they began to fear they could not control such a large number of foreign settlers. Further colonization of Texas was banned, and Mexican troops were stationed throughout the region. Texians were furious. They were especially angry when, in 1834, Santa Anna seized control of the Mexican government, set aside the Mexican constitution of 1824, and established a military dictatorship.

Once in power, Santa Anna sent his brother-in-law, General Martin Perfecto de Cos, to crush any rebellion in Texas. In response, Texians took up their long rifles and defeated General Cos at San Antonio. As part of his surrender, General Cos agreed to remove all Mexican forces from Texas.

SANTA ANNA PLANS REVENGE

Santa Anna was enraged. He regarded the defeat as a disgrace to Mexico and a blow to his personal pride. He planned revenge. He supervised the preparations for a battle in Texas, but he made serious errors. His solders were not taught how to shoot properly. Santa Anna also failed to provide his army with doctors, drugs, or ambulances. His personal caravan, though, was well equipped. It included a fancy carriage, a large silk tent, and a set of monogrammed china.

When Santa Anna reached San Antonio, which was across the San Antonio River from the Alamo, he demanded complete surrender from the men in the fort. He allowed none of his assistants to speak out against his attack plans. On the afternoon of March 6, 1836, when the Alamo had been captured and her men lay dead, Santa Anna sent a report to his minister of war in Mexico. In it he stated that six

In this painting by William Huddle, Sam Houston, wounded but victorious, offers his hand to the defeated Santa Anna after the battle at San Jacinto.

hundred Texians had been killed. This was an obvious overstatement, but Santa Anna felt such figures would impress Mexicans.

CAPTURED!

When Texian Sam Houston and a band of volunteers heard of the tragedy at the Alamo, they were determined to outwit Santa Anna. Through a series of carefully planned actions, Houston was able to surprise the Mexican forces at San Jacinto, Texas, on April 21, 1836. After the Texians' victory, Santa Anna was discovered hiding in tall grass. He was disguised in a leather cap, faded blue cotton jacket, and red slippers, and he claimed to be a private in the Mexican Army. Other Mexican prisoners recognized

him, however, and called out, "El Presidente!"

When he was brought before Sam Houston, Santa Anna referred to himself as the "Napoleon of the West", and reminded Houston to be "generous" to the defeated.

An angry Houston replied, "You should have remembered that at the Alamo!"

Houston decided to spare Santa Anna's life in the belief that the captured dictator could be of more value to Texas if he remained alive. Santa Anna was ordered to return all his soldiers to Mexico and to sign a treaty recognizing the independence of Texas. In Mexico, Santa Anna was foced to retire as dictator, but he continued to take part in the govern-ment of Mexico in various ways.

L. Tom Perry Special Collection, Harold B. Lee Library, Brigham Young University, Provo, Utah

A Day on the Trail

William Henry Jackson painted this scene of Scott's Bluff, the wagon train pass, in Nebraska. Since wagons were often full of supplies needed for the six-month trip (and they were uncomfortable to ride in), most pioneers walked.

Editor's Note: *The following article describes a typical day on the California Trail. Such a day might be June 20, 1852, and our typical pioneer group might include the Keegan family. If their crossing was on schedule, they would be close to the western border of present-day Nebraska, where all emigrants hoped to arrive by late June. The setting is the prairie, because pioneers spent far longer crossing America's vast grasslands than they did either the mountains or the desert.*

The sun has not yet risen, but Mrs. Keegan is awake already and starting her breakfast fire. The other women in this wagon train of 15 families also are out of bed. The two men who had guarded the cattle, horses, sheep, mules, and oxen during the night are herding the animals back to camp. The animals must be guarded constantly to prevent them from stampeding, being stolen, or wandering off and getting lost.

By the time the sun comes up, the rest of the travelers also are awake. Breakfast consists of coffee, milk, bacon, and biscuits. After eating, it is time to clean up, milk the cows, repack the

By Jerry Miller, illustrated by Tim Foley, *Cobblestone,* © by Carus Publishing Company. Reproduced with permission.

wagons, and harness the teams. The two men who will serve as today's scout and hunter ride off on their horses.

Whips crack, mules bray, oxen low, and the day's march begins. Mr. Keegan walks beside the family's team of six oxen. Nine-year-old Joe Keegan and his 12-year-old sister, Meg, also walk. Mr. Keegan's brother, Ezra, rides the family's saddle horse as he herds the train's cattle and sheep.

Mrs. Keegan rides in the wagon with three-year-old Helen. Except for mule drivers, only small children, sick people, or women caring for them ride in wagons. The 4-by-10-foot wagon

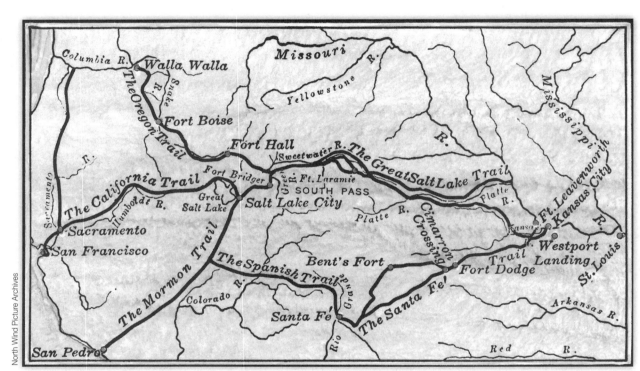

North Wind Picture Archives

Western Trails, 1800s

Pick a Trail

During the mid-19th century, up to 300,000 emigrants traveled on the Oregon, California, and Mormon trails to the American West. Those going to Oregon and California usually left from Independence, Missouri, while the Mormons left from their headquarters in Nauvoo, Illinois. The trails came together on the Platte River in present-day Nebraska. Later the Mormons split off at Fort Bridger, Wyoming, and crossed the Rocky Mountains into present-day Utah. Farther west, in present-day Idaho, emigrants going to California headed southwest.

In contrast to other western trails, the Mormon Trail was "two-way." Many Mormons, for a variety of reasons, including missionary work, also traveled east on the trail. This probably was helpful to those traveling west, because it gave them a chance to visit with seasoned trail veterans along the way.

There also was a southern route west, the Santa Fe Trail, which extended from Missouri to Santa Fe, New Mexico. This trail differed in that it primarily was a trade route, not a migration route, so it was used mostly by traders, not by settlers.

Nancy Carter/North Wind Picture Archive

Chimney Rock (in present-day Nebraska) was visible on the horizon for three to four days. Such landmarks gave travelers an idea of where they were along the trail and reassured them that they were not lost.

Why Oxen?

Pioneers had to choose which kinds of animals would pull their wagons on the Trail. Horses were fast but not strong enough for the long journey. Horses also made tempting targets for thieves. Even worse, horses often became sick from eating tough prairie grass and drinking bad water along the trail. Mules were sturdier but hard to control. Also, pioneers needed eight to ten mules to have enough strength to pull a loaded wagon.

Oxen, large male cattle, traveled only two miles per hour, but they were stronger than mules or horses. They would make good farmworkers when they got to the West. Most pioneers harnessed their wagons to four or six oxen.

beds already are piled high with enough food for a six-month trip, plus tools, furniture, cooking supplies, clothes, medicine, family heirlooms, and every other necessity. The Keegans' wagon also contains a butter churn filled with cream from the morning milking. Each day, the wagon's jolting churns the cream into butter.

The prairie is flat but rough, and riding in a wagon is uncomfortable. It is better to walk alongside the oxen. They move at a steady two miles an hour, making it easy to keep pace. Walkers can avoid the dust, pick wild-flowers, and enjoy exploring the prairie dog villages or strange rock formations along the trail.

Today, the Keegans are thrilled by the sight of Chimney Rock rising high above the prairie. But they also pass several wooden crosses marking fresh graves. Seeing the graves brings chills to Mrs. Keegan. What if her husband dies on this trip? What if she, like so many other mothers before her, has to leave a child in one of those lonely graves? There is no doctor on the trip, and no cure for deadly **cholera**.

Cholera is an infectious disease of the small intestine usually caused by bacteria in bad water.

How Did Pioneers Get Along On the Trail?

Most wagon trains chose a captain to act as their leader. Travelers also wrote rules about how to behave, solve disagreements, and punish crimes. There were even rules about the order of the wagons on the trail. All of the rolling wagons kicked up a lot of dust. That made traveling at the end of the train uncomfortable. Many groups agreed to have the wagons change places every day. That way, everyone had a turn in the front of the line, where it was less dusty.

After five hours spent covering 10 miles, it is time for the noon break. Lunch is the same as breakfast, except for some fresh greens Meg picked on the prairie. Suddenly, 12 Sioux Indians frighten everyone by riding into camp, demanding to be fed. The wagon train is crossing their land, and they intend to collect a toll—coffee, bacon, and bread. Mrs. Keegan and the other women hurry to feed the Indians while Joe and Meg stare in wonder. These strange men in blankets and animal skins are the first Native Americans they have seen.

Two hours after they stop, the people and animals begin their march again. It is hot and dusty. Everyone is tired. Joe, daydreaming about dinner, hopes there will be antelope or bison to eat instead of bacon. But that is not likely. The men do not have any experience

Gates Frontiers Fund Wyoming Collection within the Carol M. Highsmith Archive, Library of Congress, Prints and Photographs Division

Cooking three meals a day out in the open was a new experience for most emigrant women. A chuck wagon (left) was like a kitchen on wheels for transporting food and cooking equipment for the wagon train.

May be reproduced for classroom use. *Toolkit Texts: Short Nonfiction for American History, Westward Expansion*, by Stephanie Harvey and Anne Goudvis, ©2016 (Portsmouth, NH: Heinemann).

By Jerry Miller, illustrated by Tim Foley, *Cobblestone*, © by Carus Publishing Company. Reproduced with permission.

Music provided a few moments of entertainment for emigrants along the trail.

Traveling across the country by covered wagon was a hazardous undertaking. At night, emigrants would arrange the wagons in a big protective circle, which also provided a corral for the livestock.

hunting on the prairie. Besides, wild animals have started to avoid the heavily traveled trail. Maybe on Sunday's half-holiday from travel, his mother will put some beans on to cook during the preaching. Everyone likes beans, but they take a long time to cook, and fuel is scarce.

After another eight miles, it is time to camp for the night. The wagons are set up in a circle, forming a temporary corral for the livestock. The horses are unhitched and unharnessed. Meg and Joe hurry to gather "buffalo chips." This dry manure is used as fuel because there is seldom any wood to be found on the prairie. The men feed and water the animals and check their hooves—if the wagon train is to reach California, its animals must be well cared for. The women walk to a nearby stream and wash themselves, the children, and some clothing and diapers.

Dinner is coffee, milk, pickles, fresh bread with butter—and bacon. After dinner, the leader of the train and tomorrow's scouts study their guidebooks and discuss possible camping spots and river crossings. Joe listens to stories at one campfire; Meg and her friends sing hymns at another. Finally, the bone-tired travelers enter their tents, and the night herders ride off to work. A wolf howls in the darkness.

Tomorrow will be much like today—a mixture of monotony, hard work . . . and new adventures.

Granger, NYC

By Jerry Miller, illustrated by Tim Foley, *Cobblestone,* © by Carus Publishing Company. Reproduced with permission.

A ROCKY RIDE

May be reproduced for classroom use. *Toolkit Texts: Short Nonfiction for American History, Westward Expansion*, by Stephanie Harvey and Anne Goudvis, ©2016 (Portsmouth, NH: Heinemann).

During the 1800s, the stagecoach was a good—but uncomfortable—way for a person to travel out West. Pulled by four to six horses, a stagecoach was a wagon that carried passengers to towns along a set route.

Leather straps held the body of the carriage. These acted as shock absorbers for springs. Most coaches had three seats, with each seat holding three passengers. People in the front seat sat with their back to the driver. People in the other two seats faced the horses. A 10th passenger could sit on the outside seat with the driver, if invited to do so by the driver. Most travelers had only about 15 inches to squeeze themselves into if the coach was full.

Passengers paying more were allowed to ride all the way. Those paying less had to walk at bad places on the road. They might even have had to help push the wagon up hills!

Stagecoach trips began early in the day. Most drivers started work at three or four

Above: A stagecoach in South Dakota, 1889.
In spite of all of the hardships, most travelers found the journey to be a rewarding one, especially for the outstanding scenery they passed every day.

o'clock in the morning. They had to be brave, good at handling horses and guns, and able to drive well at top speed (about 8 to 10 miles an hour).

The drivers traveled through unfriendly areas. They faced bandits, dry spells, heavy thunderstorms, and swollen or overflowing rivers. Early snow, prairie fires, and wild animals were other dangers on the trail.

The stages rolled day and night for more than three weeks during each trip. The trip was hot and dusty. Stations along the route, spaced about 10 to 15 miles apart, did not offer much comfort. The food was bad, and they did not have good toilets.

Some of the best stagecoach drivers became famous—and they were not all men. Mary Fields made history in the Old West. She was a black woman who was born a slave in Tennessee. She went west, and made a living by hauling wagonloads of freight and U.S. mail. She earned the nickname "Stagecoach Mary." The fact that she was a good shot with a six-gun helped her protect her cargo.

Charley Parkhurst, always better with horses than with people, was known as one of the safest and fastest drivers in California. The stagecoaches that Charley drove were always on time, and none of the passengers were ever injured. Only when Charley died of cancer in 1879 was it discovered that Charley was a woman in disguise!

Overland stage operations ended when the transcontinental railroad was finished in 1869. The final use of stagecoaches on the frontier took place between 1890 and the late 1920s. After that, the road was paved, and the stagecoach was replaced with a Ford automobile.

CIRCLING THE WAGONS

Many people think that the **idiom** "circle the wagons" refers to a time when settlers gathered together to protect themselves from attacking Native American warriors. But in fact, many Native American tribes were friendly and welcomed these newcomers.

> An **idiom** is a phrase that has a different meaning than the literal meaning of each word.

Instead, the phrase refers to the wagon trains that transported cattle as they searched for land to ranch or farm. At night, pioneers would bring the wagons into a circle to create a corral around the herd. This kept the cattle from wandering off or getting injured by wild animals.

Oxen being yoked up in a corral of covered wagons near Scott's Bluff, Nebraska, in a painting by W.H. Jackson.

May be reproduced for classroom use. *Toolkit Texts: Short Nonfiction for American History, Westward Expansion,* by Stephanie Harvey and Anne Goudvis, ©2016 (Portsmouth, NH: Heinemann).

What's For Dinner?

Has your family ever taken a long car trip? Did you eat at restaurants or shop along the way? What if you had to pack your car with ALL the food you needed for a cross-country trip?

Pioneers often cooked over their campfire in the evening (above).

On the trail, pioneers could not stop in restaurants or grocery stores. There weren't any. The pioneers had to pack their wagons with everything they needed.

The pioneers chose their provisions (the food they brought with them) carefully. Flour was the most important item, because they ate bread every day. Salted meats such as bacon and beef jerky, beans, pickles, dried vegetables and fruits, hard coneshaped loaves of sugar, crackers, and coffee—all these were on the packing list.

Everybody carried a large supply of hardtack, or sea biscuits. Hardtack didn't taste very good, but it stayed fresh for a long time. Pioneers dipped their hardtack into coffee or milk to soften it up.

Milk was poured into a churn on the wagon each morning. As the churn bounced, the cream turned into butter.

Sometimes the pioneers shot antelope, buffalo, or small animals for fresh meat. In the summer, children picked berries

Chuck wagon,
Texas, 1907

for pies, or wild onions, dandelions, and watercress for stews. But usually they ate from their provisions.

What utensils did pioneers pack in the "cook's box"? Most boxes held a small stove, a kettle, tin cups, spoons, bread pans, a rolling pin, and a large iron frying pan called a spider (named for the little legs it sat on).

Breakfast was early. Often children ate warm johnnycakes (first called journey-cakes—can you guess why?) and bacon. Sometimes they had rusk (dried cornbread cereal), porridge, or mush.

Lunch? Cold leftovers (no time for a fire), more bacon and bread, pickles, or thick layers of dried bean jelly spread onto crackers or hardtack.

Mothers cooked most evenings, so supper was hot and tasty. Some favorite foods were

- hot flour bread dipped in bacon grease and fried
- bread on a stick—dough baked on a stick that was stuck into the ground near the fire
- bean soup
- watchagot stew—dried vegetables, beans, and leftovers stirred together in a large kettle

Dessert? Pioneers loved fried fruit pies, sugar toast, and coffee cake. On special occasions, pioneers baked celebration pie (mashed beans, sugar, milk, and spices) or fried sugar doughnuts.

Next time you're on a trip and you dig into a burger and fries at a fast-food restaurant, think about what the pioneer children ate on the trail. Anybody ready for watchagot stew?

200 lb flour

30 lb pilot bread
(like unsalted crackers)

75 lb bacon

10 lb rice

5 lb coffee

2 lb tea

25 lb sugar

½ bushel dried beans

1 bushel dried fruit

2 lb baking soda

½ bushel corn meal

½ bushel ground parched corn

Small keg of vinegar

Food for the Journey
It was recommended each adult pack the food listed above.

Women's Voices From the Trail

May be reproduced for classroom use. *Toolkit Texts: Short Nonfiction for American History, Westward Expansion*, by Stephanie Harvey and Anne Goudvis, ©2016 (Portsmouth, NH: Heinemann).

From the very beginning of emigration to California, women and children followed the trail west. The gold rush, in particular, ensured their participation in the westward adventure.

Quite a few women recorded their experiences in diaries and letters. Following are excerpts from some of those **reminiscences**, where women expressed the fear and the joy, the worry and the wonder, that came with being part of an extraordinary adventure.

In the 1866 painting above, Frances Flora Bond Palmer (known as F. F. Palmer) depicts pioneers crossing the plains with the Rocky Mountains in the background. Palmer, an English artist who became successful in the United States, painted many places that she never visited, basing details from sketches and photographs.

Reminiscences are recollections of past events.

. . . saw a fresh made grave, a feather bed lying upon it, we afterwards learned that a man & his wife had both died a few days before, & were buried together here, they left 2 small children, which were sent back to St. Joseph by an Indian chief.

—LODISA FRIZZELL, MOTHER OF 4

We crossed the Sierra Nevadas at the head waters of the San Joaquin river. On the first of August, 1841, we camped on the summit. . . . We had a difficult time to find a way down the mountains. At one time I was left alone for nearly half a day, and as I was afraid of Indians I sat all the while with my baby in my lap on the back of my horse. . . . It seemed to me while I was there alone that the moaning of the winds through the pines was the loneliest sound I had ever heard.

—NANCY KELSEY, AGE 18

Have again struck the Platte [River] and followed it until we came to the ferry. Here we had a great deal of trouble swimming our cattle across, taking our wagons to pieces, unloading and replacing our **traps**. A number of accidents happened here. A lady and four children were drowned through the carelessness of those in charge of the ferry.

—SALLIE HESTER, AGE 14

While we were traveling along the Platte River cholera broke out among the emigrants. Mother was among the first victims. On June 24 at 2 o'clock in the afternoon mother died. . . . I remember every detail of her death and burial.

—MARY MEDLEY ACKLEY, AGE 10

The country was so level that we could see the long trains of white-topped wagons for many miles . . . it appeared to me that none of the population had been left behind. . . . And, when we drew nearer to the vast multitude, and saw them in all manner of vehicles and **conveyances**, on horseback and on foot, all eagerly driving and hurrying forward, I thought, in my excitement, that if one-tenth of these teams and these people got ahead of us, there would be nothing left for us in California worth picking up.

—MARGARET FRINK, AGE 33

Traps, in this case, are personal belongings or household goods. **Conveyances** are means of transportation.

It is just four months today since we left our dear home and friends. . . . Oh, when will the day arrive when we can say this long journey is over? You may possibly infer from this remark that I am becoming weary of this mode of life but indeed, my dear children, were you all with us and our horses fresh it would notwithstanding all its hardships be to me a perfect pleasure trip. There is so much variety and excitement about it, and the scenery through which we are constantly passing is so wild and magnificently grand that it elevates the soul from earth to heaven and causes such an elasticity of mind that I forget I am old.

—HARRIET WARD, A GRANDMOTHER

. . . saw our first Indian. We children stayed closer to camp that night, but Father said the Indians were civilized. The Indians were nude save for a throw over one shoulder, & a strap around the loins. The leaders of the tribe would wear a band of feathers around his head— when a young Indian would kill his first bird, it would be tied to his hair and he would wear it for a few days.

—MARY HITE, AGE 13

Madonna of the Trail sculpture in Lamar, Colorado. Twelve monuments were erected in the 1920s and 1930s by the Daughters of the American Revolution. Created by sculptor August Leimbach, the Madonna of the Trail monuments were intended to provide a symbol of the courage of the women whose strength helped their families survive the wilderness and establish homes in the west.

MADONNA OF THE TRAIL

May be reproduced for classroom use. *Toolkit Texts: Short Nonfiction for American History, Westward Expansion,* by Stephanie Harvey and Anne Goudvis, ©2016 (Portsmouth, NH: Heinemann).

Trail Diaries of Amelia Knight

Even when exhausted by their travels, many pioneers wrote about their journey. They knew their trip west would be one of the most important times in their life and wanted to keep a record of it. Some also recognized that the western migration was a significant moment in the life of the nation as well, and these writers realized that their personal stories were a part—however small—of a historic event.

Most of the pioneers reached their destination in California or Oregon, but all wagon trains faced almost daily hardships. In the following diary entries, Amelia Knight describes part of the two-thousand-mile trek with her husband and their seven children. Along the way, she had her eighth child. They began the journey in early April and reached Oregon in mid-September of 1853.

Saturday, April 9: Started from home about 11 o'clock and traveled 8 miles and camped in an old house; night cold and frosty.

Monday, May 2: Pleasant evening; have been cooking and packing things away for an early start in the morning. Threw away several jars, some wooden buckets, and all our pickles. Too unhandy to carry. Indians came to our camp every day, begging money and something to eat. Children are getting used to them.

Monday, May 16: We have had all kinds of weather today. This morning was dry, dusty and sandy. This afternoon it rained, hailed, and the wind was very high. . . . The men and boys are all wet and muddy. Hard times but they say misery loves company. We are not alone in these bare plains, it is covered with wagons and cattle.

Oregon Historical Society, #59564

Portrait of Amelia Knight

Wednesday, June 1: It has been raining all day long… The little ones and myself are shut up in the wagons from the rain. Still it will find its way in and many things are wet. . . . [A]ll this for Oregon. I am thinking while I write, "Oh Oregon, you must be a wonderful country."

Sunday, July 17th: We crossed swamp creek this morning, and Goose creek this afternoon. . . . Travel over some rocky ground. Here Chat [Knight's son] fell out of the wagon, but did not get hurt much.

Monday, August 8: Here we left unknowingly our Lucy [Knight's daughter] behind, not a soul missed her until we had gone some miles. . . . [J]ust then another train drove up behind us with Lucy. She was terribly frightened.

Saturday, September 10: It would be useless for me with my pencil to describe the awful road we have just passed over. . . . It is something more than half a mile long, very rocky all the way up, quite steep, winding, sideling, deep down, slippery and muddy. . . . I was sick all night and not able to get out of the wagon in the morning.

Saturday, September 17: [M]y eighth child was born. After this we packed up and ferried across the Columbia River. Here husband traded two yoke of oxen for a half section of land and a small log cabin and lean-to with no windows. This is the journey's end.

YOU'RE NEVER TOO OLD TO GO WEST. In 1846, Tabitha Brown of St. Charles, Missouri, age 66, found out that her adult children were moving west. She didn't want to be left behind, so she pulled up stakes and headed for the Oregon Territory with them. A conversation with her son Orus as she decided to go with her family went something like this:

ORUS: *The West is for young men, Maw. It's 8 or 9 months on the wagon train and there are Indians, mountains, deserts, blizzards and droughts on the way! You won't have a chance!*

TABITHA: *Nonsense, Orus. I'll take good care of myself and Captain John (her 77-year-old brother-in-law, Tabitha was a widow). We'll be no bother. I'm younger in spirit than a lot of you young folks, after all! I'm going to go with you—I'm going west.*

Orus knew he'd never been able to change his mother's mind.

Oregon Historical Society, OrHi 53563

Tabitha Brown
DETERMINED TO GO WEST

The group left on April 15 of 1846. Tabitha was traveling with her daughter Pherne and her husband and children. With Orus' family, there were 14 of Tabitha's grandchildren in the group. They joined up with a large wagon train as they passed through the Kansas Territory.

Captain John rode horseback on the journey. Tabitha had a wagon complete with her rocking chair which she sat in every evening. She helped and encouraged young mothers along the way. All was well until a fast-talking guide persuaded Pherne's family to take a short cut. Tabitha was heard to mutter "I don't like it, I just don't like it at all." Orus' family stayed on the usual route.

Tabitha's letter from the Oregon Territory, written to relatives back East told of trials and tribulations, beginning with Tabitha losing her wagon and all her belongings crossing a river. Things went downhill from there. . . .

. . . The novelty of our journey, with a few exceptions, was pleasing and prosperous until after we passed Fort Hall; then we were within 800 miles of Oregon City. We should have stayed on the old road down the Columbia River—but three or four trains of emigrants were decoyed off by a rascally fellow who came out from the settlement in Oregon, assuring us that he had found a near cut-off; that if we would follow him we would be in the settlement long before those who had gone down the Columbia. This was in August. The idea of shortening a long journey caused us to yield to his advice. Our sufferings from that time no tongue can tell. (He left a pilot with us who proved to be an excellent man; otherwise we never would have seen Oregon.) He left us to the depredations of Indians, wild beasts, and starvation—but God was with us. We had sixty miles of desert without grass or water, mountains to climb, cattle giving out, wagons breaking, emigrants sick and dying, hostile Indians to guard against by night and by day to keep from being killed, or having our horses and cattle arrowed or stolen. We were carried south of Oregon hundreds of miles into Utah Territory and California; fell in with the Clammette and Rogue River Indians; lost nearly all our cattle; passed the Umpqua mountains (twelve miles through). I rode through in three days at the risk of my life, having lost my wagon, and all I had but the horse I was on.

Our family was the first that started into the Canyon. The canyon was strewn with dead cattle, broken wagons, beds, clothing, and everything but provisions of which we were nearly destitute. Some people were in [the] Canyon two and three weeks before they could get through; some died without any warning from fatigue and starvation; others ate of the flesh of the cattle that were lying [dead by the wayside].

[The group became destitute . . .]

Mr. Pringle and Pherne [her daughter] [unreadable comment] insisted on my going ahead with their Uncle John and try to save our own lives. They were obliged to stay back for a few days to recruit their few worn-out cattle. They divided their last bit of bacon, of which I had three slices, a tea-cupful of tea;

By Anne Goudvis. May be reproduced for classroom use. *Toolkit Texts: Short Nonfiction for American History, Westward Expansion*, by Stephanie Harvey and Anne Goudvis, ©2016 (Portsmouth, NH: Heinemann).

Tabitha traveled through harsh, rocky terrain on her journey to Oregon.

By Anne Goudvis. May be reproduced for classroom use. *Toolkit Texts: Short Nonfiction for American History, Westward Expansion*, by Stephanie Harvey and Anne Goudvis, ©2016 (Portsmouth, NH: Heinemann).

the last division of all we had—no bread. We saddled our horses and set off, not knowing that we should ever see each other again. Captain Brown was too old and feeble to render any assistance or protection to me. I was obliged to ride ahead as a pilot, hoping to overtake four or five wagons that left camp the day before. Near sunset came up with two families that left camp that morning. They had nothing to eat, and their cattle had given out. We camped in oak grove together for the night; in the morning I divided my last morsel with them, and left them to take care of themselves. I hurried Captain Brown to ride fast so as to overtake the wagons ahead. We passed through beautiful valleys, and over high hills; saw but two Indians at a distance through the day. In the afterpart of the day Capt. Brown complained of sickness, and could only walk his horse at a distance behind mine; he had a swimming in his head and a pain in his stomach. About two or three hours before sunset, he became delirious, and fell from his horse.

The school that Tabitha started later became Pacific University. Old College Hall was built in 1850 as Pacific's first university building. Today, it is one of the oldest educational buildings still in use west of the Mississippi River.

[Tabitha somehow gets the old man back on his horse and they continue . . .]

The sun was now setting, the wind was blowing, and the rain was drifting, upon the side of distant mountains—poor Me! I crossed the plain to where these mountain spurs met Ravines, betwixt the points. Here the shades of night were gathering fast, and I could see the wagon track no further. I alighted from my horse, flung off my saddle and saddle bags, and tied him fast with a rope to a tree. The Captain asked what I was going to do. My answer was, I am going to camp for the night. He gave a groan, and fell to the ground. I gathered my wagon sheet, that I had put under my saddle; flung it over a firm projecting limb of a tree, and made me a fine tent. I then stripped the Captain's horse, and tied him; placed saddles, blankets, bridles, etc. under the tent; then helped up the bewildered old gentleman, and introduced him to his new lodgings upon the naked ground. His senses were gone; I covered him as well as I could with blankets, and then seated myself upon my feet behind him, expecting he would be a corpse before morning. Pause for a moment and consider my situation—worse than alone; in a strange wilderness; without food, without

By Anne Goudvis. May be reproduced for classroom use. *Toolkit Texts: Short Nonfiction for American History, Westward Expansion*, by Stephanie Harvey and Anne Goudvis, ©2016 (Portsmouth, NH: Heinemann).

fire; cold and shivering; wolves fighting and howling all around me; darkness of night forbade the stars to shine upon me; solitary—all was solitary as death—but the same kind Providence that ever has been was watching over me still. I committed my all to Him and felt no fear. As soon as light had dawned, I pulled down my tent, saddled the horses; found the Captain so as to stand upon his feet—just at this moment one of the emigrants that I was trying to overtake came to me—he was in search of venison—half a mile ahead were the wagons I was trying to catch up with. We were soon there, and ate plentifully of fresh venison. Within 8 or 10 feet of where my tent was set fresh tracks of two Indians were plain to be seen, but I did not know they were there. They killed and robbed a Mr. Newton but a short distance off, but would not kill his wife because she was a woman. The Indians killed another man on our cut-off; the rest of the emigrants escaped with their lives. We then travelled on, and in a few days came to the foot of the Calapooia Mountain. Here we were obliged to wait for more emigrants to help cut a road through; here my children and grandchildren came up with us—a joyful meeting. They had been near starving. Mr. Pringle tried to shoot a wolf, but he was too weak and trembling to hold his rifle steady. They all cried because they had nothing to eat. Just at this time [unreadable comment] came to [us] with a supply, and they all cried again.

[The letter continues . . .]

SIGNED—

Tabitha Brown

Arriving in Oregon with little or nothing to her name, she supported herself and Captain John by cooking, sewing and caring for pioneer children. Tabitha began teaching at a school the settlers built. At one point, when her son Orus wanted to help her out, independent Tabitha reported to her family

I own eight cows, six calves, four horses, this log cabin and the frame house across the way. I also own eight lots and have about $1000 saved up.

The school she started, Tualatin Academy, was granted a charter in 1854 and became Pacific University. Not bad for a lady too old to go west.

History as Adventure

An Interview with Author Frances Jenner

Imagine if your research took you on a 2,000-mile journey, alongside rushing rivers in the rugged wilderness. Meet Frances Jenner, a historical fiction author who experienced the California Trail on horseback, on foot, and by car to bring her character's journey to life for readers.

Why did you decide to research and write about a pioneer journey? Tell us about your idea that "history is (or needs to be) an adventure."
I was a teacher librarian and worked with students in schools for many years. For one project about the American west, each student wrote their own pioneer journal. We researched material from historical accounts, original diaries, maps, and visual images. Traveling the trail metaphorically with our students became an adventure. They began to see the process of learning about history as an adventure in itself.

We students and teachers discovered that days on the California and Oregon trails brought tremendous challenges.

Based on our research, we filled our journals with historically accurate stories of survival as we traveled the country from Independence, Missouri, to California or Oregon in the 1850s. We wrote about fording rivers, surviving buffalo stampedes, and drinking bad water. We crossed deserts and mountains, faced starvation, cholera, and even death. Yet, our characters, like the pioneers, somehow survived.

The birth of my novel *Prairie Journey* happened right in our library with all 75 students standing by as they birthed their own journal stories. And during this process, I learned that when students engage in history as a narrative adventure, they sustain their curiosity and develop a love for history.

How did you know where to begin? Tell us about your research and writing process.
When I began the process of expanding my journal into a historical fiction novel, I set out to do more in-depth research.

By Heather Anderson. May be reproduced for classroom use. *Toolkit Texts: Short Nonfiction for American History: Westward Expansion*, by Stephanie Harvey and Anne Goudvis, ©2016 (Portsmouth, NH: Heinemann).

I read books with specific maps of the trail, pioneer diary accounts, and information on animal, plant life, and weather patterns during 1848–1860.

The new knowledge motivated me to seek out other ways to research. I had learned that wagon trains traveled about 15 miles a day and that the journey took six to seven months, but when I looked at the maps and saw the names of specific places like Ayr Ruts or Alcove Spring, these places were a mystery to me. I decided to travel the California trail, all 2,000 miles of it, to experience the sounds, smells, and sights of each place where Savannah's (the novel's main character) wagon train would travel. Then my readers and I could get a true sense of the trail.

I made five research trips with my husband, Doug. We traveled by car, but like the pioneers, we followed and hiked along the trail's rivers. Our travels lead us to museums and forts where we talked to historians and museum staff. In museums we saw replicas of covered wagons filled with food supplies, trunks carrying bedding, pots and pans and dishes, and found artifacts left on the trail—a rusted pair of scissors, a broken oxen yoke, a horseshoe.

I wrote my first draft of *Prairie Journey* before we traveled the trail. But once I had seen the land along the trail, I got a much better sense of how to place the events in the story. I redrafted the story after our travels and it started to become more alive. I revised the manuscript several more times, transforming it from a journal to a verse novel and then in its final form to a novel with verse woven into the narrative, as it was published.

What were some of the adventures you had along the way?

We had one adventure when we visited Chimney Rock. Our guide told us that Chimney Rock was sacred to the Sioux Indians. I felt drawn to this place and didn't want to leave.

There was an extra horse for me to ride back. As we trotted behind the wagon, I imagined Savannah's wagon train, the bulls bellowing, whips cracking, and the shouting of "wagons ho."

PRAIRIE Journey

by Frances Bonney JENNER

Mariah Fox Hausman

I turned to look back. There was Chimney. I gave it one last look. I thought about how the pioneer journey was so full of surprises that often threatened lives. Cholera came suddenly. River crossings turned dangerous. Wagon accidents occurred haphazardly. And yet, along with the danger, there was the adventure and exhilaration of not knowing what might happen.

I was in my own world when I heard a gunshot ring out. Rattlesnake!

Our guide saw the rattlesnake just ahead and beside the road. The wagon's horses and my mare might have bolted if the snake struck. He grabbed his rifle, took aim, and killed that rattler with just one shot. He stopped the wagon and jumped off to make sure the snake was dead. It was.

The guide gave me the rattles. I still have them.

Tell us about the parts of the story where the young girl, Savannah, encountered Native Americans on her journey.

One of my purposes in writing *Prairie Journey* was to show that relationships between pioneers and Native Americans were often positive, especially during the early years of the western migration. Most tribes were friendly to the pioneers during

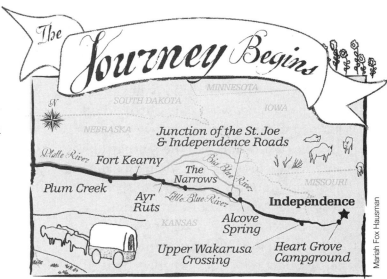

The Journey Begins

Junction of the St. Joe & Independence Roads
Fort Kearny
Platte River
The Narrows
Big Blue River
Plum Creek
Ayr Ruts
Little Blue River
MISSOURI
Independence
KANSAS
Alcove Spring
Upper Wakarusa Crossing
Heart Grove Campground
MINNESOTA
SOUTH DAKOTA
IOWA
NEBRASKA
N

Mariah Fox Hausman

this time and many pioneers treated them with friendship in return. I chose to set my story in the year 1850 for this reason.

I read many original diary accounts of pioneers and Native Americans being friendly to each other. In one diary account, 17-year-old Eliza McAuley traded bread and sugar for a pair of moccasins with a Shoshone man named Poro in 1852. Eliza had been previously afraid of Native Americans, but she began to trust them and learn their language after living near the tribe and trading back and forth with Poro.

I used Eliza's diary account as a historical basis for building a scene in which Savannah trades with Two Whistles, a young Cheyenne girl about her age. In my imagination, I thought Savannah and Two Whistles might welcome the opportunity for a relationship. And trading bread and a small mirror for moccasins seemed the best way for each to open up to the other. Eliza's diary account showed me that it was accurate to believe that Two Whistles and Savannah could experience a reciprocal exchange, no matter that they came from different worlds.

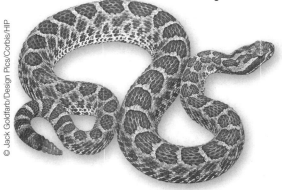

By Heather Anderson. May be reproduced for classroom use. *Toolkit Texts: Short Nonfiction for American History, Westward Expansion*, by Stephanie Harvey and Anne Goudvis, ©2016 (Portsmouth, NH: Heinemann).

What is your next project?

I am currently researching and writing a historical fiction novel about the early life of Billy the Kid in the 1870s. Billy was bright, gregarious, gifted, the lead singer in the school musical and a skilled dancer. He also learned to speak Spanish fluently as a young teen. How such a talented young man became a legendary outlaw who died before his 22nd birthday is the story of my book.

As a researcher, I continually read everything that has been written about Billy. Part of doing research is to sort out what is true. I have to continually fact-check what I read about Billy.

Two Whistles
An Excerpt from *Prairie Journey*

A young Indian girl sat just outside a tepee. Sunlight shone like golden corn, warming her brown skin and she reached her hands out to us, opened them up and they held beads, the colors of a prairie sunset. She took one, sewed it onto a moccasin, looked up, then, from her sewing and spoke to us, in Cheyenne, someone said.

She whistled then
Whistled two times

A mountain man standing by said, "She's called Two Whistles."
We smiled, and he said, "My name's Carson."
"Mr. Carson, tell her our names," I said, and let him know who we were.
He told her, and she smiled at us. And held out the moccasins she had in her hands. "She wants to trade," Mr. Carson explained. "She just finished them."
Two Whistles smiled.
I kneeled beside her, she placed the moccasins in my hands and I touched them and they felt soft and smelled of grass, earth and sky. I handed them to Katherine, she buried her face in them. "They smell sweet."
"Do you want them?" I asked.
"They're for you, Savannah."
I put them on and felt how they wrapped around my heels, my toes so snug. Made me feel safe. And soft. Two Whistles had made them, wanted me to have them. "But I have nothing to trade," I said. Then Katherine had an idea. "Your Mother's bread, baked fresh."
"They're worth more," I told her. Then remembered my small mirror, a doll's mirror it was. I had it in my deep dress pocket. I gave it to her and she made the sun glitter on her cheeks, and then on ours.
Mr. Carson translated for me and Two Whistles said it was a very good trade. Later, that afternoon, Mother agreed to make fresh loaves, one for us and one for Two Whistles. And around dusk, Katherine and I carried the loaf to Two Whistles and she received the loaf holding it warm in her hands, lifting it to her nose, breathing in its freshness. I noticed she wore the mirror around her neck on a thin piece of soft rawhide.
She gave me the moccasins and I felt them all over with my fingers, then slipped my feet into them slowly . . .

Like a new beginning
mine now
perfect fit.

By Heather Anderson. May be reproduced for classroom use. *Toolkit Texts: Short Nonfiction for American History, Westward Expansion*, by Stephanie Harvey and Anne Goudvis, ©2016 (Portsmouth, NH: Heinemann).

Quilts

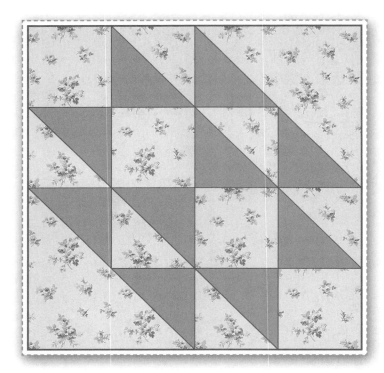

Stitching Stories

Floral pattern: © tommaso lizzul/Shutterstock/HIP

Pioneers spent many months getting ready for their long journey west. Men prepared the wagons, animals, farm equipment, and tools. Women salted meats, dried fruits and sweet corn, and bought barrels of sugar and flour. They packed everything that their family would need to live on the trail and in their new home, from dishes to clothing.

Women and girls also sewed—for their family that would travel and their family that would stay behind. Before they left, they often made a special quilt for their relatives and friends as a going-away gift. They stitched their names and the date into the quilt to help loves ones remember them.

They also sewed many quilts, as many as three for each family member, to use on the trip. Quilts were used as bedding, of course, but also as padding for hard wagon seats. They served as insulation inside the wagon to keep out the rain and wind. They were wrapped around dishes and valuables to keep them from breaking.

These quilts served a variety of purposes, but they also allowed pioneer women to express themselves. Women made quilts while on the long trip to remember family and friends back east. Quilters also created new patterns, such as Hovering Hawks and North Wind, to tell the story of their journey. Long after the trip, pioneers could remember the stories of the homes they left and of the trip they made.

Quilt patterns, such as Hovering Hawks (above) and North Wind (below), helped illustrate the stories of pioneers' journeys west.

By Heather Anderson. May be reproduced for classroom use. *Toolkit Texts: Short Nonfiction for American History, Westward Expansion,* by Stephanie Harvey and Anne Goudvis, ©2016 (Portsmouth, NH: Heinemann).

Women (left) gathered together to make quilts for their family before their long journey. Quilts made on the trail often told the story of the journey. The quilt pattern below, called Blazing Sun, uses circles to allude to wagon wheels and the harsh sun.

Work and Play

May be reproduced for classroom use. *Toolkit Texts: Short Nonfiction for American History, Westward Expansion,* by Stephanie Harvey and Anne Goudvis, ©2016 (Portsmouth, NH: Heinemann).

The Trail Through the Eyes of Young Pioneers

I was driving as usual and we had an old pig that was expecting babies that day, and she had to ride in the buggy, as father was very anxious to save the little pigs. They all died in consequences of the rough road.

—Rachel Emma Woolley, age 11, 1848

The trail west was full of discovery, danger, difficulty, excitement, and hard work for young pioneers. Ten-year-old Joseph Fish captured a typical scene when he later wrote his autobiography: "As the company stretched out across the broad prairies it presented a picturesque appearance. Bare-footed children, here and there, were wending their way along the line of march. Women, some with sunbonnets, some with hats, traveled along through the hot dust and over the parched plains. Men with long whips walked beside the lolling oxen that were dragging their heavy loads towards the setting sun."

Pioneers (above) resting on the long trail

Many young women also helped drive teams of oxen west. Ann Cannon, age fifteen, was a teamster: "In the spring of 1847, we took up the journey west . . . and I took turns driving an ox team, as the young man who started to drive it went back." Mary Field, another fifteen-year-old, said she drove and "yoked and unyoked the oxen, and helped cook and care for the children."

Dozens of young boys were in charge of teams for the entire thirteen hundred miles or helped part-time. One part-time teamster was six-year-old Robert Sweeten. Another was nine-year-old Joseph F. Smith, who treated his oxen like friends: "My team leaders' names were Thom and Joe. We raised them from calves. They were more intelligent than many a man. Thom was my favorite and best and most willing and obedient servant and friend. He was choice."

Children performed many other chores along the trail, including gathering buffalo chips (dried dung) for fuel. Buffalo chips were often all the pioneers had to cook with in the dry, arid regions of western Nebraska and Wyoming, where wood was scarce or nonexistent. Gathering chips was almost always the duty of children and women. Some hunted for wild ducks, geese, antelope, and deer.

Nebraska State Historical Society

From a young age, children took on many responsibilities, such as gathering buffalo chips for fuel.

Many families with small children traveled the trail west, a journey filled with excitement and hard work.

But it was not all work and no play for the young people. They explored, fished, swam, and played games. They waded in creeks, made mud pies, and gathered flowers. Joseph Fish learned an important lesson at Chimney Rock in Nebraska: "An interesting landmark as we journeyed up the Platte was Chimney Rock. I remember when we came in sight of it we thought it was not far off and started out to go to it. . . . We traveled some distance when we gave it up and we did not get even with it until the next day. It must have been fifteen miles away."

Scenic wonders in Wyoming included Independence Rock and Devil's Gate. Independence Rock is a huge turtle-shaped rock nearly 2,000 feet long and 190 feet high. Many young people climbed up it to admire the beautiful Sweetwater River meandering through the countryside below. They danced and listened to musical instruments atop the rock. Devil's Gate, just a few miles away, also intrigued young people. It took skill and daring to climb to the top, and those who did won bragging rights.

Many youths and older people painted or chiseled their names in these rocks. Some are still visible today. Unfortunately, there were some accidents and a few deaths at both sites.

For many youngsters, the trip west was a thrilling adventure, filled with a number of firsts. Many of them shot their first rifle, drove their first team, and saw their first rattlesnake, prairie storm, firefly, desert, buffalo, and wolf. They stood guard for the first time, picked up their first buffalo chips, rode their first horse, and swam in their first river.

One rule was seldom violated on the trail, however: The fun began only when the chores were completed. "At night when we camped," Rachel Woolley remembered, "we would rush for the river to bathe off the dust." Romania Bunnell had memories of music: "I remember the pleasant evening gatherings of the young folks by the bright camp fire where sweet songs floated forth."

The trail provided a glimpse of life and death almost daily. Emigrants, young and old, worked, played, and

May be reproduced for classroom use. *Toolkit Texts: Short Nonfiction for American History, Westward Expansion,* by Stephanie Harvey and Anne Goudvis, ©2016 (Portsmouth, NH: Heinemann).

perished. Especially during the bad cholera years of 1849 to 1852, the death rate in some companies was twenty percent. Long after the pain, dreary toil, and hunger had grown dim, however, the travelers still remembered the music, dancing, discovery, storytelling, singing, cooking, eating, praying, playing, and swimming.

In general, adolescent pioneers endured the trek better than adults and young children. Ruth May, a thirteen-year-old from England, recalled, "Of course to me as a child, this had been a delightful pleasure jaunt, and I remember it only as fun."

Barefooted children often played games and explored, after chores were completed.

Books on the Trail

Children traveling on wagon trains didn't have the opportunity to go to school. But pioneers packed along as many books as possible, and many children read books whenever they could. When a wagon's load needed to be lightened to cross a river or a mountain, many families left behind clothes or household goods. They rarely discarded precious books.

Mormon Migration

Most American pioneers migrated westward voluntarily. The story of the Mormons, however, is very different. They went because religious **persecution*** forced them to flee their homes. Between 1846 and 1869, about 70,000 Mormons traveled west, some even coming from as far away as the British Isles.

After they had been pushed from their homes in New York, Ohio, and Missouri, by the mid-1800s the vast unclaimed West seemed to offer Mormons the only opportunity for a permanent settlement. Led by Brigham Young, the first Mormon pioneers left their headquarters at Nauvoo, Illinois, in February 1846. Their 1,300-mile journey did not end until they reached Utah and its Great Salt Lake on July 24, 1847. Even today, Mormons worldwide celebrate July 24 as Pioneer Day.

In many ways, the Mormons were like other emigrants. They shared the same trail experiences and followed the same daily routines. They planned carefully what to bring, and made difficult decisions about what to leave behind. Once on the trail, they moved from one source of water to another, crossing prairies, plains, rivers, deserts, and mountains. Their food, wagons, animals, sicknesses, triumphs, and tragedies were typical.

But in other ways, the Mormons differed from other pioneers. In addition to their quest for religious freedom, they moved west as "villages on wheels," giving them a special sense of community. Generally poorer than most pioneers, they traveled without professional guides and often were on their own. They believed they were doing God's will, and that gave them the courage to go on.

Most other pioneers were not concerned about those who would follow. The first Mormons, however, built special camps along the way and improved the trails to help those who would be traveling west after them.

*****Persecution** means oppression or ill treatment based on religion, race, or beliefs.

FAST FACT
By the spring of 1847, the Mormons had built more than 80 sprawling farm towns throughout southwestern Iowa.

In south-central Iowa, for example, the Mormons established two rest and supply stations, Garden Grove and Mount Pisgah, 33 miles apart. They planted more than 2,000 acres of crops and built log homes at these stations, which saved the lives of many later Mormons who had accidents or fell sick while crossing Iowa.

The Mormons also were careful to kill animals only for food, not for sport, and they were mindful of the environment, refusing to chop down scarce trees and avoiding overgrazing. They made an effort to treat fairly the Native Americans they met along the trail. Because of this, they seldom had any trouble with the tribes.

As they moved farther west in Iowa, the Mormons clustered in one place, called Grand Encampment, just southeast of where Council Bluffs is today. The camp, with great squares of wagons on hilltops, stretched for miles just east of the Missouri River. Between mid-June and early July 1846, thousands of Mormons gathered there.

The Mormons built a ferry across the Missouri River and slowly crossed into what is now Nebraska, settling in the northeast corner of present-day Omaha. They called this city Winter Quarters. It was laid out with wide streets and a six-foot-high picket fence hemming the city in against the river. Cannon and mortars were set up on the hills to the north. Although the Omaha and Oto-Missouri tribes, living 20 miles south in villages by the Platte River, were friendly, precautions were necessary.

In contrast to Garden Grove and Mount Pisgah, Winter Quarters was planned carefully and built to be more permanent. It had two general stores and a welfare store for the poor. A flour mill was constructed at the north end of town. It also had a workshop where washboards and baskets were manufactured for sale in Missouri. The Council House served as city hall, schoolhouse, church, and social center.

By Stanley B. Kimball and Gail George Holmes, illustrated by Jeff Crosby, *Cobblestone,* © by Carus Publishing Company. Reproduced with permission.

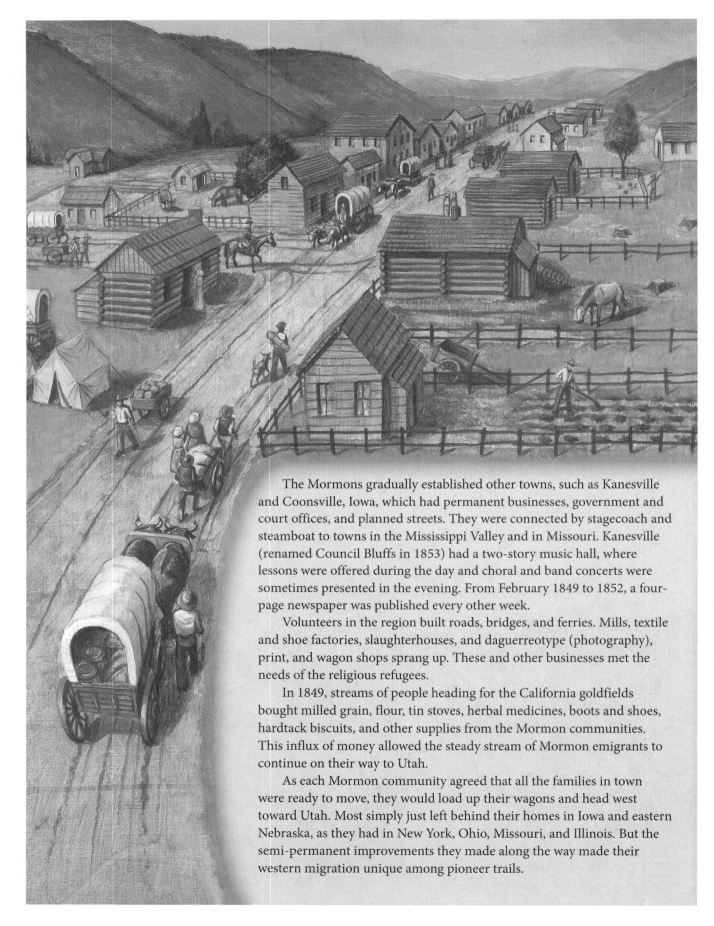

The Mormons gradually established other towns, such as Kanesville and Coonsville, Iowa, which had permanent businesses, government and court offices, and planned streets. They were connected by stagecoach and steamboat to towns in the Mississippi Valley and in Missouri. Kanesville (renamed Council Bluffs in 1853) had a two-story music hall, where lessons were offered during the day and choral and band concerts were sometimes presented in the evening. From February 1849 to 1852, a four-page newspaper was published every other week.

Volunteers in the region built roads, bridges, and ferries. Mills, textile and shoe factories, slaughterhouses, and daguerreotype (photography), print, and wagon shops sprang up. These and other businesses met the needs of the religious refugees.

In 1849, streams of people heading for the California goldfields bought milled grain, flour, tin stoves, herbal medicines, boots and shoes, hardtack biscuits, and other supplies from the Mormon communities. This influx of money allowed the steady stream of Mormon emigrants to continue on their way to Utah.

As each Mormon community agreed that all the families in town were ready to move, they would load up their wagons and head west toward Utah. Most simply just left behind their homes in Iowa and eastern Nebraska, as they had in New York, Ohio, Missouri, and Illinois. But the semi-permanent improvements they made along the way made their western migration unique among pioneer trails.

A Mormon family at their home in the Great Salt Lake Valley in 1869.

From The New York Public Library

FAST FACT
Waiilatpu is a Native American word meaning "place of rye grass."

A Higher Call

NARCISSA WHITMAN was one of the first women to make the difficult journey overland to the Oregon country in the early 1830s. She wasn't part of a wagon train, though. She and her husband, Marcus, were Presbyterian missionaries. They believed they were answering a call from God to bring Christianity to the Native Americans living in the "uncivilized wilderness."

The Whitmans built their mission at **Waiilatpu**, near present-day Walla Walla, Washington. At first the local Cayuse Indians welcomed the Whitmans. The chief gave them land, and the Whitmans built a home and a schoolroom, planted a garden and an orchard, and held religious services for the Cayuse. The Cayuse were used to wandering in search of their food, but Marcus taught them how to plow and plant. Soon, the Cayuse began to see the value of staying in one place.

Over the next few years, a growing number of emigrants wound down the trail and stopped at the Waiilatpu mission. After the difficult journey over the Rocky Mountains, the travelers needed to buy food and repair their equipment. The mission became an important stop before pioneers continued on the last leg of their journey into the Willamette Valley. The Cayuse became angry at the steady stream of white people crossing their lands.

In the fall of 1847, a wagon train arrived, carrying many people sick with measles. Before long, all the children and some adults at the mission became ill. The disease spread among the Cayuse, who began to die in great numbers. They believed that Marcus was deliberately poisoning them so that he could take their land.

On the morning of November 29, 1847, a small group of Cayuse appeared at the crowded mission and killed the Whitmans and 11 others. Twelve people escaped, and 49 others were held captive for a month before being ransomed. The mission's days came to a close. But during the 11 years the Whitmans spent at Waiilatpu, some 13,000 emigrants had turned a trapper's path into the famous Oregon Trail.

ROUGH AND TUMBLE

Growing Up in a Mining Town

Mining towns in the western frontier were often high in the mountains at the end of narrow, winding roads. Most of the towns could be reached only by mule-drawn wagons. Anne Ellis remembers her log cabin in the silver-mining town of Bonanza, Colorado. "The ceiling of our cabin was usually covered with canvas—in this, dirt would collect, making it sag in places. Mountain rats also made their nests just on top of the canvas. Once, a rat ran along the canvas and Mama saw the shape of his body and stuck a fork into him."

All mining towns had a place called an assay office, where the miners brought samples of what

Children (above) helped hunt for ore, creating collections of colorful minerals. A quartz mining site in Gold Hill, Nevada around 1866 (right).

Top and bottom: Library of Congress

The Comstock Lode in Nevada contained silver of exceptional purity, triggering a rush of thousands of miners to the area. Working the Comstock Lode was extraordinarily dangerous. Apart from the risk of cave-ins and underground fires, miners had to worry about underground flooding. When miners penetrated through rock, steam and scalding water would pour into the tunnel, and miners had to jump into cages, risking death if the hoisting mechanisms failed to lift them quickly enough. This cutaway of a hillside shows tunnels and supports, shaft, and miners with their tools engaged in various activities.

they had found. The assayer put the ore into a special cup and heated it to find out what it was. Leigh Turner in Ouray, Colorado, and her friends thought the cups were beautiful—colored with blues, greens, yellows, and browns. "We children hunted these, compared collections, and [traded] with each other." Sometimes the miners gave the kids mineral samples that they brought from the mines.

Living in a mining town could be dangerous. Children sometimes "forgot" their parents' warnings. In the spring, melting snow turned little creeks into raging rivers. If a child was missing, the first place people searched was the creek.

Boys tried to be like the miners by drilling holes in the rocks. One boy would hold the drill against the rock while the other hit the drill with a hammer. It's a wonder there weren't more smashed fingers.

In 1893, the United States government stopped buying large amounts of silver. Many silver mines had to shut down. Mining families moved on to other places and other jobs. Many of the children remembered the times in the mining towns as some of the happiest days of their lives.

All images: History Colorado. Miner's Candlestick: #H.6995.6. Miner's Hat: #GTL.PROP.101. Tin Lunchbox: #H.6200.673. Ore bucket photo: Harry H. Buckwalter Photograph Collection ph.00057 (scan #20030697).

INTO THE MINE

Deep in the heart of the Colorado mountains in the 1870s, mines twist and turn.
It is pitch-black inside the mountain. There are no stars to light the way.
This is a dangerous place for miners, but gold, silver, and other minerals are precious.
Miners do their best to come prepared for the perilous conditions.

So what do they need to enter the mine?

Miner's Candlestick

In the mountains of Colorado, men used candles to light their way. In the mid-1800s, miners secured candles to their caps or to the rocky walls of the mine using a clump of clay. Sometime in the 1860s, miners invented a miner's candlestick by bending the end of a spike to hold a candle. The spike then could be jabbed into a wooden support beam to light the way. Later, miners began using a hook on the candlestick to attach the candle to their hats, creating a kind of headlamp.

Miner's Hat

In the 1800s, miners did not have hard hats to protect their heads. Instead they wore caps made of cloth or felt. Some hats had a metal plate to attach a candle or an oil lamp to light the way through the dark tunnel.

Miner's Lunch Pail

The lunch pail usually had two or three compartments. The lower compartment contained tea that could be heated by a candle. The second compartment held their meal, usually meat, potatoes and vegetables. The third compartment usually held dessert. The miner attached a metal tea cup to the lid of the bucket.

Ore Buckets

While some mines had tunnels entering the side of a mountain, many of the shafts went straight down. It was quite dangerous to transport minors up and down the deep, dangerous pits. In large mines, cages built on platforms were used to lower men. In small mines, men rode in ore buckets. The bucket was large enough for a man to climb inside, and often, another miner or two stood on the rim of the bucket for the jerky ride down!

Miner's Code of Signals

Each mine had a hoister, a man in charge of raising and lowering the ore buckets down the mineshaft. The hoister had to be able to communicate with the miners below. A signal code using bells was used in each mine to relay messages.

May be reproduced for classroom use. Toolkit Texts: Short Nonfiction for American History, Westward Expansion, by Stephanie Harvey and Anne Goudvis, ©2016 (Portsmouth, NH: Heinemann).

BABY DOE

THE SILVER QUEEN

They once called me The Silver Queen of Colorado. My name is Elizabeth Doe, but the miners who were digging for gold near our mine in Central City, Colorado, thought I was so beautiful that they started calling me "Baby" Doe. Even after I divorced my husband Harvey, and married Horace Tabor, they still called me Baby Doe. Horace and I were called The Silver King and Queen of Denver, Colorado. We lived in a huge mansion paid for by the millions of dollars Horace made from his silver mines. It was a good life, a grand life, with beautiful clothes and fancy parties and traveling.

But I never forgot where I came from. I was a Wisconsin girl, born there in 1854. My mother despaired of me because I was a tomboy, lively and interested in everything, even though she also said I was the prettiest of all her seven children. I met Harvey Doe and we were married in 1877. Harvey's father owned a half interest in the Fourth of July Mine in Central City, Colorado, so we decided it was time to start a new life of adventure, away from Wisconsin. "We'll go west and make our fortune overnight in gold," Harvey told me. "People do it all the time there!" But Harvey didn't know how to work hard and the mine wasn't producing well. So I put on miner's clothes and went to work right beside him. Some of the people in Central City disapproved of me, but I didn't care.

Harvey just couldn't seem to work hard enough to support us, and we drifted apart. When I finally divorced him, I moved to a boarding house in Leadville, Colorado. There I met Horace Tabor, who had made his fortune with silver mines and was now lieutenant governor of Colorado. We fell in love right away. As soon as he divorced his wife Augusta, we were married. Horace said to me, "You're always so [happy] and laughing, and yet you're so brave."

Horace became a U.S. senator, and we moved to Denver and into our mansion. Many of the society folks there did not approve of us because of the scandal of being divorced. They said I was too friendly and didn't behave like a proper lady should. They made up terrible rumors and gossip about us, but we loved each other very much and it didn't matter. When some of my proper female neighbors complained about the nude statues in our gardens, I had my dressmaker come and make dresses for those statues! We also had two daughters, Elizabeth and Rose Mary. It was a wonderful life.

Sadly, it did not last. In 1893, the value of silver fell and we were ruined. Suddenly we had no money. We moved into a small rented cottage near the

A portrait of Elizabeth Tabor, better known as Baby Doe.

Two children sit on a hill overlooking the Matchless Mine in Leadville, Colorado.

Matchless Mine in Leadville, which we still owned. In 1899, Horace became ill. Just before he died, he told me to hold onto the Matchless Mine. He thought it would make millions again someday when silver went up in price once more. After Horace died, the girls and I moved into a tiny shack near the mine which was once the tool shed. The girls left home, but I stayed in my shack.

It's been nearly 35 years now and I'm still holding on to the Matchless as Horace told me to. Someday it will be worth millions again, I'm sure. I don't take charity. I pick up chunks of valuable ore and trade with shopkeepers for my food (even though I've heard some people whisper that my ore is worthless and the shopkeepers are accepting it as payment just because they feel sorry for me). When I'm cold, I wrap my feet in burlap sacks, tied with twine. When I'm sick I make my own medicine. I write in my diaries and keep the fire going. They even made a movie about me in 1932, but I refused to see it. That life, the life of Baby Doe Tabor, the Silver Queen, is over now.

On February 20, 1935, Baby Doe wrote in her diary: "Went down to Leadville from Matchless—the snow so terrible, I had to go down on my hands and knees and creep from my cabin door to 7th Street. Mr. Zaitz driver drove me to our get off place and he helped pull me to the cabin. I kept falling deep down through the snow every minute. God bless him." The storm continued for days, and when neighbors finally checked on her, they found Baby Doe Tabor, a tiny 81-year-old woman, lying dead from a heart attack, her body frozen on the floor of her cabin. She was buried next to Horace in Denver.

By Marcia Amidon Lusted. May be reproduced for classroom use. *Toolkit Texts: Short Nonfiction for American History, Westward Expansion,* by Stephanie Harvey and Anne Goudvis, ©2016 (Portsmouth, NH: Heinemann).

GO FOR THE GOLD!

Miners: Library of Congress. Pan and pick: © Photodisc/Getty Images/HIP.

There were many miners with one goal: To find GOLD in California!

Washing and panning for gold (above) in Rockerville, South Dakota

Discovery at Sutter's Mill

One January day in 1848, a worker named James Marshall spotted some shiny bits in the gravel of the American River at Coloma, California. He showed them to his boss, the owner of Sutter's Mill lumber company. When tests proved that it was gold, Sutter tried to keep the discovery secret. But news spread. His workers left the lumber mill, squatters took his land, and his business failed.

The '49ers Come to California

By 1849, California's population exploded with gold seekers. Some newcomers came overland from the East Coast in wagon trains. Others braved long sea voyages around Cape Horn at the tip of South America to reach San Francisco. By the end of 1849, the population of San Francisco was 100,000, as compared to 800 in the beginning of 1848.

By Gloria W. Lannom, *Appleseeds,* © by Carus Publishing Company. Reproduced with permission.

Mining gold was backbreaking, dirty, dangerous, and sometimes violent. Some miners worked by hand. They used picks, shovels, and pans to sift gold-bearing sand and gravel from rivers and streams. Hard-rock mining required machinery, high-pressure hoses, and water to crush and move huge quantities of rock. Deep holes scarred valuable farmland.

Miners "staked a claim" to specific land where they looked for gold. But claim jumpers frequently took over other miners' claims. And thieves stole their finds. Some miners camped inside their hillside tunnels to protect their claims.

Miners took their gold dust, flakes, and nuggets to people called assayers. They weighed and tested it for purity. Some who thought they had gold learned it was worthless iron pyrite.

Why is gold valuable?
It's beautiful, rare, useful, and durable, and it doesn't rust or tarnish. Gold can be cast, carved, pressed, rolled, polished, and hammered thinner than any other metal. Most important, though, people worldwide believe it has value.

A **sluice** is a long box for rinsing gravel and ore to sift out gold.

May be reproduced for classroom use. *Toolkit Texts: Short Nonfiction for American History, Westward Expansion*, by Stephanie Harvey and Anne Goudvis, ©2016 (Portsmouth, NH: Heinemann).

Library of Congress

Gold miners in a miners' camp

Miners needed tools, food, and clothing to survive. Storekeepers gladly provided supplies at sky-high prices. They demanded payment in gold. Many businessmen became far richer than even the luckiest miners. Peddler Levi Strauss is a good example. He sold tent canvas. But then he made more money selling rugged denim work overalls. He later founded a company that manufactured blue jeans. (And you know what they're called today!)

Gold Rush miners were also called prospectors, gold-seekers, Argonauts (after the gold-seekers of Greek mythology), or forty-niners (after the year 1849).

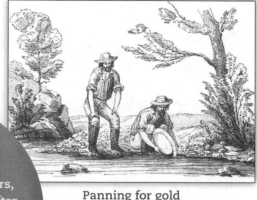

Panning for gold

Entering a mine shaft

THE ILLUSTRATED

MINERS' HAND-BOOK

AND

GUIDE TO PIKE'S PEAK,

WITH A

NEW AND RELIABLE MAP,

SHOWING

ALL THE ROUTES, AND THE GOLD REGIONS

OF

WESTERN KANSAS AND NEBRASKA.

ILLUSTRATED WITH APPROPRIATE ENGRAVINGS.

BY PARKER & HUYETT,

Third Street, opposite the new Post Office, and 65 Chesnut Street,

SAINT LOUIS.

1859.

Preparing equipment

Miner's handbooks were created to guide gold seekers. According to the *Guide to Pike's Peak*, "There appears to be a regular deposit of gold. This is true of every creek coming out of the mountains, and of every canon and valley from Pike's Peak to Laramie Plains."

Cooking at camp

All images: Library of Congress

By Gloria W. Lannom, *Appleseeds*, © by Carus Publishing Company. Reproduced with permission.

A prospector on the porch of his cabin near Eagle Creek, Murray, Idaho, 1889

You can pan for gold in the gold country today. The winter snowmelt makes rivers flow strongest in April, and they carry lots of material to sift.

Lasting Impact of the Gold Rush

Machinery and lumber suppliers did well, too. Two men who exchanged miners' gold for dollars established what is today one of America's largest banks. Sea and land transportation improved. Hotels, entertainment halls, and gambling houses flourished.

Not everything was "golden," however. As veins of gold-bearing rock played out, many miners ended up penniless and left.

The Gold Rush lasted only a few years, but it changed California from frontier territory to a prosperous statehood. In September 1850, California became the 31st state in the United States, entering as a free state where slavery was prohibited. Today, abandoned mine tunnels and rock and gravel piles left from dredging are silent reminders of this history-making period.

Toolkit Texts: Short Nonfiction for American History, Westward Expansion, by Stephanie Harvey and Anne Goudvis, ©2016 (Portsmouth, NH: Heinemann).

May be reproduced for classroom use.

Population of California Before and After the Gold Rush

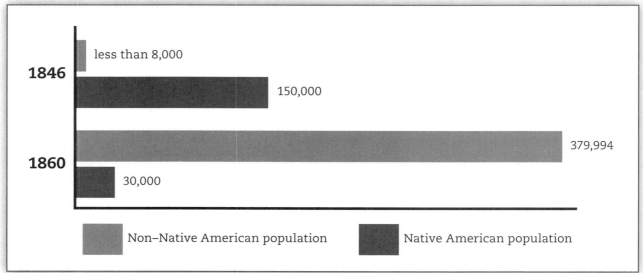

1846
less than 8,000
150,000

1860
379,994
30,000

Non–Native American population
Native American population

During the Gold Rush, gold seekers flocked to California in large numbers. As a result, Native Americans were often forced off their land.

The Discovery at Sutter's Mill

John Augustus Sutter was a wealthy landowner in California in 1848. After his foreman, James W. Marshall, reported his discovery of gold while working at the mill stream, the men agreed to keep the news secret. They knew that news of the discovery would bring gold seekers to the Sutter lands. In the following account, Marshall describes the discovery that changed America's history.

From James W. Marshall's Account, 1848

One morning in January in 1848, it was a clear cold morning; I shall never forget that morning, as I was taking my usual walk along the race, after shutting off the water, my eye was caught by a glimpse of something in the bottom of the ditch. There was about a foot of water running there. I reached my hand down and picked it up; it made my heart thump for I felt certain it was gold. The piece was about half the size and shape of a pea. Then I saw another piece in the water. After taking it out, I sat down and began to think right hard. I thought it was gold, and yet it did not seem to be of the right color; all the gold coin I had seen was of a reddish tinge; this looked to me like brass. I recalled to mind all of the metals I had ever seen or heard of, but I could find none to resemble this.

Suddenly the idea flashed across my mind that it might be iron pyrites. I trembled to think of it! This question could soon be determined. Putting one of the pieces on hard river stone, I took another and commenced hammering it. It was soft and didn't break; it therefore must be gold.

James Marshall standing in front of Sutter's sawmill, in Coloma, California, where he discovered gold.

Library of Congress

About a week's time after the discovery I had to take another trip to the fort; and to gain what information I could respecting the real value of this metal, took all we had collected with me and showed it to Mr. Sutter, who at once declared it was gold, but thought with me, it was greatly mixed with other metal. . . . After hunting over the whole fort and borrowing from some other men, we got three dollars and a half in silver, and with a small pair of scales we soon cyphered it out that there was no silver nor copper in the gold, but that it was entirely pure.

This fact being ascertained, we thought it our best policy to keep it as quiet as possible til we should have finished our mill, but there was a great number of soldiers in and about the fort, and when they came to hear of it, why, it just spread like wildfire, and soon the whole country was in a bustle.

So there, stranger, is the entire history of the gold discovery in California—a discovery that hasn't as yet been of much benefit to me.

May be reproduced for classroom use. *Toolkit Texts: Short Nonfiction for American History, Westward Expansion*, by Stephanie Harvey and Anne Goudvis, ©2016 (Portsmouth, NH: Heinemann).

Library of Congress

First Transcontinental Railroad

At a place called Promontory, a tiny settlement on the shore of Utah's Great Salt Lake, two train locomotives idled nose to nose. One train was from the East, the other from the West. A large crowd had gathered. After six years of difficult, laborious work, tracks had been laid over nearly 1,800 miles from Omaha, Nebraska, to Sacramento, California. It was May 10, 1869, and the United States was about to be connected by rail.

The railroad president got ready to hammer in the spike that would finally connect east and west. He swung and missed. The next official also missed! Still, the crowd cheered, and other important people took their turns. The spikes, of silver, iron, and gold, were hammered in place. The first transcontinental railroad was completed!

The Union Pacific locomotive from the East, called the 119, crossed over onto Central Pacific tracks. Then it backed up to allow the Jupiter,

On May 10, 1869, the two lines finally met at Promontory Point (above).

the locomotive from the West, to chug across onto Union Pacific tracks. Everyone cheered again, and celebrations lasted all afternoon.

Why was a transcontinental railroad so important? This was a time before the invention of the airplane or the automobile. Some tracks and railroads had been built, but they only connected cities east of the Mississippi River. It took months to get over land from points along the Mississippi River to the West Coast.

The idea of a transcontinental railroad emerged as large groups of people began to settle California and the western territories. A group of businessmen predicted that a railroad that extended across the West could be quite profitable.

At first, building the railroad seemed impossible. In 1862, President Abraham Lincoln signed a bill that gave the railroad companies special land grants and government bonds to help pay for the job. Even so, the owners of the Central Pacific and Union Pacific railroad companies had to raise even more money.

Both companies had tremendous difficulty getting their supplies on site. The Central Pacific had to ship their equipment from the Atlantic Coast, an expensive and time-consuming effort. Work on the Central Pacific was slowed as it approached the snow-covered Sierra Nevada, a range of steep, rocky mountains through which the tracks had to be laid.

The Union Pacific also had problems. At first, they had to ship their supplies and equipment up the Missouri River by steamboat, and then

Large work crew laid tracks for the railroad, which cut through the heart of Native American lands.

North Wind Picture Archives

May be reproduced for classroom use. *Toolkit Texts: Short Nonfiction for American History, Westward Expansion,* by Stephanie Harvey and Anne Goudvis, ©2016 (Portsmouth, NH: Heinemann).

A large work crew lays track for the railroad as soldiers and Native Americans meet nearby.

carry them overland by stagecoach and wagons. Later, they were able to send supplies along the tracks they had laid, but all the carrying, pushing, and pulling had to be done by men with picks and shovels, wheelbarrows, wagons, and mules.

The first transcontinental railroad was one of the last major projects to be constructed primarily by hand in the United States. It took the labor of thousands of men—many of them Chinese immigrants—to complete this incredible task.

Although the official date for the opening of the railroad was November 6, 1869, when the Union Pacific and Central Pacific railroads joined on May 10, 1869, the dream of a transcontinental railroad became a reality. Suddenly, a journey from the East Coast to California took a week instead of months. The railroad opened the door to settlers from the East and from other countries eager to make lives for themselves in California and other points in the West. The age of the stagecoach and wagons gave way to the era of the "iron horse."

By Mark Clemens, *Cobblestone*, © by Carus Publishing Company. Reproduced with permission.

137

The First Transcontinental Railroad

In 1860, the United States had more than thirty thousand miles of railroad, all of it east of the Mississippi River. The railroad in the East enabled easy and fast transportation. The West had only horse and wagon travel. In 1862, Congress approved funds for the first transcontinental railroad. The building of this railroad was an amazing feat of engineering and construction. The newspaper accounts below describe the Chinese immigrants who worked on the Central Pacific; the Irish and other immigrants who worked on the Union Pacific; and the meeting of the two railroad lines at Promontory Point, Utah, in May 1869.

From the Alta California, *1868*

When the first blue-clad Chinese workers appeared at the roadbed of the Central Pacific, the muscular Americans laughed at them because they looked so small and frail. They quickly proved their worth as Mr. [Charles] Crocker has wisely hired thousands, even sending to China itself for recruits.

We have witnessed their great efficiency in cutting through snowdrifts fifty feet high. They have lowered in baskets 2,000 feet down cliffs to hand-drill holes for blasting powder. We have been told of their work in carving tunnels through mountains—fifteen tunnels in all, the longest measured at 1,659 feet. Above all, these pigtailed coolies, drinking their hourly tea brought to them in buckets, have gained the respect of everyone.

From the New York Daily Tribune, *1868*

Mr. [Greenville] Dodge, the Chief Engineer of the Union Pacific, has forged more than 8,000 workers—many of them Irish immigrants—into a formidable army. They have fought off the depredations of Cheyenne war parties. . . . A train of 24 cars is needed to supply this army its daily needs. Each train is shunted into a siding when a fresh supply train comes through.

Five men work on each 700-pound iron rail, ten men to a pair of rails. Thirty seconds is allowed for each pair of rails, two rail lengths every minute, three blows to each spike, 10 spikes to the rail; this meant 400 rails, 4,000 spikes, and 12,000 hammer blows for a single mile of track!

From the New York Daily Tribune's *Front Page*

May 11, 1869

Promontory Summit, Utah, May 10—The last rail is laid! The last spike, the golden one, driven! The Pacific Railroad is completed!

The point of junction is 1,086 miles west of the Missouri River, and 600 miles east of Sacramento City.

The Celestials' Railroad

On the Utah prairie where a thousand workers had gathered for the ceremony, four Chinese men carried an iron rail toward the track. It was the last link in the railroad that within moments would span the continent.

From Gold Fields to Railroads

The date was May 10, 1869. The Union Pacific locomotive stood to one side and the Central Pacific to the other. The Chinese workers were known as "coolies," "heathens," and, because they called China the Celestial Kingdom, "Celestials." Few of their fellow railroad workers bothered to learn their names. On the job, they were all called "John Chinaman." No one knows their names today. But it was on the backs of the Chinese workers that the first transcontinental railroad was built.

For the Chinese, the work began as an experiment. Many Chinese men had come to America during the first California gold rush. When they did not strike it rich in the goldfields, they sought other work—but faced discrimination instead.

Then in 1863, Central Pacific and Union Pacific railroad tycoons agreed to build a coast-to-coast link. The Union Pacific would head west from Omaha, Nebraska, while the Central Pacific would extend east from Sacramento, California. The two companies mapped the routes, raised the money, and hired the workers.

Despite all their hard labor, not one Chinese worker was present for this photo taken at the joining of the Union Pacific and Central Pacific railroads.

May be reproduced for classroom use. *Toolkit Texts: Short Nonfiction for American History, Westward Expansion*, by Stephanie Harvey and Anne Goudvis, ©2016 (Portsmouth, NH: Heinemann).

Within a year, the Union Pacific was well into Nebraska, but the Central Pacific had bogged down at the edge of the Sierra Nevada mountains. In California, most men were busy searching for gold or silver. To complete his contract, railroad magnate Charles Crocker needed help. Over the protests of his workers, Crocker turned to Chinese workers.

Impressive Workers

In February 1865, 50 Chinese men were transported by flatcar to the rail's end in the Sierra foothills. While other workers jeered and threatened to strike, these laborers calmly set up camp, boiled rice provided by the company, and went to sleep. Up at dawn, with picks and shovels in hand, they worked 12 hours straight without complaint. Crocker was impressed by their work ethic. By sundown, Crocker had telegraphed his office in Sacramento: "Send more Chinese." Within a few months, 3,000 Chinese workers were pushing the Central Pacific eastward. By the end of 1865, more than 6,000 Chinese were working on the railroad.

Library of Congress

Wearing wide-brimmed hats, Chinese workers labored on the tracks as the Central Pacific pushed eastward from Sacramento.

As the Central Pacific soared toward Donner Summit at the top of the Sierras, the Chinese took jobs no one else would touch. They hung like dolls from ropes draped over the edges of cliffs and tapped holes into the sides of mountains. After inserting dynamite, they jerked the ropes and were yanked upward. If they were lucky, they cleared the explosion and lived to tap

This tea carrier brings refreshment to Chinese workers.

A Temporary Stay

The Chinese were unique in America's westward expansion because they were one of the few immigrant groups that did not come to settle permanently. Drawn for many of the same reasons as Americans who were looking for a better life or religious freedom, immigrant groups from around the world established small communities throughout the West. Most Chinese migrants, however, were men who had left their families behind in China. Their intention was to work hard, save their money, and return to their homeland.

Library of Congress

Snow didn't stop work on the railroad. Here, Chinese laborers dig a train out of a drift near Ogden, Utah.

Chinese workers dined on oysters and cuttlefish brought in by rail from San Francisco. They ate vegetables and rice and drank only tea. Crossing Donner Summit at 7,000 feet, many other workers took sick or quit, but the Chinese kept going.

Mobs of white workers tormented the Chinese at every camp along the way. But across Nevada and into Utah, the Central Pacific inched toward the Union Pacific. And on April 27, 1869, Central Pacific crews, by then 90 percent Chinese, laid 10 miles of track in a single day— a new record.

Left Out of History

By the time the two railroads met at Promontory, Utah, the Central Pacific employed 12,000 Chinese workers. Together with the Union Pacific crews, they watched as railroad tycoons drove in their golden spikes. But when the cameras recorded the event, the Chinese workers were left out of the picture.

On May 10, 1869, the single word "Done!" was telegraphed across the continent. Finished with their monumental task, the Chinese laborers rode the Central Pacific back across the track they had laid. Some went back to "Chinatown" communities in Sacramento, San Francisco, and other cities. Others went to Canada, where they helped build the Canadian Pacific Railroad, or worked on routes in California. Many spread out across the West, finding work or staking claims in mining towns such as Deadwood, South Dakota, and Tombstone, Arizona. Their labor and sacrifice had connected the east and west coasts of the growing nation.

more holes. If not, they fell into the gorge below.

Chinese workers blasted tunnels with nitroglycerin when other workers would not touch the explosive liquid. They graded hillsides. They chopped trees. They carried dirt in wheelbarrows, filled huge gorges with it, leveled it, and laid railroad ties evenly across it. Other workers then laid the iron rails and hammered them down while the Chinese went ahead to prepare the next mile.

Healthier Habits

Most other workers ate stale meat and drank brackish water or whiskey. But even high in the mountains,

May be reproduced for classroom use. *Toolkit Texts: Short Nonfiction for American History, Westward Expansion,* by Stephanie Harvey and Anne Goudvis, ©2016 (Portsmouth, NH: Heinemann).

Placing Out

kansasmemory.org, Kansas State Historical Society

When a child of the streets stands before you in rags with tear-stained face, you cannot easily forget him.
—Charles Loring Brace

The Children's Aid Society, founded in 1853, worked to place homeless and orphaned children from eastern cities into rural homes in the Midwest. The children were given new clothing and sometimes a small suitcase for their few personal belongings. They were then escorted to the train station, where they waited for their assigned seats.

Journey to a New Life

The trains usually left on a Tuesday so that they would arrive at various locations over the weekend. Placing-out agents accompanied the children on the rides. They passed out bibles to them and tried to comfort them as they journeyed west. Often they sang to the children to help relieve their anxiety.

Sometimes as many as 40 children rode on the orphan trains (above) with just two or three adults.

Orphan Train ad from the *Tecumseh Chieftan* newspaper.

The journey usually lasted three or four days. The children were not allowed to leave the train except to change trains or pass the time during a layover. They slept in their seats. One young girl said, "I didn't cry. I guess I was too angry to cry. We were going too far, too fast."

As the train neared its destination, the children changed their clothes and washed their faces. The girls wore new dresses. The boys wore white shirts, neckties, and suit coats. They were urged to make a good impression on the many people awaiting their arrival.

Families Needed

The townsfolk had already read about the orphan train riders in local newspapers. They were encouraged to come and view the children on the stage of the local meeting hall. As the children were lined up in rows, an agent would give a brief account of each. The agent would then explain the rules to the crowd: Placements were on a trial basis. Legal adoption was not required. Foster parents were asked to treat the children as members of the family. This meant feeding, clothing, and housing them, as well as sending them to school, church, and Sunday school. Children were expected to work as contributing members of the household.

Often the children were pulled, pushed, and shoved about as townspeople tried to decide which one to choose. Even in small towns, large numbers of people came to watch the selection process. One onlooker said, "It was a pathetic sight to see them tired young people-weary, travel-stained, confused by the excitement-peering into those strange faces."

Placements were sometimes very emotional. Lee Nailling was an eight-year-old boy traveling with his two younger brothers, Leo and Gerald. Gerald was chosen first. As he was being carried away by a woman, he realized that his brothers were staying behind. He stretched out his arms and began

Toolkit Texts: Short Nonfiction for American History, Westward Expansion, by Stephanie Harvey and Anne Goudvis, ©2016 (Portsmouth, NH: Heinemann).

May be reproduced for classroom use.

screaming for them. Lee choked back tears as he watched his two-and-a-half-year-old brother disappear into the crowd.

Children who were not selected would return to the train to be taken to the next stop on the line. Many of them could be seen boarding the train with bewildered or dejected looks on their faces. Some children traveled from location to location, feeling increasingly alone and unwanted, until there were no other children left.

Mixed Outcomes

Those who were selected were taken to farmhouses, cabins, sod houses, and shopkeepers' homes. Many of the children were adopted by loving families who nurtured and cared for them, but some of them did not fare as well. Some were chosen merely to assist in farm chores or to be domestic (household) servants. Some were selected to replace a child who had died. Others were chosen to look after an older couple. Some children who were unhappy with their homes ran away and drifted from farm to farm looking for shelter or work. Others were sent back to New York. Still others made the best of their unhappy situations until they were grown.

Many of the orphans ended up leading pleasant lives. One young girl wrote to the Children's Aid Society, "When I lived in New York, I had no bonnet. Now I have more bonnets than

Homeless children in New York City warming themselves over a steam grate.

May be reproduced for classroom use. *Toolkit Texts: Short Nonfiction for American History, Westward Expansion*, by Stephanie Harvey and Anne Goudvis, ©2016 (Portsmouth, NH: Heinemann).

I can wear. I get no whippings and I have a father and mother and brothers and sisters here, and they are kinder to me than my own ever were. I think I will never be happier than I am now."

Many orphans adjusted to their new lives and grew up to be prominent citizens in their communities. Andrew Burke and John Brady were sent to the same Indiana town on the same day. They were lonely, street-tough, unpromising boys, but a judge picked John because "I had a curious desire to see what could be made of such a specimen of humanity." John became the governor of Alaska Territory, and Andrew went on to become the governor of North Dakota.

The lives of many of these children were changed for the better by the orphan train movement. The bond that formed between them and their new parents is perhaps best illustrated

Children's Aid Society placement card. When a child was placed, a contract was signed between the Children's Aid Society and the guardians taking the child. At right is a typical contract.

Terms on Which Boys are Placed in Homes

Applications must be endorsed by the Local Committee.

- Boys under 15 years of age, if not legally adopted, must be retained as members of the family and sent to school according to the Educational Laws of the State, until they are 18 years old. Suitable provision must then be made for their future.

- Boys 15 and 16 years of age must be retained as members of the family and sent to school during the winter months until they are 17 years old, when a mutual arrangement may be made.

- Boys over 16 years of age must be retained as members of the family for one year, after which a mutual arrangement may be made.

- Parties taking boys agree to write to the Society at least once a year, or to have the boys do so.

- Removals of boys proving unsatisfactory can be arranged through the Local Committee or an Agent of the Society, the party agreeing to retain the boy a reasonable length of time after notifying the Society of the desired change.

by a letter from Mrs. Sally Highland, dated June 5, 1865. "If he were our own son," Highland wrote to the Children's Aid Society, "we could not love him more than we do. We have given him our name. We call him Charlie Highland. He thinks we are his parents and we want him to. I love him so much that it would break my heart to part with him."

The story of the orphan trains is one of immigration and westward expansion. Between 1854 and 1929, more than 100,000 children were sent on orphan trains to rural America. Descendants of the orphan train riders probably number in the millions. Hundreds of riders themselves are still alive to tell their tales.

A photograph of Toni Weiler, as a little girl, shortly after arriving in Nebraska on the Orphan Train.

Nebraska State Historical Society

Where Did They Go?

In September 1854, the first leg of the journey for the first group of orphan train riders began with a boat ride from New York City to Albany, New York. After switching to a train and then another boat, the forty-six children boarded a train for Dowagiac, Michigan. For many years, the states of Michigan, Ohio, Indiana, Illinois, Iowa, Missouri, and Kansas were the main stops for the Children's Aid Society. These states were largely agricultural and needed farm labor. Over the years, orphan trains stopped in forty-seven states. Some children also went to Canada and South America.

Orphan Train Newspaper Accounts

The Orphan Train was a program that transported orphaned and homeless children from crowded Eastern cities of the United States to foster homes in rural areas of the Midwest. The orphan trains operated between 1853 and 1929, relocating about 200,000 orphaned, abandoned, or homeless children. Below are two newspaper accounts of the arrival of orphan trains, as well as one personal recollection of an orphan who was adopted by a family in the Midwest.

The Cawker City Public Record
Mitchell County, Kansas
April 8, 1886

One of the most interesting events that has recently occurred in Cawker was the distribution of boys from New York City last Saturday. As previously announced, Mr. Charles Fry, Children's Aid Society, of New York, was to arrive on Friday night with a company of boys for the purpose of finding homes and employment with farmers and others. Early in the evening a telegram was received stating that sixteen boys would arrive on the train which was an hour late. The Young Ladies' Aid society holding a social at the time in the Hall, decided to wait and welcome the new immigrants, who upon their arrival were escorted to the Hall and given a supper. They were then quartered at the hotels under the care of the agent and his assistant, Mr. Rudolph Heig. The committee previously selected to receive names of applicants for boys reported about thirty names, and the distribution under the management of Mr. Fry, the agent of the society, began on Saturday morning at ten o'clock. The Hall was crowded by the curious sight-seers and applicants for boys. The boys were seated on the stage facing the audience and presented altogether a different appearance from the ideas formed of them by some. They were an intelligent lot of little fellows and neatly clad, the most of them having been in the society's Home four or five years, and have had good training and discipline. All but two can read and write, one of the exceptions being between three and four years old, the ages of the party ranging up to seventeen years. The good humor of the audience was evoked by the chubby baby's comical and pleased expression. This little orphan fell to the lot of Mr. and Mrs. Chas D. Brown, and quite a scene was enacted on the stage when their selection was made and the little one threw his arms around the neck of his adopted mother. "His lines are fallen in pleasant places."

The mode of distribution was for the Agent to call the name of an applicant and let him select his boy after talking to him and learning his wishes. Where two applicants wanted the same boy the choice of guardian was made by the boy himself. Those who have taken the younger boys are expected to treat them as their own in the matter of schooling and providing for them; the eldest boys are to remain one year and are then expected to decide for themselves. The boys and one girl were distributed as follows:

Willie Bailey, 12 yrs old, to L.A. Rees
Willie Howard, 12 yrs old, to Daniel Shook
Jas K.P. Smith, 12 yrs old, to W.H. McClaskey
Eddie Bean, 12 yrs old, to H.M. Reynolds
Chas Sommers, 12 yrs old, to Jas M. Doak
Chas Martin, 12 yrs old, to A. Grimes
Wm VanWoessell, 10 yrs old, to Wilson Moore
Andrew Tarbitt, 10 yrs old, to J.A. Hazeltine
George Fox, 12 yrs old, to Mrs. E. Bowman
Robert Chadwick, 12 yrs old, to Chas E. Bishop
Joseph Gathier, 17 yrs old, to Wm F. Donaldson
Richard M. Brown, 16 yrs old, to C.H. Hawkins
James Freeman, 4 yrs old, to Chas D. Brown
Robert Duval, 16 yrs old, to Thos Shaw
Thomas Pugh, 16 yrs old, to Gordon Kerr
Mary Chadwick, (no age), to Mrs. L.M. Leggett

Since the distribution as above, there have been two changes. It is the desire of the Society's agent, as well as the local committee who assisted, that if further changes are necessary, the committee be advised so that the boys can be cared for. The committee endeavored to do the best for the welfare of the boys, and there being nearly double the number of applicants as there were boys, there must of necessity be some disappointment by many who would have given good homes to the little fellows. It was noticeable that the audience took great interest in the boys being provided with proper homes. Any information, or correspondence in regard to the boys will be given attention to at this office.

Star-Courier
Columbus, Kansas
June 21, 1894

THE ORPHANS

As was announced in last week's papers, eighteen orphan children from New York City arrived in Columbus on the five o'clock train Friday morning. They were in care of Messrs. King, Tice, and Mrs. Elston. After bathing and breakfast at the Middaugh hotel, the little ones were as wide awake and bright as if they had not traveled nearly 2,000 miles to find homes in the West. At an early hour many of the kind hearted citizens of Columbus and Cherokee County thronged the office and halls of the hotel to see the children and to choose from them such as they desired. Every mother's heart was touched at the sight of the little ones as at nine o'clock they were led onto the stage at the opera house. There was the chubby, dimpled baby, at once "Monarch of all he surveyed," the little boy still in kilt skirt, his brother in the proud triumphal period of his first pants—all unconscious of how much this occasion meant for them; there were the restless, typical boys of the period, and the older and thoughtful who were evidently pondering these things. It was a beautiful tribute to kindred love when little brothers tenderly said "good bye," and two little brothers (mere babies) positively refusing to be separated, one kind hearted man took them both. One could not look upon scenes like that and not have his faith in humanity strengthened. There were more demands for children than the supply. Some ladies even came in the afternoon, hoping that some child might be left; but they were all taken before leaving the opera house. We append the names of the children and their kind benefactors.

> Willie Vancura, age six years, with S.W. Alcenz, Neutral.
> Joseph Vancura, age thirteen years, with Thomas Haines, country.
> Anna Vancura, age eleven years, with Casper Christienson [correct spelling Caspar Christiansen], country.
> Joseph Fertig, age ten years, with Wm. McMillen, Tehama, P.O.
> John Fertig, age thirteen years, with C.W. Willey, Tehama, P.O.
> Edward Burns, age seventeen years, with H.P. Adams, country.
> Jacob Leperdoff, age fifteen years, with Jacob Stebbins, country.
> Thomas Finn, age sixteen years, with C.D. Arehart, Baxter Springs.
> Thomas Smith, age fifteen years, with Mayor Wiswell, Columbus.

May be reproduced for classroom use. *Toolkit Texts: Short Nonfiction for American History, Westward Expansion*, by Stephanie Harvey and Anne Goudvis, ©2016 (Portsmouth, NH: Heinemann).

Harold Walker, age two years, with Dr. Scammon, Columbus.

Elmer Davis, age six years, with Reuben W. Hefflin, Columbus.

Clarence Brown, age four years, and Matthew Brown, age seven years, with
   J.W. Goul, Cherokee.

John Kline, age eight years, with Mrs. Nancy Dagger, Weir City.

Charles Custed, age seven years, with Mr. S.O. Goodrich, Columbus.

Scott Mosher, age nine years, with Mrs. William Taylor, Columbus.

Frank Mosher, age eleven years, with Mrs. Ed Scammon, Miami.

Willie Mangan, age 17 years, with R.L. Risbow, Columbus.

Ophan Train Personal Account

JEAN SEXTON

I rode the train to Missouri and lived a happily ever after life.

In Brooklyn, New York in 1912, an Irish carpenter, who was the father of five children, died as the result of an industrial accident. Six months later, a sixth child was born to the thirty-five-year-old widow who was working hard to keep her family together. When the baby boy was eleven months old, his mother died. The grandparents were unable to care for the six orphans, so they were taken to the Children's Aid Society.

In 1914, along with other homeless children, they boarded an Orphan Train to find new homes in the Midwest. I was the fifth child, three years old, and was separated from my sister and brothers when I was adopted in southwest Missouri.

My foster parents were Walter and Margaret Landreth, a childless couple who lived twelve miles east of Neosho. Missouri. They soon became Mama and Daddy because I did not remember my biological parents. Daddy was a farmer and I was a tomboy. I loved going with Daddy whether it was to feed the cattle or gather walnuts. Daddy wanted me to have a pony, but Mama objected, saying that she was afraid I would get hurt. They finally compromised and I was soon riding a beautiful new bicycle. I would have had fewer black and blue marks if I had been riding a pony.

Mama was often called upon to help where there was illness and at these times I would get to stay with my grandmother. She loved me and we had fun together, but one day when she heard me practicing my whistling, she warned, "Whistling girls and crowing hens always come to a sad end."

In 1918, one of Daddy's nieces, Mary, came to live with us after her mother died during the flu epidemic leaving ten children. Mary was six months younger than I and we grew up together as sisters, sometimes, mistaken for twins. With Mama's help, we had many parties for our friends with taffy pulls and parlor games. An aunt and uncle joined in the fun by helping with decorations and entertainment.

Mama wanted us to have fun but she insisted that we learn cooking and housekeeping. She used many adages in her teaching, such as: "Anything worth doing is worth doing well," "A stitch in time saves nine," and "To have friends, you must show yourself friendly." She also lived by these rules.

Mr. J. W. Swan of Sedalia, Missouri, a very kind and considerate agent for the Children's Aid Society, visited often, but Daddy did not appreciate his visits. He did not want anyone doubting his care of his little girl. When I was sixteen, Mr. Swan came for his last visit and gave me the address of my brother, who lived in Colorado. My brother and I soon found our sister and baby brother, who had been adopted by Mr. and Mrs. Stoneberger of Auburn, Nebraska. The following summer, the three of them came to Missouri and we had a wonderful reunion. After that, we kept in touch and had many good times together.

I believe the secret of a happy life is keeping busy, making many friends and being a friend to all.

I believe you will agree that my story has a happy ending.

EXODUSTERS

D ramatic change rarely happens overnight. Even after slavery was abolished in 1865, African Americans in the South faced constant oppression and discrimination. They were denied education and the right to vote, they were cheated out of their crops, and they were subjected to acts of violence. Blacks had hoped for better lives and greater opportunities after the Civil War, but soon many realized that they would not find that life in the South. As it had for so many others in search of a better future, the West beckoned to African Americans.

The Great Exodus

In the spring of 1879, a mass migration of some 6,000 black people from the South began heading for Kansas,

The Homestead Act of 1862 helped create more than 372,000 farms and enabled African Americans, such as the Shores family (above), to start new lives out West.

Nebraska, and other parts of the West. Eventually, an estimated 15,000 to 20,000 blacks were persuaded to move west, mostly on foot but sometimes by boat up the Mississippi River. They became known as the Exodusters.

A former slave, Jerry Shores, and his family followed this movement west. They traveled with three wagons in one of the first emigrant trains to Nebraska. Shores drove one wagon, his son drove another, and his 16-year-old daughter drove the third one, which included taking care of her own team and greasing the wagon's wheels.

Opportunity for Land

The Shores family settled on a homestead claim in Nebraska. In 1862, in an effort to encourage people to settle the West,

President Abraham Lincoln had signed the Homestead Act. For many former slaves, the act offered their best opportunity to own land and their own homes.

The requirements of the Homestead Act were relatively simple. Any person 21 years of age or older and head of a household was entitled to 160 acres of uninhabited federal land. Within six months of living on a chosen parcel of land, or "claim," the homesteader had to start building a permanent house and making improvements to the claim. After living on the claim for five years, the land would belong to the homesteader.

Building a "Soddy"

Since Nebraska was mostly treeless prairie land, it was nearly impossible for the Shoreses to build any kind of wooden

Benjamin "Pap" Singleton became a spokesperson for the Exodusters and recruited African American settlers to join him in establishing a colony in Kansas with advertisements that promised great opportunities.

HISTORICAL SOCIETY.

Ho for Kansas!

Brethren, Friends, & Fellow Citizens:

I feel thankful to inform you that the

REAL ESTATE

AND

Homestead Association,

Will Leave Here the

15th of April, 1878,

In pursuit of Homes in the Southwestern Lands of America, at Transportation Rates, cheaper than ever was known before.

For full information inquire of

Benj. Singleton, better known as old Pap,

NO. 5 NORTH FRONT STREET.

Beware of Speculators and Adventurers, as it is a dangerous thing to fall in their hands.

Nashville, Tenn., March 18, 1878.

This photograph shows John Summer and his family standing in front of their home in Dunlap, Kansas. The home was built in the 1880s. Many homesteaders eventually upgraded their houses from sod to something more permanent.

structure. But good, cheap material was available: The earth and grass under their feet, which some settlers referred to as "prairie marble," could be used to build a sod house, or "soddy." Like many other pioneer families on the prairie, the Shoreses immediately went to work on their soddy to keep the family safe and protected from the weather.

The first step was to find a level plot of land. They cleared it of grass, smoothed it out with a spade, and packed it down to make a hard earth floor. A one-room sod house was usually 16 by 20 feet, and once the site was ready, the builder could begin laying sod bricks around the perimeter of the house.

To build a sod house, it was important to have the right kind of grass—one with dense roots that would hold the soil together. Buffalo grass, wheat grass, and several other varieties made the best sod for building. Then the sod would either be cut into bricks or, thanks to the invention of the steel breaking plow, plowed into strips 12 inches wide and four inches thick. The strips were then cut into bricks about three feet long. These bricks might

weigh as much as 50 pounds apiece. The average sod house weighed almost 90 tons!

Once the Shoreses had their sod bricks, they placed them side by side lengthwise and grass side down to make a wall two feet thick. Every few layers, they laid them in the opposite direction to make the walls stronger. Sometimes they used loose dirt and mud to fill cracks between the bricks.

As the walls grew higher, the builders positioned wooden frames where the windows and door would go. Then they laid sod all around the frame, leaving a gap at the top (filled with rags or grass) to allow room for the sod to settle without crushing the glass in the window. Wooden pegs held the frames in place in the sod walls.

Once the walls were the correct height, the builders placed a wooden ridgepole from one end of the sod house to the other to support a roof. A sod house roof was sometimes made out of lumber covered with shingles or tarpaper, but often it was simply covered with more sod bricks, cut thinner than the ones used for the walls.

Plagued With Problems

Sod houses were sturdy, fireproof, warm in the winter, cool in the summer, and above all, cheap to construct. But what was it like to live in one? The roof often leaked, especially since Nebraska sod contained sand, which made it easier for water to filter through. Sod roofs held on to water, and even after a rainstorm was over, the soggy material would drip for days. If the ridgepole decayed, the entire roof might collapse in a mess of mud and lumber.

Snow often made its way into the house through the smallest crack or crevice, and many builders would let the sod walls settle for as long as six weeks before smoothing them and coating the inside walls with plaster. The floors in most sod houses were simply packed dirt, which sometimes got covered with carpets if the family had any. If they had more money, they might build a floor of split logs or even wide wooden planks from a sawmill.

Some pioneer women complained that nothing was ever clean in a sod house. Fleas, rats, mice, and snakes were a constant problem because they liked to live in the cracks between the bricks. Women learned to cook with lids on their pots to keep mud—or worse—from falling into the food. Beds had to go in the center of the room beneath the ridgepole, where they were most likely to stay dry. After a long, soaking rain, the family would have to take almost everything in the house outside to dry in the sunshine.

For all its hardships, life in a soddy on the Nebraska prairie was the first taste of freedom for black families like the Shoreses, who had suffered under slavery in the South. Even with the mud and the bugs, the sod house was their first real home, built with their own hands—a symbol of their new life in the West.

There's No Place Like Home

Not every family who settled in the West lived in a soddy. The luckiest families lived in simple but sturdy one-room log cabins, which had been introduced by Swedish immigrants. But even in locations with plenty of trees, a log cabin took time to build. A family might first spend several years in a dugout, which was a shelter made by digging into the side of a hill and hollowing out a room. Some settlers dug partial rooms into hillsides and then finished the front of the house with a wall of sod bricks. Still other settlers lived in tents or Indian-style tipis.

Sod houses lasted only about six or seven years. A sturdier, yet still very simple, dwelling was the one-room log cabin, but it required land with plenty of trees.

Log house: Library of Congress. Background: © Robert Glusic/Corbis/HIP.

By Marcia Amidon Lusted, *Cobblestone,* © by Carus Publishing Company. Reproduced with permission.

Benjamin 'Pap' Singleton

Father of the Black Exodus

In Vicksburg, Mississippi, African Americans wait in line to board steam boats that will take them north.

kansasmemory.org, Kansas State Historical Society

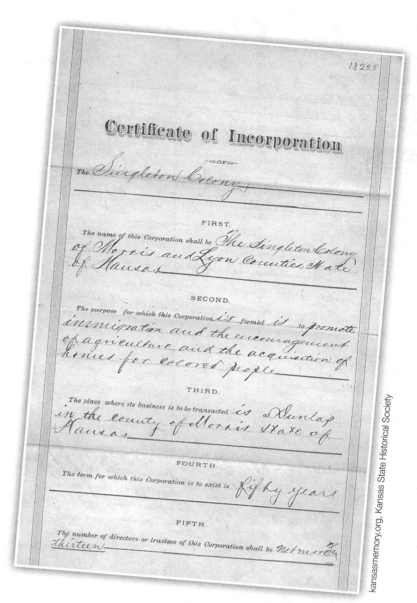

kansasmemory.org, Kansas State Historical Society

This certificate of incorporation laid out the details of the Singleton Colony's town company, including its purpose, term of duration, and number of directors.

By the end of 1865, slavery had been abolished, but racial inequality still existed in the South. Benjamin "Pap" Singleton felt he had a possible solution to this problem. He urged black Americans to go west with him to Kansas. There they could form their own independent communities. Singleton led planned, agency-organized movements to Kansas. But by 1879, the unplanned, mass exodus of African Americans to Kansas overwhelmed his efforts.

Singleton was born into slavery in Nashville, Tennessee, in 1809. He was trained at an early age to be a carpenter and coffinmaker. Sold several times, Singleton escaped each time and returned to Nashville. He finally escaped to Canada to avoid being sold again. Singleton eventually returned to the United States and made Detroit, Michigan, his home. While in Detroit, he ran a boarding house that offered a safe haven to runaway slaves. After the Civil War, Singleton returned to Tennessee. He was living in a Union camp for run-away slaves when the Thirteenth Amendment, which abolished slavery, was passed in 1865.

Incorporated means organized and maintained as a legal unit. The Singleton Colony was incorporated in 1879.

As the map indicates, Benjamin Singleton came and went from Nashville, Tennessee, until his plans for migrating west took him to Kansas.

May be reproduced for classroom use. *Toolkit Texts: Short Nonfiction for American History, Westward Expansion*, by Stephanie Harvey and Anne Goudvis, ©2016 (Portsmouth, NH: Heinemann).

The **promised land** is a place thought to bring satisfaction and happiness.

Former slaves were now legally free. But they needed something that would help them to maintain that freedom. Singleton understood that land ownership meant independence for African Americans. They would no longer need to rent themselves out as laborers to larger landowners. They would be their own bosses.

Still, immigrating to land-rich Kansas was not Singleton's original plan. His first choice was to find farmland within Tennessee. However, the price at that time for productive farmland was sixty dollars per acre. Newly freed slaves could not afford to purchase land at that price. Migrating to Kansas became Singleton's substitute plan. In the early 1870s, he visited the southeastern part of that state looking for possible land sites to obtain. In 1874, Singleton helped organize the Edgefield Real Estate and Homestead Association to help move former slaves west.

There were several reasons Kansas was considered to be the promised land by Singleton and his followers. The legendary abolitionist John Brown had lived there. African Americans believed they would receive fair treatment there. Kansas governor John St. John also let it be known that his state would welcome all homesteaders, black and white.

In August 1876, Singleton wrote to Governor St. John. He informed the governor of the possibility of African Americans' settling in Kansas. With the support of the Edgefield Real Estate and Homestead Association, Singleton and an associate visited Kansas again in 1877. After gathering information, Singleton returned to Nashville. He placed advertisements in local newspapers to announce an informational meeting. He praised Kansas as an immigration site. "During my visit I saw some excellent selections of land and plenty of fine water with a healthy climate," he told those attending the meeting.

In 1878, agents of the association began bringing former slaves to Kansas on a regular basis. One year later, the Singleton Colony (named for Singleton) in Dunlap, Morris County, became incorporated. Benjamin Singleton's dream of establishing an African American farming community was realized. He had earned the nickname "Father of the Black Exodus."

> **An abolitionist** was someone who supported the end of slavery.

More Famous African American Pioneers

Pap Singleton was just one of a number of African Americans who dreamed of owning land. The following are some others who found a new life and success in the West.

Henry Adams (1843–?)
This former Georgia slave and Civil War veteran lived most of his adult life in Louisiana. He was a strong supporter of black migration. He also was an active member of the Colonization Council, an African American organization. The council held meetings to discuss the plight of southern blacks during the 1870s. It encouraged former slaves to immigrate to Liberia in West Africa and Kansas in the United States. (Adams was last heard from in 1884. His whereabouts after that and the circumstances of his death are unknown.)

George Washington (1817–1905)
Born a slave but raised by a white couple, Washington spent his youth in Missouri. As a young man, he moved with his foster parents to the Oregon Territory. He bought land there and put it in his foster parents' name. By doing this, Washington got around territory laws prohibiting African Americans from owning property. In 1872, the Northern Pacific Railroad laid tracks across his land. Washington decided to establish a town that would eventually be called Centralia, Washington.

Library of Congress

Homesteaders in front of their home in Nicodemus, Kansas.

Nicodemus Stakes a Claim in History

In 1877, 350 former slaves moved from Kentucky to northwest Kansas. The town in which they settled was given the name Nicodemus. It was named after the first slave to purchase his freedom in the United States. W.R. Hill, a white town builder, and W.H. Smith, an African American homesteader, were partners in organizing this all-black settlement.

Hill and Smith were joined by five African American ministers who had been living in Topeka, Kansas. In April 1877, the group founded the Nicodemus Town Company and sought settlers from Kentucky to move to Kansas.

A Challenging Start

The first 350 recruits arrived in Nicodemus in September 1877 with high hopes. They were soon disappointed. They found themselves surrounded by a treeless landscape. Some of the town organizers even were living in **dugouts**. As many as sixty families returned to Kentucky. Those who stayed had brought only a few belongings with them. Their supplies soon ran out. Fortunately, some Osage Indians stopped at Nicodemus while on a hunting trip and gave the settlers food to survive the winter.

Growth and Progress

Though the first year was a struggle, several other groups of settlers soon joined the original bands. By 1885, the population of Nicodemus had grown to nearly seven hundred people. The town had two newspapers, livery stables, a post office, a general store, a doctor, hotels, restaurants, schools, and churches. From the late 1800s to the 1940s, the largest number of black farmers and African American-owned farmland in Kansas was in Graham County, of which Nicodemus was the central city.

In 1887, residents of Nicodemus raised money to try to help bring a railroad through their town. Trains and railroads meant progress.

> DUGOUTS ARE PITS DUG INTO THE GROUND AND USED AS SHELTER.

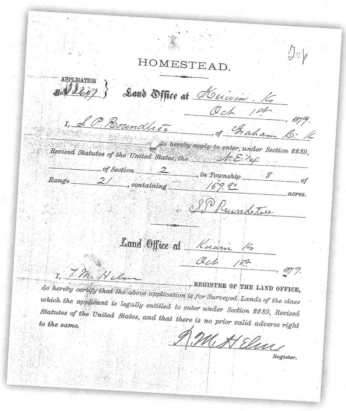

This October 1, 1879, homestead application was submitted by S. P. Roundtree, as one of the Founders of Nicodemus.

The townspeople of Nicodemus, Kansas, gather on Main Street around 1885. Today fewer than 30 people live in the town.

By Angela Bates-Tompkins, *Cobblestone*, © by Carus Publishing Company. Reproduced with permission.

Settlements Throughout the West

From the late 1870s to 1910, all-African American settlements were established throughout the western frontier. Kansas proudly boasted a half dozen, including Votow and Singleton in the southeastern part of the state. Singleton was organized by Benjamin "Pap" Singleton. Dunlap, in central Kansas, also was organized and assisted by him. Settlers from Kentucky founded Morton City, in southwestern Kansas.

Oklahoma boasted the most all-African American towns, with more than two dozen. The town of Boley was one of Oklahoma's largest. It was established in 1904. Boley still remains today, but with a mixed population. Edward P. McCabe assisted in organizing and establishing the towns of Liberty and Langston City.

The history of Colorado's all-African American settlement, Dearfield, has been recorded in a documentary. One of the most noted all-African American towns in the far western United States was Allensworth, California. It was founded and organized by James Allensworth. He was a former chaplain and buffalo soldier with the 9th Cavalry. Unfortunately, little evidence remains of these all-African American towns. Nicodemus, Kansas, which is currently being preserved, is the exception.

This black and white photograph shows a group of African American students and their teacher, in front of the Fairview School in Nicodemus, Kansas in 1915.

The townspeople hoped that a train station would carry people and goods to the town. The railroad bypassed the town, however. Many settlers became discouraged and began to leave. Some merchants moved their businesses to the newly organized railroad town of Bogue, just six miles to the west.

Economic Decline and Population Loss

Difficult years followed, but Nicodemus residents still hoped to succeed. A drought came, making it hard to grow crops. When the crops did flourish, locusts ate them.

In the 1930s, the United States was faced with the Great Depression. In Nicodemus, as elsewhere in the country, people lost their jobs and new jobs were almost impossible to find. Townspeople left for what they hoped would be new starts in better places.

May be reproduced for classroom use. Toolkit Texts: Short Nonfiction for American History, Westward Expansion, by Stephanie Harvey and Anne Goudvis, ©2016 (Portsmouth, NH: Heinemann).

Despite the decline in population, Nicodemus remains a cultural center for African American life. And although people left the town, they did not forget. Hundreds of people are drawn to Nicodemus for the annual Emancipation Celebration, held during the last weekend of July. Descendants of those first settlers come from all over the United States to reconnect with family and friends. Children whose ancestors settled this land in the 1870s use the swings on the playground and play basketball on the court near the town hall. Throughout the celebration, old men and women reminisce about their childhoods in the small town. Everyone reconnects with distant relatives who are linked by this special place. "You have your first cousins and aunts and uncles," said Jamie Alexander, a Nicodemus descendant. "And then there's always someone who your grandma says, 'That's your cousin.'"

A Unique Legacy Prevails

In 1976, Nicodemus was put on the National Register of Historic Places as a National Historic Landmark. In 1991, efforts by the Nicodemus Historical Society resulted in a proposal to establish Nicodemus as a National Historic Site/Park. The bill was passed by Congress and signed by President Bill Clinton on November 12, 1996. The town is now receiving funds to help restore its five historic buildings.

The National Park Service is providing assistance in interpreting the town's rich African American history and its unique contribution to the economic, social, and political development of Kansas and the West.

NPS Photo

Nicodemus is the oldest and only remaining all-African American town west of the Mississippi River. On August 1, 1998, Nicodemus was dedicated as a National Historic Site.

By Angela Bates-Tompkins, *Cobblestone*, © by Carus Publishing Company. Reproduced with permission.

Arthur Chapman, "Out Where the West Begins"

On an early December night in 1911, journalist Arthur Chapman was trying to come up with a topic for his regular newspaper column. As he was thinking, he saw an Associated Press dispatch about an ongoing disagreement between the Governors of several Western states. They were arguing over which state should be considered the state where "the West" begins. The AP story inspired Chapman to write a cowboy-style poem for his column. He titled it "Out Where the West Begins."

On December 3, 1911, the poem was published for the first time in Chapman's column in the Denver Republican. It was soon reprinted in other newspapers across the country. Over the next five years, "Out Where the West Begins" became one of best known poems in America. In 1917, it was published in a book of Chapman's poetry, Out Where the West Begins: And Other Western Verses.

> Out where the handclasp's a little stronger,
> Out where the smile dwells a little longer,
> > That's where the West begins;
>
> Out where the sun is a little brighter,
> Where the snows that fall are a trifle whiter,
> Where the bonds of home are a wee bit tighter,
> > That's where the West begins.
>
> Out where the skies are a trifle bluer,
> Out where the friendship's a little truer,
> > That's where the West begins;
>
> Out where a fresher breeze is blowing,
> Where there's laughter in every streamlet flowing,
> Where there's more of reaping and less of sowing,
> > That's where the West begins.
>
> Out where the world is in the making,
> Where fewer hearts in despair are aching,
> > That's where the West begins.
>
> Where there's more of singing and less of sighing,
> Where there's more of giving and less of buying,
> Where a man makes a friend without half trying,
> > That's where the West begins.

FOLLOWING THE HERD

For the men who became ranchers and cowboys, the West offered a place where success was measured by talent and skill, not the color of one's skin. Consider this story of an unlikely friendship across the racial divide.

Charles Goodnight was a former Confederate soldier who had returned to cattle ranching in Texas after the Civil War (1861–1865). Initially, Goodnight drove his cattle to places across the South where the beef would be sold as food for Indians. In 1866, Goodnight and his partner, Oliver Loving, were the first to lead a cattle drive on a route through the Southwest that later

became famous as the Goodnight–Loving Trail. Hired to help on that drive was Bose Ikard.

Ikard had been born into slavery, but after emancipation, he began hiring himself out as a cowboy. In a profession that required loyalty, bravery, honesty, and hard work, Ikard excelled. He quickly became Goodnight's trusted right-hand man on cattle drives, and soon the former slave and the ex-Confederate developed a close personal friendship.

Where Cattle—and Cowboys—Roamed Free

In the period following the Civil War, America's Southwest was sparsely settled. Before the invention of barbed wire, which eventually would make it possible to fence in the land, great herds of longhorn cattle roamed freely there. These cattle were descendants of animals that had arrived in the Americas with the first Spanish explorers in the 16th century.

A handful of scattered ranchers lived on vast tracts of open land that were sometimes as large as 500,000 acres. Cattle ranching was not a new idea. Spanish settlers had trained their Native American slaves to tend their cattle in the 1500s. Known as vaqueros, or cowherders, these Native Americans were the first cowboys. Their influence was so strong that many of the trade words they used—such as corral, rancho (ranch), rodear (rodeo), la reata (lariat), and bronco—still are used today.

Round-Up!

But it wasn't until the late 1860s that cattle ranching became an important industry in the Southwest. That's when ranchers began rounding up some of the wild longhorns to sell to

Library of Congress

A trail drive took two to three months because the herd had to be moved slowly so the cattle would not lose weight.

May be reproduced for classroom use. *Toolkit Texts: Short Nonfiction for American History, Westward Expansion,* by Stephanie Harvey and Anne Goudvis, ©2016 (Portsmouth, NH: Heinemann).

kansasmemory.org, Kansas State Historical Society

A. CASTAIGNE

Many cowboys feared drowning at river crossings because few of them knew how to swim.

meatpackers and manufacturers in the North and East, where there was a market for them. The manufacturers used the cattle's hides, horns, hooves, and tallow, or fat. Texas ranchers hired cowboys to care for and protect their herds during the long drives north.

The ranchers' plan was to drive the cattle north to the nearest railhead on the Kansas Pacific line. The first attempt to use the railhead at Sedalia, Missouri, ended in failure because the farmers along the Missouri sections of the trail refused to let the Texas cattle cross their land. They feared the cattle might carry diseases that would kill their own livestock.

The ranchers tried again the next spring, in 1867. This time they drove their herds west of Missouri farming country to a railhead at

Abilene, Kansas. A forward-thinking businessman, Joseph McCoy, had built stockyards here. He encouraged Texas ranchers to bring their herds to Abilene for shipment north. Records show that more than 35,000 head of cattle were loaded onto railroad cars in Abilene that year.

As word of the successful trail drives spread, more than three million head of cattle moved through Abilene over the five-year period from 1867 to 1872. It became the first cattle town in Kansas.

Call of the Open Range

Cattle driving was hard work. A drive could take two to three months to complete. Cowhands spent that time alongside the animals, riding 12 hours in the saddle, breathing in the dust the cattle kicked up, and sleeping under

A *railhead* was the place where railroad tracks began or ended.

149 MESS SCENE ON "ROUND UP"

Serving as kitchens on wheels, chuck wagons provided cowboys with meals along the trail.

the stars at night. They endured all kinds of weather as they guided their herds across raging rivers and through difficult canyons. And they had to be constantly on the alert for stampedes.

Yet, men were drawn to this life. No one asked questions about a cowboy's past life. Jobs were scarce after the Civil War. Some cowboys were former Civil War soldiers who were looking for an opportunity to put the conflict behind them and start a fresh life. And, with little discrimination in this line of work, approximately 5,000 black men found employment as cowboys. Some, such as Ben Hodges and Bill Pickett, even became famous for their riding and roping skills.

Progress brought an end to the cattle drive era. By the 1890s, railroads reached all the way to Texas, making trail drives unnecessary. Later, improvements in meatpacking technology and the invention of refrigerated boxcars made it possible for ranchers to ship just the meat, and not the live cattle. Some ranchers, including Goodnight, branched out into cattle breeding. Goodnight even crossed bison with cattle to create a "cattalo" herd. And while increasing numbers of homesteaders and barbed-wire fences also helped bring an end to this way of life, the life of a cowboy on the open range remains one of the most classic images of America's West.

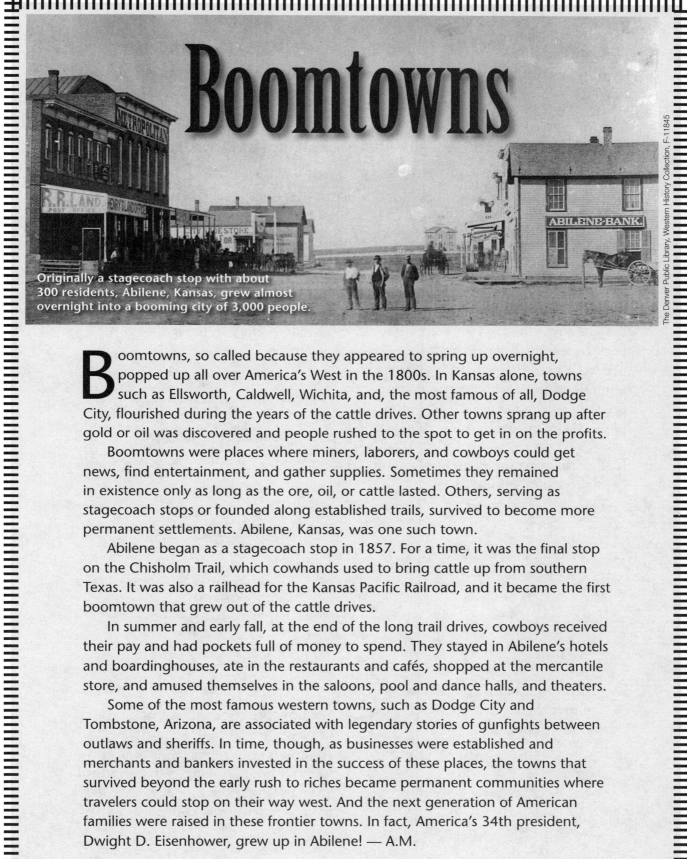

Boomtowns

Originally a stagecoach stop with about 300 residents, Abilene, Kansas, grew almost overnight into a booming city of 3,000 people.

Boomtowns, so called because they appeared to spring up overnight, popped up all over America's West in the 1800s. In Kansas alone, towns such as Ellsworth, Caldwell, Wichita, and, the most famous of all, Dodge City, flourished during the years of the cattle drives. Other towns sprang up after gold or oil was discovered and people rushed to the spot to get in on the profits.

Boomtowns were places where miners, laborers, and cowboys could get news, find entertainment, and gather supplies. Sometimes they remained in existence only as long as the ore, oil, or cattle lasted. Others, serving as stagecoach stops or founded along established trails, survived to become more permanent settlements. Abilene, Kansas, was one such town.

Abilene began as a stagecoach stop in 1857. For a time, it was the final stop on the Chisholm Trail, which cowhands used to bring cattle up from southern Texas. It was also a railhead for the Kansas Pacific Railroad, and it became the first boomtown that grew out of the cattle drives.

In summer and early fall, at the end of the long trail drives, cowboys received their pay and had pockets full of money to spend. They stayed in Abilene's hotels and boardinghouses, ate in the restaurants and cafés, shopped at the mercantile store, and amused themselves in the saloons, pool and dance halls, and theaters.

Some of the most famous western towns, such as Dodge City and Tombstone, Arizona, are associated with legendary stories of gunfights between outlaws and sheriffs. In time, though, as businesses were established and merchants and bankers invested in the success of these places, the towns that survived beyond the early rush to riches became permanent communities where travelers could stop on their way west. And the next generation of American families were raised in these frontier towns. In fact, America's 34th president, Dwight D. Eisenhower, grew up in Abilene! — A.M.

By Andrew Matthews, *Cobblestone,* © by Carus Publishing Company. Reproduced with permission.

It's Knot Easy

When pioneers collected their belongings and headed west, they bundled up everything they owned with ropes. Ropes were an important part of life, and special knots had special purposes.

Farmer's Halter Loop

Most pioneers did not have fancy halters for their animals. Instead, they looped a rope around an animal's neck to lead it. Farmers and pioneers needed a knot that would keep their animals secure without choking them. So, they used a farmer's halter loop. Now it is your turn to attempt one.

1. Lay the rope on a flat surface and make a large loop.

2. Turn one end up and tuck it behind the large loop so it is now on the right side of the loop.

3. Tuck the end back over the top of the large loop and through the small loop on the left side.

4. Pull the knot tight.

See how the rope slips through the knot when you pull the curly end? An animal can move its neck in this loop without choking. What kinds of animals might the pioneers have led by a rope with this knot?

HAULING LOGS.

Timber Hitch

Pioneers of the 1800s did not have bulldozers. When they hauled logs, they tied a rope to them with a timber hitch knot and dragged the wood across the ground. The timber hitch tightens itself when the rope is strained by the weight of a log. But when the rope is loose, the knot comes undone easily. That was important because tree branches and rough bark made it hard to untie knots. You can try tying this knot around a broom handle.

1. Loop one end of the rope up and over the side edge of the broom handle. Leave the other end loose for dragging.

2. Bring the first end back up around the bottom of the broom handle and tuck it over and behind the second end.

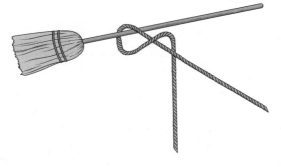

3. Wind the first end around the diagonal part of the rope several times.

4. Now pull on the second end of the rope. It should hold the broom handle tight.

Let go of the rope and notice how loose the knot becomes. It is nice to have a knot that stays tight when you need it that way, but also comes undone easily when necessary.

Pioneers used different knots for hunting, hitching animals to posts, hoisting goods up and down, anchoring heavy objects, and lashing poles together. What are some ways that we use knots today?

Home on the Range

"Home on the Range" is a classic western song, sometimes called the "unofficial anthem" of the American West. The lyrics were originally written by Dr. Brewster M. Higley of Kansas in a poem entitled "My Western Home" in the early 1870s. The song quickly became a favorite by settlers, cowboys, and others and spread across the United States.

Oh give me a home where the buffalo roam,
Where the deer and the antelope play,
Where seldom is heard a discouraging word,
And the skies are not cloudy all day.

Home, home on the range,
Where the deer and the antelope play,
Where seldom is heard a discouraging word,
And the skies are not cloudy all day.

How often at night when the heavens are bright,
With the light from the glittering stars,
Have I stood there amazed and asked as I gazed,
If their glory exceeds that of ours.

Oh give me a land where the bright diamond sand,
Flows leisurely down in the stream;
Where the graceful white swan goes gliding along,
Like a maid in a heavenly dream.

Where the air is so pure, and the zephyrs so free,
The breezes so balmy and light,
That I would not exchange my home on the range,
For all of the cities so bright.

Swing Your Partner:

Frontier Fun

THE DANCE AFTER THE HUSKING.

American artist Winslow Homer created this engraving "The Dance After the Husking" in 1858.

O n the frontier, families usually lived many miles apart. Lonely pioneers often used work as an excuse to visit.

If settlers needed to clear land, they planned a logrolling. People came from miles around. The men worked all day cutting trees and rolling logs. Sometimes the workers divided into teams. Each tried to roll logs faster than the others. The work was sweaty and hard, but the rolling contests made it fun. The workers' wives came, too. They brought food to cook and gossip to share.

If settlers needed to husk corn they planned a husking bee. Newly picked ears of corn were piled high. Neighbors divided into two teams. Everyone talked, joked, and laughed as they husked. Working quickly,

Families gathered pumpkins and husked corn together during the harvest.

each team tried to husk the most corn. Any lucky fellow finding a red ear of corn was allowed to kiss a girl. Sometimes a young man would bring a red ear from home hidden in his pocket. Then he pretended to find it as he husked.

Together, neighbors completed other big jobs such as barn building and wood chopping. Women gathered for spinning parties, apple peeling, and chicken or goose plucking. They especially enjoyed quilting bees, where they traded pieces of fabric and stitched while they chatted and sang.

But fun was not always connected to work. Dances were popular, and even logrollings and husking bees ended with lively dancing and fiddle music. Everyone from toddlers to grandparents learned to polka, waltz, and square dance.

Peggy Bell grew up on the Montana frontier. She wrote in her journal about a dance she went to when she was eight: "The men . . . danced with me and another little girl . . . . [We] were so light that when they swung us around, they lifted us off the floor . . . . Everybody danced until daylight."

Frontier churches were used for worship as well as picnics, baptisms, choir practices, and funerals. Weddings often lasted for two days with feasting, games, and dancing.

At the fair each fall, settlers brought samples of their best crops, animals, and homemade items. They competed for prizes in each category. Twelve-year-old Iowa pioneer Sarah Gillespie wrote: "We all went to the fair. We had a good time. I got two premiums [prizes] – one on cake and one on bread."

Many children thought the Fourth of July was the most fun day of the year. Early in the morning, people headed to town in flag-trimmed wagons decorated in red, white, and blue. The town band led a big parade down the main street, and citizens gave patriotic speeches. There were picnics, games, and races. There might also be a pie-eating contest, a tug of war, greased poles to climb, or oiled pigs to catch. Later, fireworks lit up the sky, and folks danced long into the night.

These celebrations made the lives of hard-working frontier families much more enjoyable. They created memories that lasted a lifetime.

Logging was hard and dangerous work, but log-rolling contests made it fun. In the summertime, lumber companies would sponsor these contests, each sending their best rollers. The first log-rolling world championship took place in 1898 in Omaha, Nebraska.

Library of Congress

By LeeAnn Blankenship, *Appleseeds*, © by Carus Publishing Company. Reproduced with permission.

*Pinned to Annie Oakley's dress are the numerous awards
and medals she won for her sharpshooting, 1899.*

Annie Oakley: Little Sure Shot

*The most famous female star in Buffalo Bill's Wild West show was Annie Oakley, a
sharpshooter. Born in poverty in Ohio in 1860, Annie soon learned that she could support
her family using her skills at marksmanship with a gun. Annie began shooting in contests
and exhibitions at the age of 15. She spent 17 years with Buffalo Bill's show, performing
tricks such as shooting the corks off bottles, snuffing candles, and even shooting a playing
card with the thin edge facing her. She could hit 943 out of 1,000 targets in a row.*

Library of Congress

Oakley holds a gun given to her by William F. "Buffalo Bill" Cody, 1922.

Annie Oakley *(continued from previous page)*

Annie also changed the look of female performers by popularizing "cowgirl" frontier costumes, which she sewed herself. She always wore a skirt, but often wore buckskin leggings underneath to show that she was an athlete and to make it possible for her to move easily. Her blouses had fringe or beading, and she wore a cowboy hat. Annie met Queen Victoria, who called her "a very clever little girl," during one of Buffalo Bill's European tours, and became an international superstar. She also met the legendary Lakota Sioux chief Sitting Bull, who adopted her and gave her the name "Watanya Cicilla," or "Little Sure Shot." During World War I, Annie made an offer to the government to create a company of expert female sharpshooters. The government ignored her, so she raised money for the Red Cross by giving shooting exhibitions at Army camps around the country. Annie died in 1926.

Bandit Heroes

Jesse James was the most famous outlaw in the James-Younger Gang. In 1882, Jesse James was killed by a member of his own gang who hoped to collect a reward on James' head. James became a legendary figure of the Wild West after his death.

Jesse James was a lad
who killed many a man.

He robbed the Glendale train.

He stole from the rich
and he gave to the poor.

He'd a hand and a heart
and a brain.

This ballad glorifies the deeds of America's most famous criminal, Jesse James. Through such songs and myths, and from books, newspapers, and tall tales, the legend of American outlaws grew. To many Americans in the period following the Civil War, Jesse James was a hero, representing manliness, courage, cunning, and daring. Outwitting and outfoxing his pursuers, protected by friends, James became the Robin Hood of the prairie.

In the second half of the nineteenth century, Jesse James's exploits—both real and fictitious—captured the public's imagination. Outlaws thrilled and fascinated people in a manner similar to the way in which sports heroes and movie actors fascinate us today. The exaggerated writing of reporters, novelists, and advertisers helped Americans accept thugs as heroes.

During the Civil War, William Quantrill, a murderous Confederate gang leader, led a group of thugs on a spree of violence, much of it against innocent civilians in Kansas, Nebraska, and neighboring states. As members of Quantrill's unit, brothers Jesse and Frank James learned how to fight and survive on the run. But in a folksong, the ruthless Quantrill was a "bold and daring" patriot, a Robin Hood from the mountains who

May be reproduced for classroom use. *Toolkit Texts: Short Nonfiction for American History, Westward Expansion*, by Stephanie Harvey and Anne Goudvis, ©2016 (Portsmouth, NH: Heinemann).

descended with his band to the prairie to rob the rich and divide it "with widows in distress."

∾

Oh, Quantrill's a fighter,
a bold-hearted boy,

A brave man or woman
he'd never annoy.

He'd take from the wealthy
and give to the poor.

For brave men there's never
a bolt to his door.

∾

In the history of western bandit outlaws, the Robin Hood myth emerges over and over again. (See page 183.) Cole Younger, Jesse James, Pretty Boy Floyd, and other outlaws and bandits all became the subjects of western folktales and ballads.

After the war, many ex-Confederate fighters carried on their own war. They rode into former

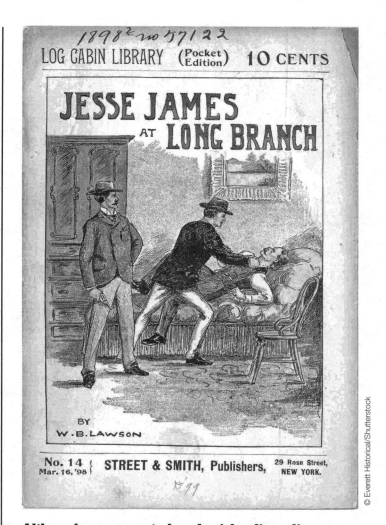

Although exaggerated and misleading, dime novels such as this one offered an exciting view of the Wild West.

Passengers on a train are robbed at gunpoint.

By Roger A. Bruns, *Cobblestone,* © by Carus Publishing Company. Reproduced with permission.

The outlaws and lawmen mentioned in this article lived mostly in the West—that is, the territories west of the Mississippi River. This map shows states as they are today and the areas where these outlaws and lawman were most active.

pro-Union towns in Kansas and Missouri and caused trouble for innocent people. Some of them, like the James gang, turned to robbing banks and trains.

In the early 1870s, the James gang became national news. A newspaper writer named John Newman Edwards, a former Confederate army officer, became the gang's most vigorous defender and promoter. In his articles, he made it seem as if the vicious gang members were as honorable as King Arthur and his knights.

Sheriffs and marshals across the West had no luck trapping or even tracking the gang. But in April 1882, Bob Ford, a local gunman who had joined the gang, shot and killed Jesse James. Ford had decided to kill James for the reward money.

Some people refused to believe that James had died. One story held that he had arranged his own fake funeral and had actually sung in the choir. Another story claimed that James later graduated with honors under an assumed name from the University of Michigan.

This movie poster advertises for The Great Train Robbery, a popular movie about a group of cowboy outlaws who hold up a train and rob the passengers.

Many bandit heroes followed James, including the Dalton brothers, the Doolin gang, Butch Cassidy and the Sundance Kid, and, in the twentieth century, men such as John Dillinger and Pretty Boy Floyd. They had all heard stories about James and the other western heroes and wanted to be considered in the same category.

In ballads and songs, the legends of these outlaws grew. They were portrayed as misunderstood trailblazers who had been laid out by treachery and fate or as heroic badmen who had taken up stealing horses and robbing stages, trains, and banks mostly for honor and pride. Newspapers, magazines, and cheap novels expanded on these images, shaping Americans' sympathetic view of the western bandit hero. ★

Robin Hood is a heroic outlaw in English folklore. According to legends, he was a skilled archer and swordsman. He is often portrayed as "robbing from the rich and giving to the poor" alongside his band of Merry Men. The legend of Robin Hood continues today.

By Roger A. Bruns, *Cobblestone*, © by Carus Publishing Company. Reproduced with permission.

My name is Bass Reeves, and I was born a slave in Crawford Country, Arkansas in 1838. My name isn't even all my own. I was owned by William Steele Reeves, an Arkansas state legislator, and because I was his slave, I was given his last name. When I was only about 8 years old, William Reeves moved us to Texas. I stayed there, becoming the personal companion and servant for his son George. When George went to fight for the Confederates during the Civil War, I even went along with him. When I heard that slavery might be ending, I decided it was time to move out on my own. Some say I left because I beat up George after a fight over a card game. Folks can believe what they want, but I yearned for freedom. So I headed out for a place where I thought I could find that freedom: Indian Territory. They call it Oklahoma now. There I lived with the Cherokee, Creek, and Seminole Indians. I learned to be a pretty fair shot with a pistol and a rifle (I could shoot equally well with either hand), and how to speak some of the tribes' languages.

When the the 13th Amendment to the U.S. Constitution made me a free man in 1865, I headed home to Arkansas, married, and became a farmer. My wife Nellie and I eventually had 10 children. But I was not meant to be a farmer. A man named Isaac C. Parker became the judge for the Federal Western District in 1875. That meant he oversaw Indian Territory, which had become a refuge for every murderer and thief who was running from the law. There was no law in Indian Territory, so Parker decided to

Bass Reeves was one of the first black Deputy U.S. Marshals west of the Mississippi River. He arrested over 3,000 felons and shot and killed fourteen outlaws in self-defense.

By Marcia Amidon Lusted. May be reproduced for classroom use. *Toolkit Texts: Short Nonfiction for American History, Westward Expansion*, by Stephanie Harvey and Anne Goudvis, ©2016 (Portsmouth, NH: Heinemann).

By Marcia Amidon Lusted. May be reproduced for classroom use. *Toolkit Texts: Short Nonfiction for American History; Westward Expansion*, by Stephanie Harvey and Anne Goudvis, ©2016 (Portsmouth, NH: Heinemann).

send some in. He hired a new U.S. Marshall, James Fagan, and 200 deputies to go in and clean things up. Marshall Fagan had heard of me, heard that I knew the territory and could speak Indian languages, so I was hired. He told us, "Bring them in alive…or dead!"

So I rode out, usually with a wagon, a cook, and a posse man. We might cover 800 miles during a trip. I confess, I couldn't read nor write, but I could memorize the warrants on the criminals I was sent to catch. And catch them I did: 3,000 men had to answer to the law after I found them. A few I had to kill so that they wouldn't kill me. Sometimes I had to ride in disguise as a cowboy, a rustler, or even an outlaw myself. Other times I sat tall on my stallion, wearing my favorite black hat and carrying two Colt pistols, well-dressed and polite lest they think I wasn't a real deputy, and maybe also to fool them into thinking I wasn't as powerful as I really was. My pay was in fees and rewards and I supported my family well, even if I spent little time with them. The hardest manhunt of my life was actually for one of my own sons, who killed his wife. I knew he had to be brought to justice, and that I was going to be the one to do it. And I did.

For 35 years, I was one of the most successful lawmen in Indian Territory. When my time as a deputy marshal ended in 1907, I spent a few years as a policeman in Muskogee, Oklahoma, and there was never a crime on my beat in two years.

My name is Bass Reeves, and I was the first black Deputy U.S. Marshall west of the Mississippi River. People call me a frontier hero. They say I was one of the best lawmen in the Indian Territories, that I was fearless, impossible to bribe, and I could outsmart any outlaw. But what matters most to me is that I brought the law to a lawless place. Someone once asked me why I spent so much time enforcing "white men's laws." I told him, "Maybe the law ain't perfect, but it's the only one we got, and without it we got nuthin.'"

A Collection of Outlaws

In his 35 years as a deputy U.S. Marshal, Bass Reeves dealt with many infamous outlaws and brought them to justice:

Bob Dozier: Dozier was an outlaw who didn't just limit himself to one kind of crime. He held up banks and stagecoaches, rustled cattle and horses, committed murder, and even swindled people out of cash. He was also very difficult to catch. Reeves was the first lawman to actually track Dozier down, but Dozier ambushed Reeves and thought he had killed him. Reeves played dead, then when Dozier approached him, he leaped up and ordered Dozier to surrender. They ended up in a gunfight and Dozier was killed.

Belle Starr: Starr was a notorious female outlaw, known for stealing horses and cattle, bootlegging, and harboring fugitives and other outlaws. She was a friend of Frank and Jesse James, who were also well-known outlaws. Reeves didn't need to actually capture Starr. When she found out that he had a warrant for her arrest, she turned herself in rather than be chased by him.

Born in 1848, Belle Starr was known as an infamous outlaw in the Wild West.

Library of Congress

Greenleaf: Reeves also arrested a Seminole Indian outlaw named To-Sa-Lo-Nah, known as Greenleaf, who had avoided being captured for 18 years. Reeves and his posse surrounded Greenleaf's location and took him by surprise. When the outlaw saw that he was surrounded, he surrendered. Greenleaf's legendary ability to avoid capture was so famous that people actually came to see him in jail, just to see if it really was him.

Reeves didn't always apprehend just one outlaw at a time. His record was nineteen horse thieves, all captured at once near Fort Sill, Oklahoma.

Riding with the

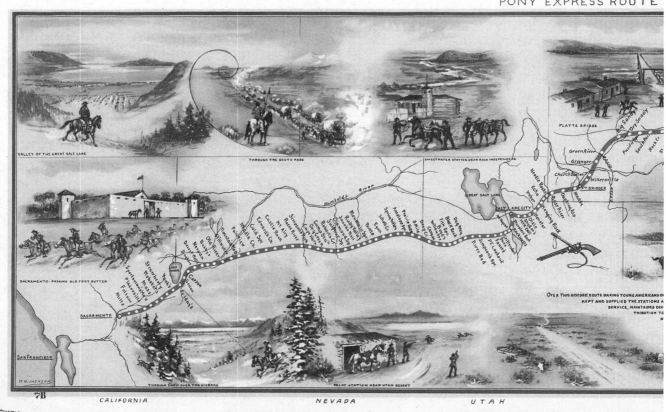

PONY EXPRESS ROUTE

WANTED
YOUNG, SKINNY, WIRY FELLOWS NOT OVER EIGHTEEN. MUST BE EXPERT RIDERS, WILLING TO RISK DEATH DAILY. ORPHANS PREFERRED.

© Nella/Shutterstock/HIP

With the notice above, a Leavenworth, Kansas, company named Russell, Majors & Waddell hoped to establish a spectacular 10-day mail ser vice from St. Joseph, Missouri, to Sacramento, California. That may not sound so impressive today, considering the speed of our text messages, e-mails, and cell phones. But in the mid-1800s, it took several weeks for news and information to make its way from St. Joseph, where telegraph service ended, to the West Coast.

Pony Express

A Map of the Pony Express route.

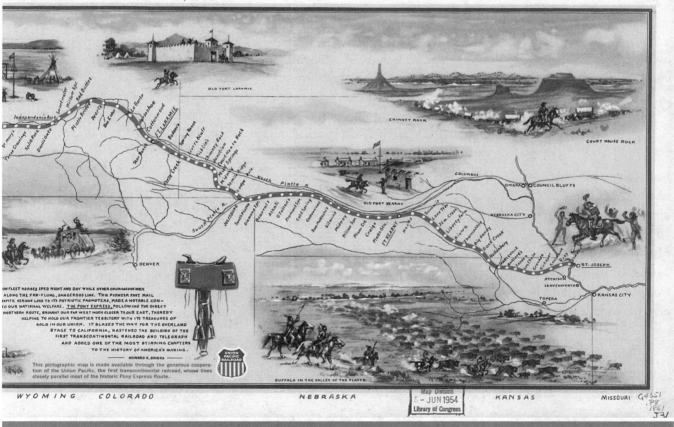

APRIL 3, 1860 — OCTOBER 24, 1861

ON FLEET HORSES SPED NIGHT AND DAY WHILE OTHER COURAGEOUS MEN ALONG THE FAR-FLUNG, DANGEROUS LINE. THIS PIONEER FAST MAIL DESPITE SERIOUS LOSS TO ITS PATRIOTIC PROMOTERS, MADE A NOTABLE CONTO OUR NATIONAL WELFARE. THE PONY EXPRESS, FOLLOWING THE DIRECT NORTHERN ROUTE, BROUGHT OUR FAR WEST MUCH CLOSER TO OUR EAST, THEREBY HELPING TO HOLD OUR FRONTIER TERRITORY WITH ITS TREASURES OF GOLD IN OUR UNION. IT BLAZED THE WAY FOR THE OVERLAND STAGE TO CALIFORNIA, HASTENED THE BUILDING OF THE FIRST TRANSCONTINENTAL RAILROAD AND TELEGRAPH AND ADDED ONE OF THE MOST STIRRING CHAPTERS TO THE HISTORY OF AMERICA'S MAKING.

HOWARD R. DRIGGS

This pictographic map is made available through the generous cooperation of the Union Pacific, the first transcontinental railroad, whose lines closely parallel most of the historic Pony Express Route.

WYOMING   COLORADO   NEBRASKA   KANSAS   MISSOURI

The Pony Express's first trip, begun on April 3, 1860, successfully delivered the mail to Sacramento in just under 10 days. After that, teenaged boys regularly made the nearly 2,000-mile trip back and forth from St. Joseph to Sacramento. They rode through blizzards and snowdrifts, over the white salt desert of Utah and the badlands of Nevada, through cloudbursts and heat waves. They fought wolves and were on the lookout for terrifying bison stampedes and Indian ambushes.

The boys traveled light, usually dressed in buckskin shirts, pants, slouch hats, and moccasins. The leather mail pouch, called a *mochila* (Spanish for "knapsack"), rested on top of a lightweight saddle. Riders were paid 100 dollars to 125 dollars per month; some got 150 dollars if the route was especially dangerous. Each rider took an oath promising not to drink liquor, fight, or use bad language.

Stations with fresh horses were spaced 10 to 15 miles apart. Riders were scheduled to take shifts of about

Because Pony Express riders had to weigh no more than 125 pounds, teenaged boys were recruited to do the job.

75 miles each, but sometimes there were no relief riders and they had to continue. One of the most famous riders, 15-year-old William Cody, later known as Buffalo Bill, reportedly stayed in the saddle for nearly 22 hours over 322 miles.

The Pony Express carried President Abraham Lincoln's inaugural address of March 4, 1861, to the West Coast in a record-setting time of 7 days 17 hours. Rider "Pony Bob" Haslam was responsible for one 75-mile leg of this journey, through western Nevada. He delivered the message despite being wounded by Paiute Indians. Getting Lincoln's words to the people in California was of vital importance: The Civil War was brewing and people on each side of the conflict were trying to convince California to support their cause.

During their 18 months in the saddle, the Pony Express riders lived by the motto "The mail must go through." An Indian war in the spring of 1860 interrupted service for a few weeks, but in the end, it wasn't the Indians or the weather that stopped the Pony Express. It was the telegraph.

On May 27, 1861, a construction crew put up the first telegraph pole in Omaha, Nebraska, connecting that city with the East. As they worked their way west, another crew headed east from California. On October 24, 1861, the two crews met in Salt Lake City, Utah. They joined their wires, thus putting the Pony Express out of business. Not even the fastest rider could outrace Samuel Morse's message machine.

The Pony Express did, however, establish the benefit of timely communication between East and West. And even more important, since riders carried the mail throughout the year, it convinced Americans that a central route across the land could be traveled in winter as well as summer. Within eight years, the tracks for the first transcontinental railroad were laid, and Americans began riding the "iron horse" to points west.

Pony Express riders changed horses at stations located about 10 to 15 miles apart along the route— approximately the longest distance a horse can go at full speed.

A Change of Worlds

CHIEF SEATTLE SIABL
SUQUAMISH/DUWAMISH SALISBAN

Chief Seattle (1786–1866) was speaking to Governor Isaac Stevens, at the signing of the treaty that surrendered the land where the city of Seattle now stands.

Chief Seattle

   To us the ashes of our ancestors are sacred and their resting place is hallowed ground. You wander far from the graves of your ancestors and seemingly without regret. Your religion was written on tables of stone by the iron finger of your God so that you could not forget. The red man could never comprehend nor remember it. Our religion is the tradition of our ancestors—the dreams of our old men, given then in the solemn hours of the night by the Great Spirit, and the visions of our sachems (chiefs), and is written in the hearts of our people.

   Your dead cease to love you and the land of their nativity as soon as they pass the portals of the tomb and wander away beyond the stars. They are soon forgotten and never return. Our dead never forget the beautiful world that gave them being. They still love its verdant valleys, its murmuring rivers, its magnificent mountains, sequestered vales, and verdant-lined lakes and bays, and never yearn in tender, fond affection over the lonely hearted living, and often return from the Happy Hunting Ground to visit, guide, console, and comfort them...

Every part of this soul is sacred, in the estimation of my people. Every part of this soil is sacred, in the estimation of my people. Every hillside, every valley, every hill and grove, has been hallowed by some sad or happy event in days long vanished. Even the rocks, which seem to be dumb and dead as they swelter in the sun along the silent shore, thrill with memories of stirring events connected with the lives of my people, and the very dust upon which you now stand responds more lovingly to their footsteps than to yours, because it is rich with the dust of the sympathetic touch.

And when the last red man shall have perished, and the memory of my tribe shall become a myth among the white man, these shores shall swarm with the invisible dead of my tribe, and when your children's children think themselves alone in the field, the store, the shop, upon the highway, or in the silence of the pathless woods, they will not be alone. In all the earth there is no place dedicated to solitude. At night when the streets of your cities and villages are silent and you think them deserted, they will throng with the returning hosts that once filled them and still love this beautiful land. The white man will never be alone.

Let him be just and deal kindly with my people, for the dead are not powerless. Dead—I say? There is no death. Only a change of worlds.

Chipeta, White Singing Bird

1843–1924

Chipeta was a Native American leader, the wife of Chief Ouray of the Ute tribe in Colorado. Chipeta, which means White Singing Bird, was raised by the Ute tribe and learned their traditional ways of life. She spoke three languages and became a talented artisan in beadwork and tanning. After marrying Chief Ouray, she became his advisor and sat beside him at council meetings, the only woman ever allowed on a Ute tribal council. Chipeta used diplomacy to try to achieve peace with settlers in Colorado and advocated for the rights of Native Americans. Both Chipeta and her husband befriended white settlers and were known for helping them through the wilderness safely.

Library of Congress

Chipeta and Chief Ouray

Yet tensions were rising as the settlers drove off the wild game that the Utes needed to survive. In addition, the U.S. government was pressuring the Utes to take up farming and convert to Christianity. Chief Ouray negotiated several treaties in which the Ute were assigned reservation land, but each new treaty reduced the land available to the tribes. Ouray maintained his patient and peaceful attitude, but this angered many Utes. In one instance, Chipeta rescued a settler family from hostile Utes during a uprising. After Ouray's death in 1880, she continued as the leader of her people.

Chipeta represented the Utes as a delegate to lobby the U.S. Congress and frequently traveled to Washington, DC. Chipeta also testified at a congressional inquiry into a Ute uprising. Years later, Chipeta met with President William Taft, who found her well-spoken and highly educated. Sadly, despite signing a treaty with the U.S. government, the Utes were forced to leave Colorado and resettle on a reservation in Utah.

Chipeta was highly respected as a wise and compassionate leader. She was inducted into the Colorado Women's Hall of Fame because of the courage and valor she demonstrated in her efforts to mediate between Native Americans and whites.

Andrew Jackson, seventh president of the United States, was both a war hero and a figure of controversy as president. More than any other president that came before him, he was elected by the people and considered himself to be a man of the people. His legacy includes founding the Democratic Party and supporting individual liberty. But he was also responsible for treaties that forced the removal and relocation of 15,000 Cherokee on the Trail of Tears, as well as other tribes east of the Mississippi River. He began negotiating policies and treaties that resulted in the harsh treatment of Native Americans even before he became president. Jackson was also a slaveholder, and supported extending slavery into the western states.

As the first frontier president, Andrew Jackson's policies forced at least 46,000 Cherokees, Choctaws, Muscogee-Creeks, Chickasaws, and Seminoles off their ancestral lands.

Jackson was born into a poor family in 1767, but quickly became a rising lawyer and politician. By the War of 1812, he was a major general in the battle against the British-allied Creek Indians. His victory over the British in the Battle of New Orleans in 1815 made him a national war hero. He went on to invade Florida in 1817 and captured posts held by the Spanish. Although his actions sparked debate in Washington, D.C., he did make it possible for the U.S. to acquire Florida as part of its territory in 1821.

Jackson's popularity led to the suggestion that he run for president, but his first attempt in 1824 did not succeed, although it did win him a seat in the U.S. Senate. But in 1829, Jackson's second try for the presidency succeeded, despite a campaign that was characterized by negative personal attacks on him and his wife.

Jackson was the first frontier president, and his administration marked a shift after presidents who came from the eastern part of the country. Jackson also used his powers of veto and did not defer to Congress. One of his most important legacies was over the expiring charter of the Second Bank of the United States. Jackson saw this bank, which had been formed as a place for federal funds and the government's fiscal agent, as a privileged institution and an enemy of the common people. Jackson successfully vetoed the rechartering of the bank.

When Jackson left the White House in 1836, he was even more popular than he had been when he was elected. He left behind a mixed legacy. While he supported slavery and the forced relocation of Native Americans, he also left behind a strong Democratic Party and a presidency that focused on the will of the people.

Andrew Jackson:
Hero or Not?

Library of Congress

Andrew Jackson, who served as a major general during the War of 1812, led American forces to victory over the British in the Battle of New Orleans.

By Marcia Amidon Lusted. May be reproduced for classroom use. *Toolkit Texts: Short Nonfiction for American History, Westward Expansion,* by Stephanie Harvey and Anne Goudvis, ©2016 (Portsmouth, NH: Heinemann).

The War's Western Roots

Library of Congress

The United States had been embroiled in a war of words and ideas long before either side fired its weapons in the Civil War. Americans had argued for decades over the issue of slavery and whether it should be allowed to expand into the West. As western territories began to apply for statehood in the first half of the 1800s, the same question kept coming up: Should the territory be allowed to enter the Union as a slave state, or as a free state where no slavery was permitted?

Slave State or Free State?

Control of the vast Southwest, over which the United States and Mexico fought a war from 1846 to 1848, stirred new concerns about the spread of slavery. In an effort to resolve these differences, David Wilmot, a Pennsylvania congressman, introduced what became known as the Wilmot Proviso. His bill would ban slavery from any land acquired from Mexico during the U.S.–Mexican War. Although Congress never passed it, Wilmot's bill divided the nation more deeply as each side—northerners against slavery

Dubbed "the Pathfinder" for his exploration of the West, John C. Frémont saw firsthand the potential for the nation's growth.

FAST FACTS

THE CIVIL WAR OFFICIALLY BEGAN ON APRIL 12, 1861, WHEN CONFEDERATE SOLDIERS FIRED ON UNION SOLDIERS INSIDE FORT SUMTER, IN THE HARBOR AT CHARLESTON, SOUTH CAROLINA.

and southerners in favor of it—became increasingly suspicious of the other's intentions regarding western settlement.

Then on the heels of the war with Mexico came the California gold rush of 1849. California's population grew enormously, thanks to gold seekers and the businesses and services that catered to them. California soon applied for statehood. However, southerners were so opposed to adding California as a free state that some of them threatened to **secede**.

To preserve the Union, leaders in Congress came up with another idea: the Compromise of 1850. This legislation eased sectional tensions by admitting California as a free state, and creating the Utah and New Mexico territories. It let settlers vote on whether to permit slavery—this choice was called "popular sovereignty"—and it established a stronger fugitive slave law that required Americans in all states and territories to help return runaway slaves to their masters.

The Kansas-Nebraska Act

The issue of slavery in the western territories refused to go away, however. In 1854, Senator Stephen A. Douglas of Illinois introduced the Kansas–Nebraska Act to organize those two new western territories under the terms decided by popular sovereignty. That overturned two earlier laws, together called the Missouri Compromise of 1820, which had banned slavery in all territories north of Missouri's southern border (except Missouri itself). When antislavery northerners and proslavery southerners flocked to Kansas to try to win the vote for their sides, violence broke out. Hundreds of people were killed or wounded.

The Kansas–Nebraska Act also led to the creation of a new political party—the Republican party. Its members believed that slavery should not expand into newly created western territories and states. John C. Frémont, who had become famous exploring the West, was the first, but unsuccessful, Republican presidential nominee in 1856.

Then, in 1857, the U.S. Supreme Court ruled in *Dred Scott v. Sandford* that the federal government could not stop slavery from spreading. Instead of settling the issue, the decision simply made many northerners angrier and convinced them that southerners would do anything to protect slavery.

A New President and a Divided Union

Meanwhile, the Republicans had gained support for their determination to keep slavery out of the West. In 1860, they tried again for the presidency. With the Democratic party divided and weakened, this time the Republican candidate, Abraham Lincoln, won.

Almost immediately after Lincoln's election, seven southern

This map shows how the Southwest initially was carved up after the Compromise of 1850.

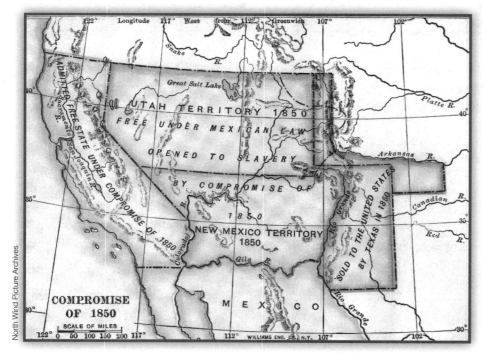

COMPROMISE OF 1850

May be reproduced for classroom use. *Toolkit Texts: Short Nonfiction for American History, Westward Expansion,* by Stephanie Harvey and Anne Goudvis, ©2016 (Portsmouth, NH: Heinemann).

Violence between pro- and antislavery settlers caused a number of deaths and prompted the nickname "Bleeding Kansas."

Sarin Images / Granger, NYC

states seceded from the Union. Although Lincoln had said that he would not end slavery in the South—just that he would stop it from expanding—some southerners refused to believe him. Those who took him seriously feared that without the growth of slavery, free states would take control of the government and have the power to end slavery altogether. Southerners worried that northerners could use the federal government to trample the right of their individual states to decide things for themselves.

The issues that sparked the Civil War came from the West, and pivotal fighting went on there. In 1860, the West was defined as the area west of the Appalachian Mountains. While many famous battles occurred along the more populated East Coast, in Virginia, Maryland, and Pennsylvania, Lincoln believed that gaining control of the Mississippi River in the West was crucial to the Union cause. So was defeating the South's ability and will to fight, which meant attacking throughout the Mississippi Valley, destroying crops and morale, and splitting the South geographically.

The plan that won the war came mainly from Lincoln — a westerner. He had been born in the Kentucky wilderness, raised on the Indiana frontier, and started a family and law practice in Illinois. The two generals who ultimately led the Union to victory were westerners, too: Ulysses S. Grant of Ohio and Illinois, and William T. Sherman of Ohio.

It is often overlooked, but the Civil War was indeed a battle between the North and the South…over the West.

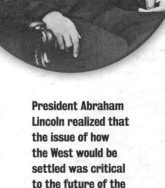

Library of Congress

President Abraham Lincoln realized that the issue of how the West would be settled was critical to the future of the Union.

WARFARE IN THE WEST

The Civil War in the West posed special challenges to both armies. It was hard to supply large groups of men across great distances. This meant that the size of the forces engaged in battle paled beside that of their more famous counterparts to the east. Rarely did western armies exceed 1,000 men, and the participants numbered a few hundred or even fewer in some of the most renowned engagements.

Difficulties of communication and distance complicated efforts to find out what was happening, let alone conduct coordinated operations. Messages often failed to reach their intended recipients, and gaps in time and space made strategic movements nearly impossible. Troops tended to follow preexisting transportation routes and often had to stay close to supply sources, especially water.

Both Union and Confederate forces had to deal with hostile Native American tribes as well as each other. Tribes sometimes formed alliances with one of the sides. As the most visible sign of government authority in the region, Union and Confederate commanders also had to maintain order. The Union possessed several prewar forts along various routes, enabling officers to gather supplies, outfit expeditions, and challenge Confederate efforts to gain control of the Southwest.

After 1862, the Southwest was not a strategic priority for either side, and Union forces, consisting mostly of state or territorial volunteers, battled various tribes to protect settlers and establish control over the region. The federal government often left the state or territorial units to their own devices. This sometimes resulted in more ferocious fighting than previously was seen in the region.

Terrain, distance, and difficulty of communication made it hard to move large groups, so mostly small groups of soldiers fought in the west.

May be reproduced for classroom use. *Toolkit Texts: Short Nonfiction for American History, Westward Expansion,* by Stephanie Harvey and Anne Goudvis, ©2016 (Portsmouth, NH: Heinemann).

North Wind Picture Archives

Caught in the Crossfire

The Civil War had raged for four bitter years, lasting from 1861 to 1865 and pitting states and often families and neighbors against each other. Ultimately it determined that the United States would continue to exist as a union of states under a single government, and that it would no longer be the largest slaveholding country in the world. The issues that resulted in the war were partly born from the Westward expansion, as the question of whether new states and territories should be free or slaveholding areas brought slavery, and whether the Union would continue to be a union, to the forefront. The war ended with the surrender of the Confederate Army in 1865, but battles of another kind would continue in the west.

The sparks that started the Civil War as settlers pushed west were not extinguished once that conflict was over. Rather, as settlers and miners streamed westward, moving into and across traditional Indian lands, battles erupted. The post–Civil War army's new mission became one of containing and controlling the Native Americans.

Fighting for Land

In the Southwest, Apaches had been struggling with Texans and the U.S. Army for decades, but smoldering conflicts had burst into flame during the Civil War. Apaches and their northern neighbors, the Comanches—taking advantage of the drain of men east as Texans joined the Confederacy—pushed back against

Although they fought fiercely (above), in the end the Indians were no match for the persistent westward movement by settlers.

Texas settlement. They also attacked the men building the Union Pacific Railroad across Kansas.

In 1862, trouble broke out farther north. Settlers pouring into Minnesota before the war had forced the Santee Sioux onto a strip of land that was too small to support them. They became dependent on government supplies. When Congress, worried about paying for the war, neglected to pay for Indian supplies, the Santee Sioux began to starve.

Young men of the tribe fought furiously to take back their lands. They killed between 400 and 800 settlers before the Minnesota militia and the Union army crushed them. Army officials condemned 303 Indians to death for the attacks, but President Abraham Lincoln pardoned all but 39 of them. They were hanged on December 26, 1862, in the largest mass execution in American history.

The Government Pushes Back

The Santee Sioux "uprising" made westerners nervous and military officials angry. The federal government began to press hard against all western Indians. In Colorado, 100,000 eastern settlers crowded Cheyenne and Arapaho Indians off their land and onto an arid reservation at Sand Creek on the Arkansas River.

Tribal leaders such as Gall (top) and Red Cloud (bottom) resisted efforts by the U.S. Army to push the Sioux off their land.

Indians who refused to go raided settlers' farms for food and supplies. On November 29, 1864, federal troops opened fire on a friendly band of Cheyennes camped at Sand Creek, killing 150 to 200 Indians, mostly old men, women, and children.

The Sand Creek Massacre infuriated the Teton Sioux, who were loosely allied with the Cheyennes and who resented the miners and soldiers who were moving through prized native hunting grounds on their way to the newly discovered gold mines of Montana. Under leaders such as Red Cloud, Sitting Bull, Crazy Horse, and Gall, the Teton Sioux fought back.

When the Civil War ended in 1865, the U.S. Army focused most of its attention and resources on the Indian wars on the Plains. In October 1867, the Apaches, Comanches, Kiowas, Cheyennes, and Arapahoes signed the Treaty of Medicine Lodge in Kansas. In exchange for annual payments, provisions, clothing, tools, and schools, they promised to stop interfering with the building of the transcontinental railroad and raiding white settlements.

The next year, the Sioux and their allies signed a similar document, the Treaty of Fort Laramie. It established the tribe on the Great Sioux Reservation, 22 million acres of land in what is now South Dakota. They also retained the

Sent to live on reservations where there were few natural resources, Indians had to rely on the U.S. government for clothing and food.

May be reproduced for classroom use. *Toolkit Texts: Short Nonfiction for American History, Westward Expansion,* by Stephanie Harvey and Anne Goudvis, ©2016 (Portsmouth, NH: Heinemann).

right to hunt in the Powder River region, in what is now western Nebraska and eastern Wyoming.

The Railroad Moves In

Almost immediately, however, surveyors for the Northern Pacific Railroad moved into Sioux territory. So did buffalo hunters and miners. Red Cloud begged the government to honor their treaty, but to no avail. In 1873, the army sent General George A. Custer into the Sioux lands to find a good place for an army post in the Black Hills. Not only did he find a spot, but followers of the expedition found something else—gold. By 1875, a gold rush was on, and miners poured into the lands the Sioux had been guaranteed by treaty.

At first the army tried to hold back miners and settlers while the government negotiated to buy more cessions. When the Sioux categorically refused

Native Americans and U.S. officials were photographed after a council meeting at Pine Ridge, South Dakota.

to sell any more land, however, the army stepped aside and simply warned easterners to arm themselves against "hostile" Indians.

In early 1876, the Sioux and their western allies joined together under Sitting Bull to stop the flood of settlers into their land. Army officials sent three columns of troops from three different directions into the Powder River region to surround the Indian camp and defeat the Sioux once and for all. Custer, commander of the Seventh Cavalry, located the Indians near the Little Bighorn River. He divided his men into four groups and led his own group into an attack, without support, on June 26. Tribal Leader Gall and his men were ready and eager for battle, however. Custer and all the men in his group—more than 250—died.

Winning the Battle, But Losing the War

The U.S. Army lost the Battle of the Little Bighorn, but the Sioux lost the war. Furious at the destruction of Custer's command, the army moved a larger force against the Sioux, who were forced either to flee to Canada or to surrender when their food ran short. By 1877, the Sioux were either in exile or on reservations.

Although they tried to resist, Native American groups throughout the West met similar fates: death, exile, or restricted living on reservations. The movement west simply could not be stopped.

General George A. Custer's defeat at the Little Bighorn River shocked the nation.

Library of Congress

North Wind Picture Archives

Buried Alive

Sarah Winnemucca Hopkins
Palurr Numu
c. 1844–1891, writing c. 1882

*Sarah Winnemuca Hopkins, a
Paiute activist and educator,
was once buried alive by her
mother, to protect her from
a group of white settlers. Her
recollections of the frightening
experience are below.*

   *She excelled at languages
and served as an interpreter
for the U.S. Army in 1860s
and 1870s. Hoping that her
work would help her people,
Winnemucca was disappointed
by the treatment she and
other Paiutes received at the
hands of the U.S. government.
She did help preserve the history
and culture of her people by writing
her autobiography,* Life Among the
Paiutes, *in 1883.*

Sarah Winnemucca Hopkins

Oh what a fright we all got one morning to hear some white people were
coming. Everyone ran as best as they could. My poor mother was left with my
little sister and me. Oh, I never can forget it. My poor mother was carrying my
little sister on her back, and trying to make me run, but I was so frightened I
could not move my feet, and while my poor mother was trying to get me along,
my aunt overtook up, and she said to mother: "Let us bury our girls, or we shall
all be killed and eaten up." So they went to work and buried us, and told us if we
heard any noise not to cry out, for if we did they would surely kill and eat us.

So our mothers buried me and my cousin, planted sage bushes over our faces to keep the sun from burning them and there we were left all day.

Oh, can anyone imagine my feelings buried alive, thinking every minute that I was to be unburied and eaten up by the people that my grandfather loved so much. With my heart throbbing, and not daring to breathe, we lay there all day. It seemed that the night would never come.

Thanks be to God the night came at last. Oh, how I cried and said, "Oh, father, have you forgotten me? Are you never coming for me?" I cried so I thought my very heartstrings would break. At last we heard some whispering. We did not dare to whisper to each other, so we lay still. I could hear their footsteps coming nearer and nearer. I thought my heart was coming right out of my mouth. Then I heard my mother say, "It is right here!" Oh, can anyone in this world ever imagine what my feelings were when I was dug up by my poor mother and father? My cousin and I were once more happy in our mothers' and fathers' care, and we were taken to where all the rest were.

I was once buried alive. But my second burial shall be forever, where no father or mother will come and dig me up. It shall not be with throbbing heart that I shall listen for coming footsteps. I shall be in the sweet rest of peace—I, the chieftain's weary daughter. Well, while we were in the mountains hiding, the people that my grandfather called our white brothers came along to where our winter supplies were. They set everything we had left on fire. It was a fearful sight. It was all we had for the winter, and it was all burnt during that night. My father took some of his men during the night to try and save some of it, but they could not; it had burnt down before they got there.

INTO THE WEST

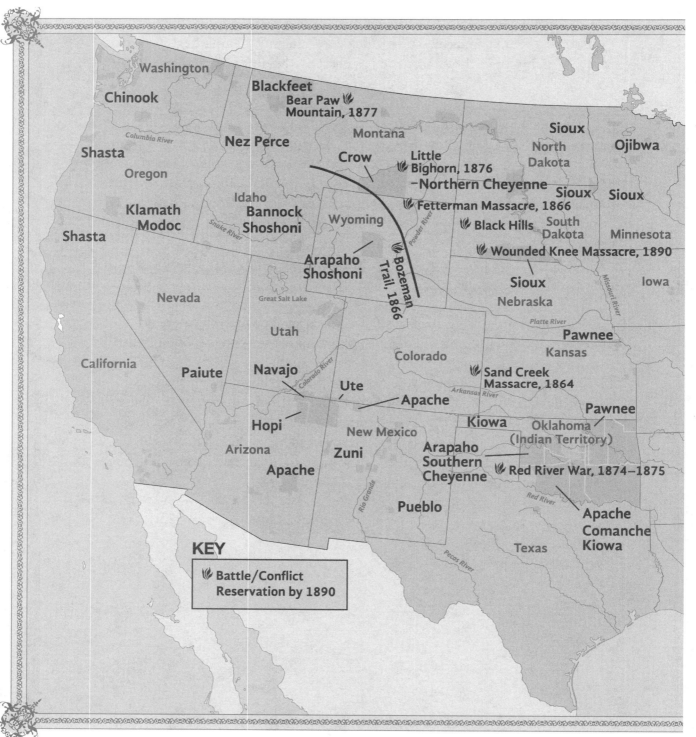

Washington

Chinook

Blackfeet
Bear Paw 🌿
Mountain, 1877

Columbia River

Nez Perce

Montana

Sioux

North
Dakota

Ojibwa

Shasta

Oregon

Crow

Little 🌿
Bighorn, 1876

–Northern Cheyenne

Sioux

Sioux

Idaho
Bannock
Shoshoni

Snake River

Wyoming

🌿 Fetterman Massacre, 1866

🌿 Black Hills

South
Dakota

Minnesota

Klamath
Modoc

Shasta

Arapaho
Shoshoni

Bozeman
Trail, 1866

Powder River

🌿 Wounded Knee Massacre, 1890

Nevada

Great Salt Lake

Sioux

Nebraska

Missouri River

Iowa

Utah

Colorado

Platte River

Pawnee

California

Paiute

Navajo

Colorado River

Ute

Apache

🌿 Sand Creek
Massacre, 1864

Arkansas River

Kansas

Hopi

Arizona

Zuni

New Mexico

Kiowa

Oklahoma
(Indian Territory)

Pawnee

Apache

Arapaho
Southern
Cheyenne

🌿 Red River War, 1874–1875

Rio Grande

Pueblo

Red River

Apache
Comanche
Kiowa

Pecos River

Texas

KEY

🌿 Battle/Conflict

Reservation by 1890

May be reproduced for classroom use. *Toolkit Texts: Short Nonfiction for American History, Westward Expansion,* by Stephanie Harvey and Anne Goudvis, ©2016 (Portsmouth, NH: Heinemann).

This map shows the locations of significant Native American conflicts, as well as the locations of western Native American groups and reservations in the late 1800s.

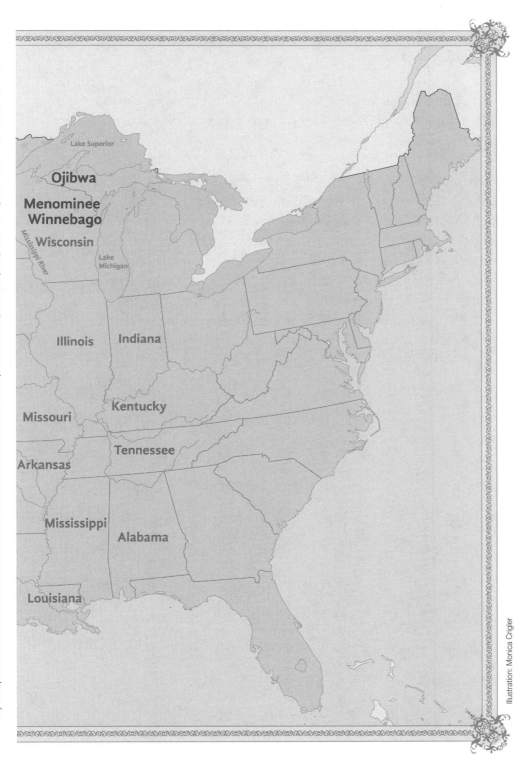

Illustration: Monica Crigler

This I Believe

Chief Joseph Inmutooyahlatlat
NEZ PERCE Tsutpeli

Chief Joseph, leader of the Nez Perce, was invited to address Congress on January 14, 1879. This excerpt from his speech made a case for his people being allowed to remain on their traditional lands.

Our fathers gave us many laws, which they had learned from their fathers. These laws were good. They told us to treat all men as they treated us; that we should never be the first to break a bargain; that it was a disgrace to tell a lie; that we should speak only the truth; that it was a shame for one man to take from another his wife or his property without paying for it. We were taught to believe that the Great Spirit sees and hears everything, and that he never forgets; that hereafter he will give every man a spirit-home according to his deserts, if he has been a good man, he will have a good home; if he has been a bad man, he will have a bad home. This I believe, and all my people believe the same.

Chief Joseph (Nez Perce)

Chief Joseph was best known for his resistance to the U.S. government's attempts to force his tribe onto reservations. The Nez Perce were a peaceful nation that spread from Idaho to Northern Washington. The tribe had maintained good relations with settlers after the Lewis and Clark expedition. Joseph spent much of his early childhood at a mission maintained by Christian missionaries.

In 1855, Chief Joseph's father, Old Joseph, signed a treaty with the U.S. government that allowed his people to retain much of their traditional lands. In 1863, another treaty was created that severely reduced the amount of land, but Old Joseph maintained that this second treaty was never agreed to by his people. A showdown over the second "non-treaty" came after Chief Joseph assumed his role as Chief in 1877. After months of fighting and forced marches, many of the Nez Perce were sent to a reservation in what is now Oklahoma, where many died from malaria and starvation. Chief Joseph tried every possible appeal to the federal authorities to return the Nez Perce to the land of their ancestors. In 1885, he was sent along with many of his band to a reservation in Washington where, according to the reservation doctor, he later died of a broken heart.

A portrait of Chief Joseph

Library of Congress

Words Do Not Pay

CHIEF JOSEPH

Chief Joseph, leader of the Nez Perce, gave this speech on a visit to Washington, D.C., in 1879.

I do not understand why nothing is done for my people. I have heard talk and talk, but nothing is done. Good words do not last long unless they amount to something. Words do not pay for my dead people. They do not pay for my country, now overrun by white men. They do not protect my father's grave. They do not pay for all my horses and cattle. Good words will not give me back my children. Good words will not make good the promise of your war chief General Miles. Good words will not give my people good health and stop them from dying. Good words will not give my people a home where they can live in peace and take care of themselves. I am tired of talk that comes to nothing. It makes my heart sick when I remember all the good words and all the broken promises. There has been too much talking by men who had no right to talk. Too many misrepresentations have been made, too many misunderstandings have come up between the white men about the Indians. If the white man wants to live in peace with the Indian he can live in peace. There need be no trouble. Treat all men alike. Give them all the same law. Give them all an equal chance to live and grow. All men were made by the same great Spirit Chief. They are all brothers. The earth is mother of all people, and all people should have equal rights upon it. You might as well expect the rivers to run backward as that any man who was born a free man should be contented when penned up and denied liberty to go where he pleases. Let me be a free man—free to travel, free to stop, free to work, free to travel where I choose, free to choose my own teachers, free to follow the religion of my own fathers, free to think and talk and act for myself—and I will obey every law or submit to the penalty.

I Will Fight No More Forever

CHIEF JOSEPH

The Nez Perce tribe refused in 1877 to resettle on a reservation. Chief Joseph led his tribe on an extraordinary 1,500-mile escape through Wyoming, Idaho, and Montana from the U.S. army. The tribe avoided capture for many months. But when winter arrived, Chief Joseph finally announced his decision to surrender to the U.S. military.

Tell General Howard I know his heart. What he told me before, I have it in my heart. I am tired of fighting. Our Chiefs are killed; Looking Glass is dead, Ta-Hool-Hool-Shute is dead. The old men are all dead. It is the young men who say yes or no. He who led on the young men is dead. It is cold, and we have no blankets; the little children are freezing to death. My people, some of them, have run away to the hills, and have no blankets, no food. No one knows where they are—perhaps freezing to death. I want to have time to look for my children, and see how many of them I can find. Maybe I shall find them among the dead. Hear me, my Chiefs! I am tired; my heart is sick and sad. From where the sun now stands I will fight no more forever.

**Lieutenant Colonel
George A. Custer**

May be reproduced for classroom use. *Toolkit Texts: Short Nonfiction for American History, Westward Expansion,* by Stephanie Harvey and Anne Goudvis, ©2016 (Portsmouth, NH: Heinemann).

ON THE LITTLE BIGHORN

Thanks to a vision Sioux leader Sitting Bull had, the Sioux and Northern Cheyenne fighters went into battle feeling confident of victory.

The Fort Laramie Treaty of 1868 established that the Black Hills would always belong to the Sioux as part of the Great Sioux Reservation. Some Sioux bands resigned themselves to life on the reservation, but others remained defiant. They refused to become dependent on the U.S. government. They wanted to live and hunt freely. But after gold was discovered in the Black Hills in 1874, the U.S. government pressured the Sioux to give up that sacred land. That led to conflicts.

REPORT OR RELOCATE

By 1875, the federal government wanted to resolve permanently the situation in the West. It ordered all Sioux to report to an agency on the reservation by January 31, 1876. Those who refused would be hunted down and forced to relocate. Some members of the Sioux, Northern Cheyenne, and Arapaho bands ignored the ultimatum. They were determined to fight to keep the Black Hills under their control. A military force of more than 2,000 U.S. soldiers, divided into three groups, was sent to deal with those "hostile" people.

North Wind Picture Archives

Surrounded and outnumbered by Sioux and Northern Cheyenne fighters, Custer and his men were all killed.

Lieutenant Colonel George A. Custer and the 7th U.S. Cavalry made up a large part of one of those forces. An experienced soldier of the Civil War (1861–1865) and frontier, Custer hoped for a stunning victory that would add to his military reputation.

"WE ARE GOING TO HAVE A LOSING FIGHT..."

In June, about 8,000 native people, including Sioux leaders Sitting Bull and Crazy Horse, had gathered in an encampment on the banks of the Little Bighorn River in southeastern Montana. The group had just celebrated its annual Sun Dance ceremony and was preparing for hunting season. On June 25, Arikara scouts traveling with the 7th Cavalry located the large encampment. Fearing that his cavalry's presence had been detected, Custer decided not to wait for reinforcements and planned an attack. The scouts tried to warn Custer that there were too many warriors in the camp. One scout, Bloody Knife, said, "We are going to have a big fight, a losing fight." Custer ignored him.

Custer divided his 600-man command into four segments. The pack train remained behind to guard the ammunition and supplies. One wing, under Captain Frederick Benteen, scouted to the southwest. Another force, under Major Marcus Reno, moved to attack the southern end of the sprawling camped village. Custer led a third wing northward along a ridge.

A HOPELESS SITUATION

Custer believed 800 warriors were in the camp, but the real number was closer to 1,800 fighters. Initially caught by surprise at the presence of the soldiers, the Sioux and Northern Cheyenne men rallied and rode out to face Reno. They quickly drove him back with heavy losses. Then, they turned to face Custer and his command of 210 troopers. With their path blocked by overwhelming numbers of warriors on horseback, the situation for Custer and his men quickly became hopeless. The cavalrymen shot their horses to use them as defensive cover, but they soon were either dead or too severely wounded to continue fighting.

Northern Cheyenne chief Two Moons, who fought in the battle, later recalled, "We circled all around him [Custer]—swirling like water around a stone. We shoot, we ride fast, we shoot again. Soldiers drop, and horses fall on them." Custer's entire command was wiped out by the evening of June 26.

Despite the victory, Sitting Bull ordered his people to break camp and scatter. He knew that the army would be looking for revenge. And he was right. A relief column of soldiers found Custer's bloody battleground the next day. They hastily dug graves for the more than 260 soldiers who were killed. The shocking news of Custer's defeat was telegraphed across the nation.

NO MORE CHOICES

Within months, many of the Sioux and Northern Cheyennes, relentlessly pursued by the army, surrendered. Some were killed or sent to prison. Others accepted that they had no choice but to live on a reservation. After avoiding capture for many months, Crazy Horse surrendered at Fort Robinson in Nebraska in the spring of 1877. He was killed before the end of the year when agents attempted to arrest him. Sitting Bull and his band escaped to Canada. They lived there until 1881, when starvation forced them to return to live on the Standing Rock Reservation.

The Battle of the Little Bighorn was an overwhelming victory for the Sioux and their allies. But it made the U.S. government determined to rein in any hostile bands of native people. More soldiers were ordered west, and the government stopped trying to persuade the Sioux to give up the Black Hills—it simply seized the land.

SETTLING ON A NAME

The United States has wrestled with how to remember the Battle of the Little Bighorn. In 1879, the government designated the battlefield a national cemetery. In 1881, the remains of the 7th Cavalry troopers were dug up and placed in a mass grave marked by a large granite memorial (BELOW). (A year after the battle, Lieutenant Colonel George A. Custer's body was moved to the U.S. Military Academy at West Point.) The National Park Service began to manage the Little Bighorn site in 1940, and in 1946, it became known as the Custer Battlefield National Monument. In 1991, the name changed again to the Little Bighorn Battlefield National Monument.

© Zack Frank/Shutterstock

All the Soldiers Were Now Killed:
Two Moon Describes Custer's Last Stand

The Battle of the Little Bighorn, commonly referred to as Custer's Last Stand, was a battle between the 7th Cavalry Regiment of the United States, led by General George Custer, against the Lakota Sioux, Northern Cheyenne, and Arapaho tribes. Sitting Bull and Crazy Horse, leaders of the Sioux on the Great Plains, strongly resisted the efforts of the U.S. government to confine their people to reservations. Tensions between U.S. government and the Sioux and other tribes had been rising since the discovery of gold on

Library of Congress

A Portrait of Two Moon

Native American lands in the Black Hills. When a number of tribes missed a federal deadline to move to reservations, the U.S. Army, including Custer and his 7th Calvary, was dispatched to confront them. Custer was unaware of the number of warriors fighting under the command of Sitting Bull at Little Bighorn. His forces were outnumbered and quickly suffered a severe defeat. Five of the 7th Cavalry's twelve companies were wiped out; Custer was killed, as were two of his brothers, a nephew, and a brother-in-law. The total U.S. casualty count included 268 dead and 55 severely wounded.

After the Battle of Little Bighorn, the United States military worked hard to end Native American resistance. Most of the tribes involved in the battle surrendered to the United States the following year. The following account of the Battle of Little Bighorn by Cheyenne Chief Two Moon was published in a magazine in 1898.

"About May, when the grass was tall and the horses strong, we broke camp and started across the country to the mouth of the Tongue River. Then Sitting Bull and Crazy Horse and all went up the Rosebud. There we had a big fight with General Crook, and whipped him. Many soldiers were killed—few Indians. It was a great fight, much smoke and dust."

"From there we all went over the divide, and camped in the valley of Little Horn. Everybody thought, 'Now we are out of the white man's country. He can live there, we will live here.' After a few days, one morning when I was in camp north of Sitting Bull, a Sioux messenger rode up and said, `Let everybody paint up, cook, and get ready for a big dance.'

"Cheyennes then went to work to cook, cut up tobacco, and get ready. We all thought to dance all day. We were very glad to think we were far away from the white man.

"I went to water my horses at the creek, and washed them off with cool water, then took a swim myself. I came back to the camp afoot. When I got near my lodge, I looked up the Little Horn towards Sitting Bull's camp. I saw a great dust rising. It looked like a whirlwind. Soon Sioux horseman came rushing into camp shouting: 'Soldiers come! Plenty white soldiers.'

"I ran into my lodge, and said to my brother-in-law, 'Get your horses; the white man is coming. Everybody run for horses.'

"Outside, far up the valley, I heard a battle cry, Hay-ay, hay-ay! I heard shooting, too, this way [clapping his hands very fast]. I couldn't see any Indians. Everybody was getting horses and saddles. After I had caught my horse, a Sioux warrior came again and said, 'Many soldiers are coming.'

"Then he said to the women, 'Get out of the way, we are going to have hard fight.'

"I said, 'All right, I am ready.'

"I got on my horse, and rode out into my camp. I called out to the people all running about: 'I am Two Moon, your chief. Don't run away. Stay here and fight. You must stay and fight the white soldiers. I shall stay even if I am to be killed.'

"I rode swiftly toward Sitting Bull's camp. There I saw the white soldiers fighting in a line. Indians covered the flat. They began to drive the soldiers all mixed up—Sioux, then soldiers, then more Sioux, and all shooting. The air was full of smoke and dust. I saw the soldiers fall back and drop into the riverbed like buffalo fleeing. They had no time to look for a crossing. The Sioux chased them up the hill, where they met more soldiers in wagons, and then messengers came saying more soldiers were going to kill the women, and the Sioux turned back. Chief Gall was there fighting. Crazy Horse also.

"I then rode toward my camp, and stopped squaws from carrying off lodges. While I was sitting on my horse I saw flags come up over the hill to the east like that [he raised his finger-tips]. Then the soldiers rose all at once, all on horses, like this [he put his fingers behind each other to indicate that Custer appeared marching in columns of fours]. They formed into three branches [squadrons] with a little ways between. Then a bugle sounded, and they all got off horses, and some soldiers led the horses back over the hill.

"Then the Sioux rode up the ridge on all sides, riding very fast. The Cheyennes went up the left way. Then the shooting was quick, quick. Pop pop pop very fast. Some of the soldiers were down on their knees, some standing. Officers all in front. The smoke was like a great cloud, and everywhere the Sioux went the dust rose like smoke. We circled all round them—swirling like water round a stone. We shoot, we ride fast, we shoot again. Soldiers drop, and horses fall on them. Soldiers in line drop, but one man rides up and down the line—all the time shouting. He rode a sorrel horse with white face and white fore-legs. I don't know who he was. He was a brave man.

"Indians keep swirling round and round, and the soldiers killed only a few. Many soldiers fell. At last all horses killed but five. Once in a while some man would break out and run toward the river, but he would fall. At last about a hundred men and five horsemen stood on the hill all bunched together. All along the bugler kept blowing his commands. He was very brave too. Then a chief was killed. I hear it was Long Hair [Custer], I don't know; and then the five horsemen and the bunch of men, may be forty, started toward the river. The man on the sorrel horse led them, shouting all the time. He wore a buckskin shirt, and had long black hair and mustache. He fought hard with a big knife. His men were all covered with white dust. I couldn't tell whether they were officers or not. One man all alone ran far down toward the river, then round up over the hill. I thought he was going to escape, but a Sioux fired and hit him in the head. He was the last man. He wore braid on his arms [sergeant].

"All the soldiers were now killed, and the bodies were stripped. After that no one could tell which were officers. The bodies were left where they fell. We had no dance that night. We were sorrowful."

Battle of Little Bighorn

The battle of Little Bighorn occurred in 1876 and is commonly referred to as "Custer's Last Stand." The battle took place between the U.S. Cavalry and northern tribe Indians, including the Cheyenne, Sioux, and Arapaho. Before this battle, the Sitting Bull had decided to wage war against the white settlers for encroaching on tribal lands in the Black Hills after gold was discovered in the area. In the spring of 1876, Sitting Bull and his tribal army had successfully battled the U.S. Cavalry twice.

The battle came about when Lt. General George Custer led a force of six hundred cavalry into Sioux land. Although his scouts warned him that an estimated eight thousand Sioux and Cheyenne had joined forces, Custer ignored their reports. He split his force and decided not to wait for a larger army force to catch up with his column. Another group of Indian forces, led by Crazy Horse, effectively trapped Custer and his men. In a desperate attempt to hold off the Indian warriors, Custer ordered his men to short their horses and stack their bodies to form a barricade to protect them from the Indians.

It took less than an hour for the arrows and bullets of the Indians to wipe out General Custer and his men. Despite having won this battle, the Indians were not victorious. Outrage over the death of the popular Custer led the U.S. government to redraw the boundaries of the Black Hills so that the land would not be part of reservation property, which left it open for white men to settle. The battle took place on June 25, but news did not reach the East until July 5.

From the New York Times, July 6, 1876

Gen Custer and seventeen commissioned officers butchered in a battle of the Little Horn—attack on an overwhelmingly large camp of savages—three hundred and fifteen men killed—the battlefield like a slaughter pen.

A Fuller Report From the Scene as General Terry Arrives.

They met a sight to appall the stoutest heart… General Custer had evidently attempted to attack the village… which was about two miles long and a mile wide. At the highest point of the ridge they found Custer, surrounded by his chosen band. Here were his two brothers and his nephew, all lying within a circle of a few yards, their horses beside them. Here the last stand had been made, and here one after another of this last survivors of Custer's five companies had met their death… Not a man had escaped to tell the tale, but it was inscribed on these barren hills in a language more elegant than words.

It is obvious that the troops were completely surrounded by a force of ten times their number… Information from Army sources leads to the conclusion that 2,500 or 3,000 Indians composed the fighting force arrayed against Custer and his 600.

Destroying a Culture

The U.S. government spent nearly 100 years trying to develop a Native American policy that would work in the West. It crafted more than 400 agreements with Native American groups between 1778 and 1871. The U.S. Senate ratified 370 treaties and negotiated another 50 treaties that were never ratified. By the time Congress ended its efforts in 1871, most native groups had been restricted to life on large reservations. Their days of moving freely over the land were over.

A New Act for Native Peoples

In 1887, Senator Henry L. Dawes of Massachusetts made a proposal.

He suggested breaking up the large communal reservation lands into many smaller sections. The U.S. government would give 160 acres of farmland or 320 acres of grazing land to each native family. This effort would cut native people's ties to large tribes and make them live more like traditional American families. The act further proposed that native children attend government-funded boarding schools. The schools would teach young Native Americans how to live in "American society."

The Dawes Act encouraged—or forced—Native Americans to adopt nonnative customs, language, and clothing. Those who supported

Senator
Henry L. Dawes

U.S. commissioners posed with a delegation of Sioux leaders who came to Washington, D.C., in 1888.

Top and bottom: Library of Congress

the act, including President Grover Cleveland, hoped that it would end the federal government's role of managing reservations and overseeing Native American welfare.

Loss of Land

Congress passed the Dawes Act, or the General Allotment Act, on February 8, 1887. Publicly, it claimed to protect native property rights. At that time, Native Americans owned about 138 million acres. By 1900, however, the amount of land had dropped to 78 million acres. Although each family was given a parcel of land to manage, the land was often dry and unsuitable for farming. In addition, many native people historically had been hunters. They didn't know much about agriculture on a large scale, and they could not afford to buy tools or farm animals without help from the government. Meanwhile, the surplus land that remained after allotment was auctioned off to settlers and railroad companies.

Loss of Culture

The boarding schools were another concern. Many Native American children died after they were exposed to diseases for which they had no immunity. School administrators assigned new names to the students. They gave the students western-style clothing to wear and unfamiliar foods to eat. Long hair, which was encouraged and admired in native families, was forbidden at the schools. Teachers and administrators punished children for speaking their native language or for practicing native traditions or celebrations. Supporters of the schools hoped that the children would forget their heritage and adopt the customs of American culture.

At first, the Dawes Act applied only to certain Native American groups. However, in 1893 Cleveland appointed Dawes chairman of a commission that negotiated with the Five Civilized Tribes (the Cherokee, the Chickasaw, the Choctaw, the Creek, and the Seminole), which had

Photographs from the Carlisle Indian School show a group of Sioux boys shortly after their arrival at the school.

Carlisle Indian School's group of "assimilated" Sioux students.

Assimilate means to conform with the customs or attitudes of a group or nation.

previously been excluded from the Dawes Act. Members of these groups registered with the Bureau of Indian Affairs, a U.S. government agency set up to oversee and control issues related to Native Americans. They received property in exchange for giving up their tribal connections, assimilating into American society, and agreeing to obey U.S. laws.

A national policy of assimilation extended into the 20th century. Then, the Institute for Government Research released a report about Native Americans in the United States. Called the Meriam Report, it exposed the poor quality of life on reservations as well as the inhumane conditions at boarding schools. Shortly after the report was filed, the Great Depression pushed the United States into a severe economic downturn. It caused difficult living conditions all over the country for most of the 1930s.

A New Deal for Natives

In June 1934, the impact of both the Meriam Report and the Great Depression resulted in another piece of legislation. It was called the Indian Reorganization Act, or the Indian New Deal, in reference to President Franklin D. Roosevelt's other national reforms. The act granted rights to Native Americans, including control of their assets (which were mainly land) and the return to self-government at the tribal level. Many tribes created their own constitutions.

In the first 20 years after the act was passed, Native Americans reclaimed more than 2 million acres. The act also established a government aid program so that native groups could receive money for land purchases and education. Native people no longer had to send their children away to boarding schools.

The Indian Reorganization Act was not perfect, and people still debate its effectiveness. By reversing the worst elements of the Dawes Act, however, it tried to address the injustices of that earlier law. It laid the foundation for the recognition of Native American rights and opened up the potential for dialogue between tribes and the U.S. government.

A White Man's Name

LUTHER STANDING BEAR, MATO NAJIN
BRULE SIOUX, LAKOTA

1868–1939, writing c.1928

Boarding schools were established for Native American children in the United States during the late 19th century to educate Native American children. Children were immersed in American culture, but this meant that they were forced to abandon their Native American identities and cultures. The experience was often harsh, especially for the young children who were separated from their families. Their long hair was cut, they were forbidden to speak their native languages, and their traditional names were replaced by new American names.

Library of Congress

Luther Standing Bear, Dakota Chief

One day when we came to school, there was a lot of writing on one of the blackboards. We did not know what it meant, but our interpreter came into the room and said, "Do you see all these marks on the blackboard: Well, each word is a white man's name. They are going to give each one of you one of these names by which you will hereafter be known." None of the names were read or explained to us, so of course we did not know the sound or meaning of any of them.

The teacher had a long pointed stick in her hand, and the interpreter told the boy in the front seat to come up. The teacher handed the stick to him, and the interpreter then told him to pick out any name he wanted. The boy had gone up with his blanket on. When the long stick was handed to him, he turned to us as much as to say "Shall I—or will you help me to—take one of these names? Is it right for me to take a white man's name?" He did not know what to do for a long time, not uttering a single word—but he acted a lot and was doing a lot of thinking.

Finally he pointed out one of the names written on the blackboard. The the teacher took a piece of white tape and wrote the name on it. Then she cut off a length of the tape and sewed it on the back of the boy's shirt. Then that name was erased from the board. There was no duplication of names in the first class at Carlisle School!

Then the next boy took the pointed and selected a name. He was also labeled in the same manner as Number One. When my turn came, I took the pointer and acted as if I were about to touch an enemy. Soon we all had names of white men sewed on our backs.

The Cutting of My Long Hair

GERTRUDE BONNIN ZITKALA-SA
YANRRON STOUX NAKOTA

1876–1938, writing in 1899

Gertrude Bonnin was born in 1876 on the Yankton Indian Reservation in South Dakota. She lived on the reservation, a place of happiness and security, until 1884, when at 8 years old was sent to a school run by missionaries in Indiana. She later wrote about her experiences at the school, where her heritage was stripped away. In this recollection, she describes her sadness at being forced to cut her traditionally long hair.

Gertrude Simmons Bonnin Zitkala-Sa [Red Bird]

Late in the morning, my friend Judwin gave me a terrible warning. Judwin knew a few words of English, and she had overheard the paleface woman talk about cutting our long, heavy hair. Our mothers had taught us that only unskilled warriors who were captured had their hair shingled by the enemy. Among our people, short hair was worn by mourners, and shingled hair by cowards.

We discussed our fate some moments, and when Judwin said, "We have to submit, because they are strong," I rebelled. "No, I will not submit! I will struggle first!" I answered.

I watched for my chance, and when no one noticed, I disappeared. I crept up the stairs as quietly as I could in my squeaking shoes—my moccasins had been exchanged for shoes. Along the hall I passed, without knowing whether I was going. Turning aside to an open door, I found a large room with three beds in it. The windows were covered with dark green curtains, which made the room very dim.

Thankful that no one was there, I directed my steps toward the corner farthest from the door. On my hands and knees I crawled under the bed, and cuddled myself in the dark corner. From my hiding place I peered out, shuddering with fear whenever I heard footsteps nearby. Though in the hall loud voices were calling my name, and I knew that even Judwin was searching for me, I did not open my mouth to answer. Then the steps were quickened and the voices became excited. The sounds came nearer and nearer.

Women and girls entered the room. I held my breath and watched them open closet doors and peep behind large trunks. Someone threw up the curtains, and the room was filled with sudden light. What caused them to stop and look under the bed I do not know. I remember being dragged out, though I resisted by kicking and scratching wildly. In spite of myself, I was carried downstairs and tied fast in a chair. I cried aloud, shaking my head all the while until I felt the cold blades of the scissors against my neck, and heard them gnaw off one of my thick braids. Then I lost my spirit. Since the day I was taken from my mother I had suffered extreme indignities. People had stared at me. I had been tossed about in the air like a wooden puppet. And now my long hair was shingled like a coward's. In my anguish I moaned for my mother, but no one came to comfort me. Not a soul reasoned quietly with me, as my own mother used to do; for now I was only one of many little animals driven by a herder.

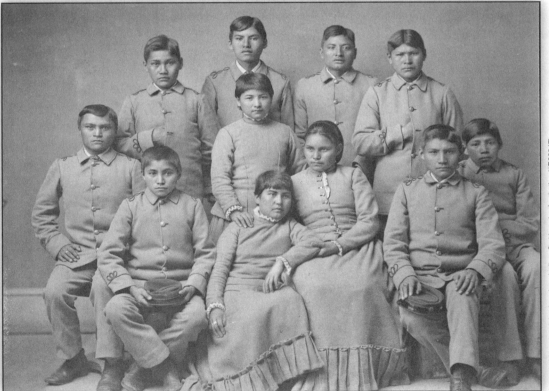

A photo of Apache children when they arrived at the Carlisle School in 1886, and the same group of children taken four months later.

A TIME OF TROUBLES

In this historical fiction account, a 13-year-old Sioux girl describes what life was like for her family on a reservation in 1880:

NO longer do the men of my tribe mount their horses and ride out on great bison hunts. The women do not prepare feasts of fresh bison meat roasted over the fire. The enormous herds are gone, and so are the days when we traveled freely, setting up our tepee camps wherever the bison led us. The white men say we must learn to farm instead of hunt. They insist we become "civilized" and adopt their ways. Our tribe must stay on this reservation, which is a small part of the land we used to roam.

We used to ride freely on the Great Plains.

Before the reservation, my people rose with the sun, ready to use the gifts of nature to meet our needs. Each day was a challenge, but we were free. Now we must depend on the white man's promise to feed and clothe us, but the government has not kept its word.

The Great Father pledged to give us cattle, tools, and seeds for farming, as well as blankets and cloth. While we learn to grow our own food, the government promises us beef, flour, beans, coffee, and other supplies. We line up to receive our rations, but there is never enough. The food is often not fit to eat. My father says dishonest agents steal provisions meant for us and sell them for a profit.

Like my father, the men of our tribe were once proud hunters providing us with meat and skins from bison, elk, and other animals. They were warriors, ready to protect their families at a moment's notice. When we moved to the reservation, they had to give up their weapons and learn to plow. But farming takes fertile land and good weather, and we have neither. Settlers take the best land, and drought and hot summer winds kill many of the crops. We have not been able to raise enough food, and now we are starving.

757. Rifle Guns, Pine Ridge Agency, Jan. 18th, 1891.

Life on reservations means living in the shadow of soldiers and cannon.

As always, my mother and the other women cook, clean, and raise children. The home is a woman's responsibility, but without fresh bison hides, Mother cannot repair our tepee or make a new one. Government officials insist we dress like white settlers, so we must now sew our garments from thin cloth instead of animal skins. Without our warm bison robes and deerskin clothing, we are always cold in the winter winds.

As if cold and hunger aren't enough to deal with, our people have been sick. We have little resistance to white men's diseases, and many people die—especially children. Officials have forbidden our

Our tepees sheltered us from winter's hardship.

We knew how to use all the parts of an animal.

medicine men from using traditional ways to treat the sick, so they must act in secret.

We children are busy doing chores and helping our parents, but we try to find a little time to play so we can forget our troubles for a while. Boys pretend to be warriors and hunters. Girls play with their dolls, and we all like to play ball and stick games. In the evening, we gather around our grandparents to hear them tell stories about their youth. They have so much wisdom to pass on to us!

Churches have set up schools on the reservation to teach us English and try to turn us into Christians. The teachers cut our hair short and give us new names. They want us to learn to live like them and hope we will help our parents give up the ancient ceremonies and customs. But when we go home after school, most of us still speak our own language and follow our traditional ways.

Some of my friends have been sent to boarding schools where they must live year-round. The white men think children are more likely to change if they are separated from their families for long periods. Students who return to their families after years at boarding school often feel like they no longer belong with their own people. This is a sad thing because we place a high value on family.

Still, some things have not changed. The Sioux will always love the earth and all its creatures. We treasure our children and respect our elders. We try to follow the right path in life, and we ask the Great Spirit to give us strength and wisdom.

Many of us long for the old days and desperately hope for a way off the reservation. You can hear our yearning in the songs we sing around the fire on cold nights. Oh, Great Spirit, please hear our cries!

Ruth Spencer Johnson enjoys writing about American history for young people.

Traditional ceremonies are still practiced but in secret.

May be reproduced for classroom use. *Toolkit Texts: Short Nonfiction for American History, Westward Expansion,* by Stephanie Harvey and Anne Goudvis, ©2016 (Portsmouth, NH: Heinemann).

Many Native Americans felt helpless as they watched their way of life and traditions disappear in the second half of the 19th century. Their survival depended on promises made in treaties, but the U.S. government consistently failed to honor those promises. The situation for many native people grew desperate.

For the Sioux, 1889 was a particularly bad year. The U.S. government had been trying for some time to get the Sioux to agree to the breakup of the Great Sioux Reservation. In 1889, the government's use of threats and pressure succeeded, and it split the large Sioux reservation into six much smaller parcels. The surplus land that resulted was made available for nonnative settlement. Then, on top of that, an influenza epidemic swept through the Great Plains that winter and **decimated** native communities.

Visions of a Better Life

Around this time, a Paiute Indian named Wovoka shared his religious visions of the Ghost Dance. While in a trance, Wovoka had seen his ancestors coming across the plains driving bison before them. Wovoka preached that the land would once again be filled with animals. People would be reunited with their ancestors, who would return to live on the earth. Until that time, Wovoka said, Ghost Dancers should live peacefully as honest and hardworking people.

Wovoka's message gave many Sioux hope that things might change. Believing that it offered a path to restore their traditional way of life, some Sioux embraced the Ghost Dance. Ceremonies usually lasted several days. Participants fasted, offered prayers, and listened to sermons. They wore special clothes—"ghost shirts"—that they believed to be bulletproof. They danced in a circle around a pole or a tree. Sometimes, a participant went into a trance, in which he or she often had visions of dead ancestors.

Settlers Grow Concerned

Word of the Ghost Dance movement reached Washington, D.C., in June 1890. The government was not overly concerned, but settlers in the Dakotas were. They spread rumors of an attack by the Sioux. The Sioux continued to dance, even when their food allotments were cut and they began to starve. They held on to the hope that change was coming.

That fall, more rumors of a Sioux attack on settlers made the Indian agents take action. Soldiers arrived at the Pine Ridge and Rosebud reservations in southern South Dakota in late November. Their presence convinced the Ghost Dancers that the army was sent to kill them. They fled to a place in the Badlands called the Stronghold. Officials then ordered the Sioux to report to their agencies and decided to take into custody any Ghost Dance leaders who had not joined the camp at the Stronghold.

Unfair Use of Force

One of the most famous Sioux leaders was Sitting Bull. He was living on the Standing Rock Reservation in northern South Dakota. He had not joined the Ghost Dance movement, but his popularity and status as a former warrior who refused to be intimidated alarmed officials. He had strongly opposed the government's push to seize additional reservation lands and its efforts to "civilize" native people. On December 15, 1890, tribal police tried to arrest Sitting Bull. A fight broke out, and Sitting Bull was killed. Despite its message of hope, the Ghost Dance movement became an excuse for the U.S. military to use alarming levels of force against the Sioux.

> **Decimated** means to kill or destroy a large part of a group of people.

Message of Hope

Library of Congress

Ghost Dance ceremonies gave the Sioux hope at a time when their future looked bleak.

May be reproduced for classroom use. *Toolkit Texts: Short Nonfiction for American History, Westward Expansion,* by Stephanie Harvey and Anne Goudvis, ©2016 (Portsmouth, NH: Heinemann).

The Ghost Dance Songs

ARAPAHO LNUNA-INA

The Ghost Dance religion was founded by the Paiute prophet Wovoka, who taught that, through dancing, the world would be renewed and the dead brought back to life. He said, "I went up to heaven and saw God and all the people who had died a long time ago. God told me to come back and tell my people they must be good and love one another, and not fight, or steal, or lie. He gave me this dance to give to my people." These peaceful ideas spread quickly through the Indian nations. It was seen as a threat by the whites, and led to the tragic massacre at Wounded Knee on December 29, 1890. The first of these three songs was composed by Nawat or Left Hand, chief of the southern Arapaho.

Portrait of Nawat

My children, when at first I liked the whites,
My children, when at first I liked the whites,
I gave them fruits,
I gave them fruits.

Father, have pity on me,
Father, have pity on me,
I am crying for thirst,
I am crying for thirst;
All is gone—I have nothing to eat,
All is gone—I have nothing to eat.

Father, the morning star
Father, the morning star
Look on us, we have danced until daylight,
Look on us, we have danced until daylight.
Take pity on us—Hi'i'i'
Take pity on us—Hi'i'i'

ENDING A WAY OF LIFE:

Wounded Knee

Major General Nelson A. Miles (on horseback, left) keeps a watchful eye on a native encampment.

Library of Congress

When the smoke cleared from the banks of Wounded Knee Creek on December 29, 1890, approximately 300 Sioux men women, and children and their chief, Big Foot, were dead. A force of U.S. soldiers, who had been tasked with arresting Big Foot and disarming his warriors, had unexpectedly opened fire from their positions surrounding the Sioux camp at the same time that Big Foot was meeting with Army officers. Even as the Sioux warriors scrambled for their guns, the army troop used rifles and larger guns to rake the camp and the tepees that housed the Sioux and their families. It was a tragic end to the Indian Wars.

When word of the events at Wounded Knee reached top U.S. military and government leaders, they publicly congratulated the soldiers for "their splendid conduct." Fighting native people in the West was generally popular in the 1800s. While the Wounded Knee Massacre is viewed as an isolated tragic event today, people in 1890 thought it was the beginning of a war. In fact, when Major General Nelson A. Miles arrived on December 31 to take

This group of Sioux from the Pine Ridge Reservation are dressed in full native regalia. Stereotypes of the Sioux as villains were reinforced by the roles they played in Buffalo Bill's popular Wild West Show.

command of the situation, he ordered soldiers to fortify the buildings at the Pine Ridge agency to prepare for an attack.

But Miles also sent letters, gifts, and negotiators to the frightened Sioux. He assured them that he wanted to make peace. He promised to arrange for them to go to Washington to explain their problems to government officials. He sent troops to camp near the Sioux to nudge them toward Pine Ridge. By January 15, 1891, all the Sioux had surrendered. War was averted.

Miles also launched an investigation into Colonel James W. Forsyth's actions at Wounded Knee. He blamed Forsyth for turning a peaceful surrender into a deadly massacre. But soldiers defended Forsyth. They said that the Sioux had planned to attack them. Some claimed that the Sioux had attacked first.

Miles did not believe the stories, but government officials in Washington did not want to punish Forsyth when many Americans supported him. They blamed the Sioux. The Secretary of War said that anger had made the Sioux attack the soldiers and that their rage blinded them from seeing that they were killing their own families. That was one way the

May be reproduced for classroom use. *Toolkit Texts: Short Nonfiction for American History, Westward Expansion*, by Stephanie Harvey and Anne Goudvis, ©2016 (Portsmouth, NH: Heinemann).

government explained the deaths of so many Sioux women and children.

When the Sioux leaders arrived in Washington for their promised visit, President Benjamin Harrison refused to talk with them. He only shook their hands. The secretary of the interior warned them to make sure they did as the government told them or face severe punishment.

Popular culture reinforced the idea that Sioux fighters had caused the "Battle" of Wounded Knee. Miles had sent 27 of the Sioux leaders to prison. In March 1891, government officials **commuted** the sentences of 23 prisoners so they could perform in Buffalo Bill's Wild West Show. In the era's most popular entertainment, the Sioux played the parts of savage villains.

Commuted means changed a punishment to a less severe one.

For the Sioux who had not been involved in the events of December 29, at first it seemed as though life would get better. The army took control of the reservations in early 1891 and encouraged native people to raise cattle. The Sioux were good with horses and cattle, and their herds did well. But nonnative settlers wanted their lands. In 1900, the government taxed native cattle, and the Sioux herds disappeared. Tribes leased their land to white ranchers, while Sioux communities fell into poverty, barely surviving on government support.

FAST FACT

TWENTY U.S. SOLDIERS RECEIVED MEDALS OF HONOR FOR THEIR ACTIONS AT WOUNDED KNEE. IN 2001, NATIVE AMERICAN GROUPS CALLED FOR THE GOVERNMENT TO RESCIND, OR TAKE BACK, THE MEDALS.

In 1968, native people in Minnesota organized the American Indian Movement (AIM). The AIM called attention to the problems of daily life for native people. Then, in 1970, Dee Brown wrote a book called *Bury My Heart at Wounded Knee.* It told in heartbreaking detail how badly the government had treated native people. It became a bestseller.

Americans learned more about the history of false promises and failed treaties between Native Americans and the U.S. government. Some tribes won legal settlements against the U.S. government. The Sioux proved that the Black Hills were taken from them illegally. They continue to fight for their return. Meanwhile, the Sioux in South Dakota are still very poor, with high rates of disease. More than 100 years ago after the Wounded Knee Massacre, the Sioux continue to face challenges.

Capturing a Vanishing World

An Apache girl with a baby in a papoose

Edward S. Curtis, Chronicling the West

By the early twentieth century, there was a growing feeling in the United States that Native Americans were a vanishing race. Much of their culture was disappearing, unrecorded.

By Marcia Amidon Lusted. May be reproduced for classroom use. *Toolkit Texts: Short Nonfiction for American History, Westward Expansion,* by Stephanie Harvey and Anne Goudvis, ©2016 (Portsmouth, NH: Heinemann).

Blackfoot teepee

Library of Congress

At the very end of the nineteenth century, a photographer and ethnologist (someone who studies different peoples and the relationships between them) named Edward Sheriff Curtis was traveling through Montana as the official photographer for an exploratory expedition. Curtis and his companions, on horseback, found themselves on a mountainside that overlooked a valley floor where thousands of teepees spread across the plain. Curtis had already witnessed some very sacred Sundance ceremonies of the Piegan and Blackfoot tribes, and had taken award-winning photographs of an Indian princess. But this moment, gazing down at so many Native Americans gathered in one place, changed him forever. Suddenly everything fell into place and he knew, beyond a doubt, that his life's work was to use his camera and pen to record the lives of North American Indians.

Curtis spent the next 30 years documenting the lives of over 80 Indian tribes west of the Mississippi River, from Mexico all the way up to Alaska. His goal was to photograph all of the remaining Indian tribes in North America. He felt he had no time to lose—a recent census had estimated the Native American population at 237,000, down from perhaps 10 million four centuries earlier. Entire tribes, languages, and traditions were being lost. His work resulted in 20 volumes of a book series called *The North American Indian*, with each volume containing 300 pages of text and 75 photographs. He also produced a silent movie about the beliefs of the Rawakiutl Indians of the Pacific Northwest.

By the time he died in 1952, Curtis' work was largely forgotten. But it was rediscovered in the 1970s, and today much of it, including many more photographs than those included in his books, are part of the collections of many important libraries, including the Library of Congress. Curtis succeeded in his life's work and left a record of a way of life that has disappeared from the American landscape forever.

A basket maker

Solomon Butcher

Like Edward Curtis, Solomon D. Butcher used his camera to record a time and place that was quickly disappearing from American history, but in his case he documented the experience of homesteaders in Custer Country, Nebraska. Beginning in 1886, Butcher traveled the area by horse and buggy, taking photographs and recording the pioneer stories of the people who had come west because of the 1862 Homestead Act in order to claim their own piece of land. He took over 1,500 photos and in 1901, published them in a book called *Pioneer History of Custer County, Nebraska.* He was especially known for his photographs of sod houses, which homesteaders built out of the prairie sod itself because of a lack of wood for building homes. Eventually the size of Butcher's collection of photographic plates became too big for him to cope with, and he donated the collection to the Nebraska State Historical Association in 1912. Butcher never knew just how important his photographs and stories would become in capturing a moment in American history when settlers were helping to create the country as it is today.

Beginning in 1900 and continuing over the next thirty years, Edward Curtis, or the "Shadow Catcher" as he was called by some of the tribes, took over 40,000 photos and recorded rare details from over eighty Native American tribal groups.

This photo by Solomon Butcher shows one of a Nebraska family in front of their sod house.

By Marcia Amidon Lusted. May be reproduced for classroom use. *Toolkit Texts: Short Nonfiction for American History, Westward Expansion,* by Stephanie Harvey and Anne Goudvis, ©2016 (Portsmouth, NH: Heinemann).

SAND CREEK'S STORY

An Interview With Ranger Craig Moore

Colorful cottonwood trees mark the location of the Sand Creek today, but in 1864 the banks of the creek were treeless.

May be reproduced for classroom use. *Toolkit Texts: Short Nonfiction for American History, Westward Expansion*, by Stephanie Harvey and Anne Goudvis, ©2016 (Portsmouth, NH: Heinemann).

A crowd of dignitaries came together in southeastern Colorado on April 28, 2007. Tribal leaders, descendants, and local residents joined with the governor of Colorado, senators, congressmen, and the director and staff of the National Park Service (NPS) to dedicate the newest national park—the Sand Creek Massacre National Historic Site.

Sand Creek's story begins with the Colorado Territory gold rush of 1858. White settlers were determined to take control of this valuable land, even though it had been guaranteed by treaty to the Indians who lived there. As settlement increased on these lands, fighting broke out between the Cheyenne and Arapaho Indians and the U.S. government. United States military officers in the territory grew concerned that the Indians in the area were either allies of the Confederacy or were being influenced by Confederate officials.

Then, on November 29, 1864, two regiments of the U.S. Volunteer Calvalry totaling 675 troops attacked a peaceful camp of Arapaho and Cheyenne Indians near Sand Creek. Led by Colonel John Chivington, these men ignored a white surrender flag and an American flag raised by the Native Americans. They killed 230 tribal members, many of them women and children, as well as important chiefs who had tried to establish peace with settlers in the region. These deaths significantly weakened the two tribes. After investigating the attack, Congress condemned it. The federal government took control of Indian affairs away from the states and territories to try to keep local militia, angry at neighboring Indians, from launching another massacre.

FAST FACTS

AS A RESULT OF THE MASSACRE, PRESIDENT ANDREW JOHNSON'S ADMINISTRATION ULTIMATELY ASKED COLORADO GOVERNOR JOHN EVANS TO RESIGN.

The Sand Creek Massacre National Historic Site protects, preserves, and commemorates the site of the 1864 tragedy.

Sand Creek Massacre National Historic Site was established to remember the Native Americans killed there. Today, the National Park Service is working to create informative programs at the site while protecting it for future generations. An event called the Spiritual Healing Run takes place each year. Participants include descendants of the Indians who were killed at Sand Creek. Visitors may hike a trail leading to the site's historical marker. Several interpretive panels, which share the history of the event and the ecology of the site, are located on the trail.

Park ranger Craig Moore is responsible for creating materials that will be used to interpret the site for visitors. Following is a conversation he had with two students from Broomfield, Colorado's Legacy High School.

WHY IS THIS HISTORIC SITE IMPORTANT TO NATIVE AMERICAN?

The site is much more than a monument. It's part of the tribe's historic migrations and part of its ancestral homeland. Prior to 1858, Native Americans had had the whole territory in which to live. Even though they'd been forced onto the arid and

At the annual Spiritual Healing Run, Cheyenne and Arapaho gather to commemorate the event, honor those who were lost, and educate future generations about the Sand Creek massacre.

May be reproduced for classroom use. *Toolkit Texts: Short Nonfiction for American History, Westward Expansion*, by Stephanie Harvey and Anne Goudvis, ©2016 (Portsmouth, NH: Heinemann).

FAST FACTS

THE BITTER IRONY OF THE SAND CREEK MASSACRE WAS THAT THE MILITIA ATTACKED NATIVES WHO WERE COOPERATING WITH THE GOVERNMENT.

useless land that was Sand Creek, the site still holds the spirits and the remains of their Native American ancestors. It's symbolic of the historic Native American struggle to preserve homelands in the West.

HOW DOES THE NATIONAL PARK SERVICE DECIDE WHICH NATIVE AMERICANS WILL BE DOCUMENTED AND HONORED AT THE SITE?

Our government was specific in the wording of the law that created the site. The park service partners with four tribes: the Northern Cheyenne, the Northern Arapaho, and the Southern Cheyenne and Arapaho tribes of Oklahoma. The law grants these tribes, as descendants of those who were massacred, certain historic, cultural, and traditional uses of the site. The park service continues to research historic documents at places such as the Colorado and Oklahoma state historical societies, the Denver Public Library, and the National Anthropological Archives. Additional information and oral history interviews are gathered from tribal elders who belong to the Indian nations represented at Sand Creek.

WHAT ISSUES DOES THE SITE CURRENTLY FACE?

We currently are trying to preserve the natural and cultural integrity of the site. This means that we're trying to leave the site in the condition in which it would have been during the actual event, and to respect the artifacts and landscape of the site. Many people are helping us do this, including scientists, historians, and archaeologists. The park service is creating signs and interpretive panels to help tell the site's story. Telling the story in a concise, educational, and accurate manner is more difficult. We're working with our Native American partners and others to create the materials in the best manner possible. Other issues include working with neighboring landowners to reduce the chance of fire.

NPS

The village at Sand Creek was under the protection of an American flag and a white flag of truce.

WHAT DOES THE NATIONAL PARK SERVICE HOPE VISITORS WILL TAKE AWAY FROM THEIR EXPERIENCE AT THE SITE?

We hope visitors will take away a better overall understanding and appreciation of the history and legacy of the Sand Creek Massacre. Through a variety of programs, we hope to instill in visitors a desire to protect and preserve Sand Creek and all of our national parks for the benefit and enjoyment of this generation and future generations. ∎

RANCH of the SWALLOWS

This illustrated map shows the location of Ranch of the Swallows.

© RYGER/Shutterstock

You know the **PILGRIMS** landed on the Atlantic coast of America in **1620**. But did you know that the **SPANISH** were already here—far to the west?

© Charles Mann/Alamy Stock Photo

Long before Paul Revere made his famous ride in 1775, travelers were riding into El Rancho de las Golondrinas (Ranch of the Swallows) in New Mexico. The ranch was a welcome stopping point for explorers, merchants, and soldiers as they journeyed along the Camino Real. This was the 1,500-mile Royal Road that led from Mexico City north to New Mexico. The ranch was the last place to camp before reaching Santa Fe. Santa Fe was the Spanish capital in New Mexico.

Spanish settlers built the ranch in the early 1700s. The first building was a small house of adobe bricks made from mud and straw. Through

the years, ranchers added more buildings around a central courtyard. The ranch offered a place for travelers to refresh themselves with water from the natural springs. And their horses could graze and rest.

Families who had moved far from their homes in Spain found comfort in familiar customs. Just as in Spain, girls at he ranch learned the skills they needed for taking care of the home. Boys learned to care for the animals, the crops, and the ranch buildings and fences.

Girls would mash the roots of the yucca plant to make soap for washing clothes. They learned to grind corn between two stones (the *mano* and *metate*) to make cornmeal for tortillas. Boys learned to irrigate by operating gates along the *acequia*, or irrigation ditch. And they helped with the cattle and sheep.

Small children could help pick the plants used in dyeing the wool and collect wood for fires and pieces of metal from the blacksmith shop to be used again. Even tiny scraps of metal could be melted down to make nails. The ranch had to make everything it needed. So, nothing could be wasted.

For generations, one family owned El Rancho de las Golondrinas. Over time, it became less important as a stopping point. But the family kept the original structures on the ranch. In the 1930s, a Santa Fe family bought the ranch and turned it into a living history museum. They moved more buildings, such as a schoolhouse and a mill with a giant waterwheel, from other old towns in New Mexico.

Today, you can see the past in the present at the Ranch of Swallows. ∎

Today, the ranch is a "living history" museum. Each year, more than 50,000 people from all over the world come to see what ranch life was like 300 years ago. Schoolchildren come to dip candles, bake bread, spin wool into yarn, and grind corn. They learn what life was like on a New Mexico ranch before George Washington was born.

© Jim Feliciano/Shutterstock/HIP

by Deborah Holt Williams, *Appleseeds*, © by Carus Publishing Company. Reproduced with permission.

© Greg and Jan Ritchie/Shutterstock

FACING THE FUTURE

A Sioux tepee on the Great Plains

Today, the Oglala Sioux Nation at the Pine Ridge Indian Reservation spreads over nearly 3,500 square miles of southwestern South Dakota. It's the second-largest Native American reservation in the United States. It's also a place where people still suffer from the U.S. government's broken promises.

"Our needs are so great," says Bryan Brewer, 2012–2014 president of the Oglala Sioux Tribe. "They all go hand in hand.

"Probably our biggest needs right now are housing, economic development, jobs, and education," Brewer says. Many of the people live in poverty, including a majority of children. Unfortunately, jobs are scarce. Unemployment hovers around 80 percent. And living off the land is harder than it was 150 years ago.

"We come from a warrior society, and we were hunters," says Brewer. "We weren't farmers."

BROKEN PROMISES

The United States made treaties with the tribe when it moved to the reservation. "These treaties have never really been honored," he continues. Among other things, the United States seized most of the Great Sioux Reservation's original land. The Black Hills, along with other areas that can support grazing and farming, were lost.

In 1980, the Supreme Court held that the U.S. government took the land unlawfully. The land's value with interest would come to roughly $1.3 billion today. Income from the land would be additional. More than money, though, the Sioux would like Congress to give back much of the land. The Black Hills remain sacred to the tribe.

"We're still fighting to get land back," Brewer says. Federally owned lands would come to about three fifths of the original treaty area.

UNMET NEEDS

The United States also has a continuing duty to provide monetary support each year. "Every year, we give them a needs-based budget," Brewer says. But Congress gives only a fraction of the full amount needed. As a result, the Oglala Sioux Nation suffers. "We're not meeting the needs of our people," he says. "We have people who are dying who can't get medical care" even for treatable diseases such as diabetes.

Housing is another huge need. The nation needs at least 12,000 more homes. Yet even people with homes lack basic necessities. "We have people who are living without electricity and without propane fuel," Brewer notes. Widespread poverty and unemployment make other troubles worse. Crime and addiction are significant problems for the tribe. Children suffer the most.

FAST FACTS

A 2009 DEFENSE FUNDING LAW "APOLOGIZES ON BEHALF OF THE PEOPLE OF THE UNITED STATES TO ALL NATIVE PEOPLES FOR THE MANY INSTANCES OF VIOLENCE, MALTREATMENT, AND NEGLECT INFLICTED ON NATIVE PEOPLES BY CITIZENS OF THE UNITED STATES." HOWEVER, THE LAW SPECIFICALLY ADDS THAT NOTHING IN IT SUPPORTS OR SETTLES ANY CLAIM BY NATIVE AMERICANS AGAINST THE UNITED STATES.

© Wollertz/Shutterstock.com

The Sioux strive to keep their traditions alive at powwows and other contemporary celebrations.

The state of South Dakota somtimes places children who need foster care into nonnative homes. "We'd like to have our own facilities to care for these children and guarantee that they would keep [connected to] their culture," says Brewer. However, that would take money—something they lack.

PROTECTING RESOURCES FOR THE FUTURE

"Our tribe right now is in debt about $100 million dollars," Brewer notes. Yet the Sioux won't do just anything to make quick money.

"We're so concerned about our environment now," he says.

For example, the reservation has shale, oil, and gas. However, errors in drilling, spills, improper waste disposal, and other activities can contaminate water. The nation also objects to plans for the Keystone XL pipeline to cross its land. "Our water is precious up here, and we have so little," Brewer says. Contamination of that resource "could destroy our way of life here."

Still, the nation has hope. "We're really working hard on economic development," says Brewer. More businesses would bring more jobs.

Tourism is one possibility. "A lot of people would like to have an Indian experience," Brewer notes. Managing some National Park Service land or having a park outside the U.S. system is also a possibility.

U.S. government funds have also let the nation buy about $60 million worth of "fractionated land." These are some of the parcels that were allotted under the 1887 Dawes Act. Many had dozens or even hundreds of co-owners— sometimes too many for people to use the land practically. The optional "buy backs" could now let the nation lease lands for income.

Perhaps most important, the Oglala Sioux people strive to retain their cultural identity. People come from far and wide for their powwows. "The powwow is a social gathering where we get together," explains Brewer.

The tribe also practices other traditions, such as the naming and the Sun Dance ceremonies. Other events include competitive dance competitions with elaborate **regalia**.

Meeting the nation's many needs remains an ongoing challenge. But, says Brewer, "We are rich in our culture, rich in our history, and rich in our population." ∎

Regalia are ceremonial objects and clothing.

RECLAIMING THE WEST

NPS

At the age of 35, Powell embarked on the epic Powell Geographic Expedition, a dangerous three-month river trip down almost 1,000 miles of the Green and Colorado rivers through the Grand Canyon.

Many people seemed to know about the West by the mid 1800s. Some said it was the Great American Desert—a land so forbidding only fools dared settle there. Others proclaimed the West the Garden of the World. As the area was settled, the amount of rainfall coincidentally increased for a while, giving rise to the saying "Rain follows the plow." According to this theory, settlers actually increased the fertility of an area by farming it.

Exploring the Unknown

Still, to most people, the West was a mystery. It was a space marked "unknown" on maps. In 1869, John Wesley Powell set out to explore it. Coming to know the West intimately, Powell worked to change the way the West was viewed and cared for.

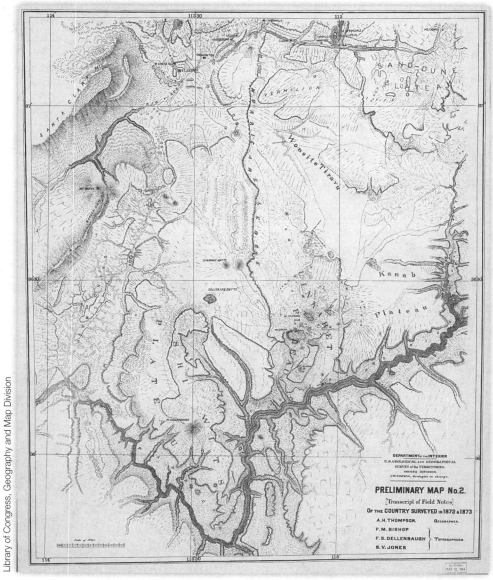

Powell created this map of the land that he surveyed in 1872 and 1873.

Largely self-educated, Powell was a professor of geology and curator of the Illinois Natural History Society Museum. Although he had lost his right arm in the Battle of Shiloh during the Civil War, in 1869 Powell led a group down the Green and Colorado rivers through the Grand Canyon, until then unexplored. The group, formed to collect specimens for the Illinois museum, suffered blistering heat, chilling rain, physical exhaustion, and food shortages. Frequently the river was difficult to navigate, causing the men to carry the boats and supplies overland.

Despite newspaper accounts of their deaths, Powell and five others successfully completed the expedition. But Powell did more than simply gather samples. He recorded valuable scientific observations, explored the Grand Canyon, and drew geological sketches of the riverbanks and surrounding plateaus. He computed the height of the canyon walls and measured the flow of its streams. He recorded the barometric pressure, temperature, and mileage.

Documenting the West

The American people proclaimed Powell a hero. Congress, recognizing his efforts, supported his work by granting him money for a geological and geographical survey of the Colorado River and its tributaries. From 1871 to 1879, Powell's surveys

Powell and Paiute chief Tau-Gu, overlooking the Virgin River in Utah, during an expedition in 1873.

NPS

explored the adjoining canyon regions of what are now western Colorado, eastern Utah, northern Arizona, and northwestern New Mexico. Mapping and naming canyons, valleys, and streams whose existence had been unknown to white people, Powell's surveys also reported on the plants, animals, fossils, soil, and water of these areas. Within ten years, Powell had made more than thirty trips through much of the territory that became Colorado, Utah, Arizona, New Mexico, Idaho, and Nevada. In 1879, he persuaded Congress to combine his work with other government surveys to form the U.S. Geological Survey to oversee western development.

Powell valued knowledge, especially when it was used for the good of humanity. Using his surveys, he studied the land and classified it by precipitation and usage. On this basis, Powell developed proposals for land reform, which he described in his 1878 Report on the Lands of the Arid Region of the United States.

In Arid Lands, as it came to be called, Powell sought to correct two widespread misunderstandings. The West, Powell explained, was not the Great American Desert. Although the forty percent of the continent west of the one hundredth meridian received less than twenty inches of rain annually, this area was fertile when irrigated. But neither, Powell emphasized, was the West the Garden of the World. Although the West was then experiencing a period of increased rainfall, Powell knew from his studies that there had been periods of drought that were sure to recur.

A Critical Resource

Because of this, Powell saw water as the West's critical resource. Homesteaders moving west were doomed to failure unless they could be guaranteed water for irrigation. Since only water could make the land valuable, water monopolies should be prevented and water rights linked to the land by law.

Settlement of the West would require new water-rights laws and forms of cooperation. Although the development of dams and canals would depend on assistance from the federal government, settlers should join together to form cooperative irrigation districts, sharing water because it was scarce. Settlers interested in livestock should receive larger homesteads than customary and band together to form pasturage districts. Careful management of the common pasturage would help prevent the over-grazing that led to soil erosion.

Powell's conservation plan ignited controversy. Many Americans believed in "rugged individualism," a lone person or family working hard and succeeding, not the cooperation Powell advocated. Many viewed modifying the Homestead Act, which gave a citizen one hundred sixty acres of free land if the person was willing to work it, as almost sacrilegious (disrespectful toward something sacred). In a time of abundance, Powell spoke of shortages.

Congress failed to pass Powell's land use program. In the 1880s, drought and wind changed the West from America's land of promise to a dust bowl. Winters and springs of blizzards and storms passed into summers and autumns of droughts and prairie fires. Wagons returned from the West with "In God we trusted, in the West we busted" painted on their sides.

To solve the West's crisis, Congress put Powell in charge of the Irrigation Survey, designed to select reservoir sites and determine irrigation projects. But in 1890, Congress stopped the survey.

Ahead of His Time

May be reproduced for classroom use. *Toolkit Texts: Short Nonfiction for American History, Westward Expansion*, by Stephanie Harvey and Anne Goudvis, ©2016 (Portsmouth, NH: Heinemann).

Although many consider John Wesley Powell the originator of conservation in the United States, it was years before his ideas were widely accepted. Even today, conservation issues are often controversial.

In 1902, President Theodore Roosevelt signed the Reclamation Act, designed to reclaim the arid West by a series of dams and irrigation projects. Following this, Utah passed an act placing ownership of water with the state. Legal disputes over the possession of water, especially where streams and rivers cross state boundaries and where water has been diverted from its natural course, have continued through the years. In 1963, for example, the Supreme Court agreed that Arizona had rights to specific amounts of water each year from the Colorado River and all water from the Gila River.

In conservation, the issue is frequently a question of whether to develop an area or preserve it. The completion of the Coolidge Dam on the Gila River in 1930 ended fifty-five years of opposition by Apache Indians who feared the destruction of their tribal burial grounds. To prevent this destruction, an $11,000 concrete slab was laid over the site.

U.S. Geological Survey

As director of the U.S. Geological Survey, Powell made his main project the creation of a national topographic map.

In 1964, Glen Canyon, an area that captivated Powell on his Grand Canyon journey, was flooded to create Glen Canyon Dam. The canyon itself was renamed and is now Lake Powell. Only John Wesley Powell could say whether this development, rather than preservation, was what he had in mind when he advocated reclaiming the West. ∎